MEMORIALIZING
MOTHERHOOD

West Virginia and Appalachia

A Series Edited by Ronald L. Lewis, Ken Fones-Wolf,
and Kevin Barksdale

TITLES IN THE SERIES

MEMORIALIZING MOTHERHOOD

ANNA JARVIS AND THE STRUGGLE FOR CONTROL OF MOTHER'S DAY

KATHARINE LANE ANTOLINI

MORGANTOWN 2014

West Virginia University Press 26506
Copyright 2014 West Virginia University Press
All rights reserved
First edition published 2014 by West Virginia University Press
Printed in the United States of America

21 20 19 18 17 16 15 14   1 2 3 4 5 6 7 8 9

ISBN:

cl   978-1-938228-93-3
epub   978-1-938228-96-4
pdf   978-1-938228-95-7

Library of Congress Cataloging-in-Publication Data:
Antolini, Katharine Lane.
Memorializing motherhood : Anna Jarvis and the struggle for control of Mother's Day / Katharine
Lane Antolini. -- First edition.
pages cm -- (West Virginia and Appalachia)
Includes bibliographical references and index.
ISBN 978-1-938228-93-3 (cloth : alk. paper) -- ISBN 1-938228-93-6 (cloth : alk. paper) -- ISBN 978-
1-938228-96-4 (e-pub) -- ISBN 1-938228-96-0 (e-pub) -- ISBN 978-1-938228-95-7 (pdf) -- ISBN
1-938228-95-2 (pdf)
1. Mother's Day. 2. Jarvis, Anna, 1864-1948. I. Title.
HQ759.2.A57 2014
394.2628--dc23
          2014025852
Art Direction by Than Saffel / WVU Press

Cover design by Kelley Galbreath
Book design by Kelley Galbreath

TO MY MOTHER, LALA, AND MOTHER-IN-LAW, RETA—
may I never take your love and guidance for granted.

AND TO MY SONS, JOHN MICHAEL AND COOPER—
may you never take my love and guidance for granted.

CONTENTS

THE CULTURAL DUALITY OF MOTHER'S DAY

M other's Day celebrated its centennial in May 2008. A century before, on May 10, 1908, four hundred members of the Andrews Methodist Episcopal Church, in Grafton, West Virginia, and a crowd of fifteen thousand people at the Wanamaker Store Auditorium in Philadelphia attended the first official observance of Mother's Day in the United States. The following year, forty-two additional states joined West Virginia and Pennsylvania in commemorating the day. The speed and extent of the observance's popularity gratified its founder, Anna Jarvis. It was obvious to her that the country's sons and daughters craved such a day of maternal tribute as she recounted how "thousands and thousands of persons in all walks of life, with the mother-hunger in their hearts, found Mother's Day a blessing, a comfort and an uplift."[1] She decided to devote her life to the day's perpetuation, and after six years of urging, Congress finally designated Mother's Day a national holiday in 1914. The Mother's Day Flag Resolution empowered President Woodrow Wilson to issue a formal proclamation calling on the American people to honor U.S. mothers by displaying the American flag on all government buildings and private homes on the second Sunday in May.

The fact that almost every state in the country, including the territories of Hawaii and Puerto Rico, hosted a Mother's Day observance by 1909 stands as a testament to Jarvis's dedication and successful leadership of her holiday movement. Her Mother's Day promotions quickly expanded beyond the United States as well, reaching grateful sons and daughters in Canada, Mexico, South America, Australia, Africa, China, and Japan by 1911. Two years before President Wilson formally proclaimed the day an official American holiday, Jarvis had already translated her Mother's Day literature into over ten different languages. She insisted, "The marvelous growth of Mother's Day in a few years to a national and international day can be attributed to the 'heart' or 'living' interest it possess for almost every home and every person of a mother-loving heart in this and other countries."[2]

1

Today, Mother's Day remains a widely observed American holiday. Over 80 percent of Americans celebrated the day in its centennial year. Most buy gifts as opposed to displaying the American flag in maternal tribute, of course. This has made Mother's Day a multibillion-dollar industry for retailers and the second-highest gift-giving day behind Christmas.[3] Yet neither Anna Jarvis's lifelong dedication to the day's observance nor its enormous commercial appeal can completely explain the holiday's longevity. Historically, Mother's Day has generated a century-long public discourse on American motherhood. To observe Mother's Day is to join the larger debate over the cultural expectations of motherhood, as the day would be meaningless without a model of motherhood to serve as a measurement of praise. Every celebration must have at its core an image of a mother deemed worthy of memorializing. The praising of your mother as a good mother on Mother's Day, in other words, depends on your understanding of what constitutes good mothering and whether or not your mother meets the established criteria. Consequently, the holiday has always provided a platform for a cultural debate over the intrinsic value of motherhood and the appropriate boundaries of the maternal role.

Since the nineteenth century, various social, commercial, and political movements have advocated the celebration of Mother's Day in order to define and harness the symbolic power of motherhood in American society, thereby revealing the observance's powerful duality as both a holiday and a cultural representation of motherhood. Through a historical analysis of the founding and celebrating of Mother's Day in the early twentieth century, this book uncovers the cultural significance of the day's duality and, in the process, draws a stronger connection between the developing scholarship on the history of holidays and the history of motherhood in American society. A wide range of disciplines influence the scholarship on holidays and on motherhood, thus leading to the further integration of the two fields. Both holidays and motherhood, for example, are studied as cultural institutions, consisting of their own constantly changing expectations and patterns of behavior, traditions, and rituals; thus, they are both a product of, and an influence on, American culture.[4] "Holidays, like other cultural products tend to offer a somewhat refractory reading of society," asserts Amitai Etzioni. "They advance our understanding of a set of specific social phenomenon and they cast light on the community or society in which they are celebrated."[5] Maternal scholarship describes a similar refractory reading offered by the social construction of motherhood. "There have always been mothers but motherhood was invented," explains Ann Dally. "Each subsequent age and society has defined it in its own terms and imposed its own restrictions and expectations on mothers. Thus motherhood has not always seemed or been the same."[6]

Both Etzioni and Dally stress the changing nature of holiday observances and maternal expectations as a key opportunity for further study. According to Etzioni, the editing and reengineering of holidays and their rituals "takes place constantly, drawing on both new and old patterns. How effective this is, and can be, is a major subject for social scientists, as it currently remains largely unstudied." For Dally, to understand the trends and traditions that define the modern institution of motherhood, we must first uncover the history: "Old trends need to be followed back. New trends can be traced back into the past and often then acquire new meaning and depth. The future emerges from the past and thus helps us understand and come to terms with the present."[7] By emphasizing Mother's Day's duality, this book illustrates the enmeshed and interdependent ideological trends, traditions, patterns, and even misunderstandings embodied within the day's historic observance, revealing the holiday's cultural significance as a symbolic celebration of motherhood.

Within the literature on holidays, Mother's Day typically falls into one of three mutually inclusive categories: the sentimental holiday, the invented tradition, and the recommitment holiday. Sentimental holidays are defined as such for their celebration of the private family rather than the community.[8] They were primarily a product of the nineteenth century, a gift from white middle-class Victorians uncomfortable with the carnivalesque celebrations of annual holidays. They preferred to observe the traditionally public fêtes as child-centered domestic occasions more reflective of their ideals of "domestic warmth, intimacy, romantic love, special affection for children and grandparents, and a familial and feminized view of religion," according to historian Elizabeth Pleck.[9] It was the Victorians, after all, who domesticated Christmas. They successfully replaced a holiday celebrated during the colonial period through public drunkenness, overeating, masquerading, and overall unruly merriment to one of private reverence, with a Christmas tree in the parlor surrounded by presents and eager children awaiting the arrival of Santa Claus.[10] Mother's Day falls easily within this sentimental classification. The traditions surrounding the holiday's observance are meant to celebrate the home just as much as they are designed to honor the mothers within it.

But because Mother's Day carried those Victorian ideals into the modern twentieth century, it can also be described as an invented tradition created to maintain a perceived continuity with the past during times of rapid social change.[11] Historians who address the issue of Mother's Day note the significance of its timing, portraying the holiday's veneration of motherhood and domesticity as an obvious backlash against the expanding public roles of women at the turn of the century.[12] Along the same argument, Mother's Day can also be viewed as a recommitment holiday for its use of specific narratives and rituals to reinforce a social commitment to shared beliefs. In this case, it is a holiday used to reaffirm traditional gender roles by glorifying women's primary commitment to their families as wives and mothers.[13]

Mother's Day as a sentimental holiday best describes its intimate celebration of home and motherhood as designed by Anna Jarvis in 1908 and designated by Congress in 1914. It also effectively represents the intent behind the day's specific spelling that remained essential to Jarvis's holiday vision. "It is a personal day—'possessive singular,'" she continually emphasized. "Mother's Day is not for the famous. It is just for tributes and to glorify your humble mother and mine."[14] Mother's Day retains its predominantly sentimental image today, one that is popularly dismissed as a creation of the floral and greeting card industries as Americans spend billions of dollars on tributes to their humble mothers each year.

INTRODUCTION

Twenty-first century Americans are not the first to criticize the holiday's cultural legitimacy. Mother's Day attracted its share of skepticism from the very start. When its sentimentalism failed to completely mask the incongruities between its message of domestic harmony and the social upheaval brought on by the industrial and urban expansion of the early twentieth century, many questioned the new holiday's relevancy as a tribute to modern motherhood. Mother's Day was in good company, however, for even established sentimental holidays such as Thanksgiving and Christmas lost some of their innocence in the face of changing sensibilities and growing commercialization. Elizabeth Pleck describes this evolution of twentieth-century holiday celebrations as postsentimental:

It is best to think of the postsentimental approach to ritual as a third layer, added on top of the carnivalesque and the sentimental approaches, and as a stance in a debate, which presumes that others will argue and make visible the merits of sentimentality. Postsentimentalism is both a way of talking about ritual and a style of practicing it. Cynical and critical, postsentimentalism uses sentimentality as a foil. . . . Instead of affirming an ideal of the family, celebrations in postsentimental times upheld a set of values that can be best described as individualist, pluralist, therapeutic, and consumerist.[15]

Pleck places the transitional phase between the sentimental and postsentimental eras in the first decades of the twentieth century, precisely the period when Mother's Day gained national recognition. As a sentimental holiday in an emerging postsentimental society, then, the value of the Mother's Day observance has never gone uncontested.

In 1927, *Parents Magazine* sponsored an essay contest addressing the holiday's cultural relevancy. The magazine offered a monetary prize for the top four letters written on the merits of Mother's Day as viewed from a mother's perspective. Sixty-eight mothers wrote essays in favor of the holiday—maudlin sentiment and all. "Despite the skepticism which this frank generation may feel about the prescribed sentimentality of Mother's Day, I should hate to see the institution abolished," wrote first-prize winner Viola Lockhart Warren of Rochester, New York. She saw a sincere value in the holiday's lesson for children:

It is to her children that the real advantage of the day accrues. It is a wholesome curb on their sense of self-importance to experience this one celebration which has not themselves as its central figure. On Mother's Day they must give her happiness and then remain in the background, where they may make an important discovery—that Mother is a separate entity, capable of gratification entirely aside from them. The young mother is so closely identified with the physical existence of her small children, that they come to think of her in terms of themselves. If Mother's Day can teach them to think of her as an individual rather than as a convenience, it will strengthen

4

her influence for the reasoning age just ahead of them. You see, to a mother, even Mother's Day must benefit the children to prove its right to survive! [16]

Nellie M. Wilson of Indianapolis, Indiana, echoed Mrs. Warren's heartfelt endorsement of the observance: "Surely Mother's Day should be set apart to teach the youngest to the eldest, that on that day, Mother is first; that is her one day in the whole year when all should do her reverence."[17]

Although outnumbered by those who praised the holiday, forty-eight mothers wrote of their overall disapproval for the magazine's essay contest. "Since I have become the mother of two normal, healthy children, my feeling revolts each year at the approach of Mother's Day, with its sentimental accompaniments," admitted Mary B. Fenelon of Big Rapids, Michigan. She criticized the holiday's exaggerated veneration of mothers. She did not want to be held in awe by her children. She wanted to be their companion, not the "object of their reverence."[18] Elinor Franklin Young of New York City agreed that the observance caused more harm than good. She believed those who had learned as children to appreciate their mothers did not require the prodding of an official holiday to express that appreciation:

> Those who observe Mother's Day merely because some unknown somebodies have decreed it necessary are either succumbing to false sentiment or acting in fear lest non-observance cause pain. And, in this connection, think of the many mothers who get an extra stab of pain on this day, hoping against hope for a greeting which does not come.[19]

Emphasizing the duality of Mother's Day as a holiday and cultural representation of motherhood allows us to build on Pleck's sentimental/postsentimental model. The 1927 magazine contest nicely illustrates how the holiday's sentimental design did not universally speak to every woman's view of herself as a mother. In this example, Mrs. Fenelon and Mrs. Young were more than postsentimental cynics of a sentimental holiday; they were vocal critics of the model of motherhood the holiday was designed to commemorate. Mother's Day lacked relevancy to their lives, at least, because its idealized measure of motherhood did not mirror their own experiences and expectations in the same way it did for Mrs. Warren and Mrs. Wilson. The women's conflicting opinions offer a brief yet provocative glimpse into the rich source of maternal history hidden within the Mother's Day narrative. It reminds us that in order to celebrate Mother's Day, we must first construct a maternal ideal worth memorializing.

MOTHERS' DAY VERSUS MOTHER'S DAY

Americans were not the first to reserve a special day of tribute for mothers. The practice dates from antiquity. The ancient Greeks honored Rhea, the mother of Zeus. The ancient Romans celebrated the mother goddess Cybele with a three-day long spring festival, known as the Hilaria, on the Ides of March. The early Christians designated the fourth Sunday in Lent as "Mothering Sunday," which may have been an adaptation of the pagan worship of Cybele, where honoring the Virgin Mary or the Mother Church replaced the honoring of the mother goddess. During the sixteenth century, parishioners in England first celebrated Mothering Sunday by returning to the church of their baptism to pay tribute. By the 1600s, the celebration broadened to include the practice of apprentices and servants returning home with small gifts for their mothers. This custom persisted into the early nineteenth century; sons and daughters returning home to visit their mothers were said to "go a mothering."[20]

The American observance of Mother's Day began in the nineteenth century. Although Anna Jarvis considered herself the true founder of Mother's Day, she was not the first to promote the idea of a maternal memorial day. Five others earned local and national notability for their sponsorship of a Mother's Day celebration before she launched her movement in 1907: Ann Reeves Jarvis (1858), Julia Ward Howe (1873), Juliet Calhoun Blakeley (1877), Mary Towles Sasseen (1893), and Frank Hering (1904). Chapter 1 traces the origins of the first calls for a Mother's Day and compares the maternal models that each of these five designed his or her day to commemorate. Their individual stories reveal how the holiday's susceptibility to conflicting maternal imagery began long before Anna Jarvis's battle to defend her sentimental observance from its postsentimental detractors. In her discussion of Mother's Day, for example, historian Stephanie Coontz recounts the time she received a handmade gift from her son for Mother's Day. The school had encouraged students to personally make, not purchase, a present for their mothers in appreciation of her special love and care as the holiday had "originally intended." She was delighted to receive the gift, of course, but she admitted that the historian in her "was a little bemused":

> The fact is that Mother's Day originated to celebrate the organized activities of women *outside* the home. It became trivialized and commercialized only after it became confined to "special" nuclear family relations. The people who first inspired Mother's Day had quite a different idea about what made mothers special. They believed that motherhood was a *political* force. They wished to celebrate mothers' social roles as community organizers, honoring women who acted on behalf of the entire future generation rather than simply putting their own children first.[21]

Essentially, the earliest promoters of the maternal holiday envisioned an observance best exemplified by the possessive plural form *Mothers' Day* rather than its possessive singular representation.

In contrast to Mother's Day's sentimental celebration of the family and a mother's central role within it, Mothers' Day venerated the full range of women's roles as mothers and the boundless reach of their maternal influences. As mothers, Reeves Jarvis, Howe, and Blakeley understood the private and public dynamics of women's maternal

*Figure I.1. Anna Jarvis. Courtesy of the International Mother's Day Shrine,
Grafton, West Virginia.*

identities and seized the opportunity to organize women around their shared maternal
experiences in a way that encouraged social and political activism. Unlike the three
earliest figures, the remaining Mother's Day promoters, Sasseen and Hering, were
not parents. Their child centered perspective of motherhood subsequently failed to
recognize the same maternal traits revered by the holiday's original possessive plural
design. They introduced instead the sentimental celebration of Mother's Day that
Anna Jarvis later elaborated and popularized throughout the early twentieth century.
Where Reeves Jarvis, Howe, and Blakely offered mothers an active role in their own
tribute, Sasseen and Hering reduced mothers to passive figures of praise.

Chapter 2 formally introduces Anna Jarvis and the work she referred to as her
Mother's Day movement to establish and protect the sentimental design of her holiday observance. The discussion begins with the relationship between Jarvis and her
mother, Ann Reeves Jarvis, and the role her mother's memory played in the promotion of Mother's Day. Although Jarvis dedicated the day to all mothers in general
appreciation for their familial devotion, she designed the day as a special tribute to
her mother. Yet when she memorialized her mother, she did so strictly as a daughter—which invariably distorted Ann Reeves Jarvis's Mothers' Day model built on
the collective strength women gained from their shared maternal experiences. The

discussion ends with Jarvis's battle to defend her Mother's Day design from political aggrandizement and commercial exploitation. In 1912, Jarvis formally structured her movement into a central organization, the Mother's Day International Association, to better coordinate, as well as protect, her work. As part of the incorporation process, she trademarked all names and emblems used by her association, thereby defining the observance as her sole intellectual and legal property.[22]

Throughout her career, the public assaults Jarvis led against the floral, confection, and greeting card industries for their holiday profiteering and copyright infringement were tailor-made for sensational media coverage. In 1922, the *New York Times* reported her endorsement of open boycotts against the florists who raised the prices of white carnations every May. A year later, the paper detailed her crashing of a retail confectioner convention to protest the industry's economic gouging of her Mother's Day sentiment. Her 1925 arrest for disorderly conduct after disrupting an American War Mothers convention in Philadelphia made the front page of Midwestern newspapers. Jarvis condemned the organization's holiday fund-raising drives featuring the sale of white carnations. The legendary stories continue to fascinate modern observers and academics. The media coverage of Mother's Day centennial celebrations focused more on the embittered founder's ill-fated crusade against commercialism than any other aspect of her Mother's Day movement. Most historical accounts share the same focus on Jarvis's life.[23] Yet this book reveals the often overlooked complexity of Jarvis's relationship with modern commercial forces and, more importantly, clarifies what both contemporary detractors and modern historians have judged as her irrational criticisms of the commercialization of Mother's Day.

INFRINGERS, CHARITY CHARLATANS, AND THE EXPECTANT MOTHER RACKET

For forty years, Jarvis waged a war against a variety of adversaries to protect her vision of Mother's Day and the model of motherhood it memorialized. This resulted in a lengthy list of people and organizations she classified as "anti-mother propagandists" for their distortion or abuse of Mother's Day. All rival promoters of the holiday, according to Jarvis, were primarily motivated by greed—even those who sought to harness the observance's popularity toward nobler humanitarian causes. She considered noncommercial organizations that economically profited from Mother's Day, either indirectly through spin-off holidays and welfare campaigns or directly through fund-raising events, as pirates looting the day's popularity for personal gain. Piracy was piracy, irrespective of any altruistic justifications for the holiday's appropriation. The "Christian pirates," in her opinion, were habitually the worst offenders of all.[24]

The second half of the book utilizes Jarvis's list of "anti-mother propagandists" to explore how noncommercial or philanthropic Mother's Day rivals reinterpreted the holiday to meet specific political, economic, or social welfare agendas. This consists of more than just the aesthetic differences commonly depicted within the existing literature; it includes original historical analyses of the divergent models of motherhood expressed through the imagery and rhetoric of the alternative celebrations. Ironically, the lesser-known rivals of Jarvis and her movement shared her condemnation of commercialization and her desire to redeem the holiday's tainted reputation. That redemption, however, required the rejection of Mother's Day's sentimental design as culturally irrelevant. For organizations wishing to educate parents on the new child-rearing techniques or for charities struggling to aid impoverished mothers and children, the sentimentality of Jarvis's Mother's Day held little value.[25] Subsequently, they sought to style the holiday to better represent their postsentimental criticisms and modern concerns.

Since the discussion is limited to only the groups who came in direct conflict with Jarvis, it is not an exhaustive study of Mother's Day's postsentimental representations, but one that builds on Jarvis's continued role in the day's contested history. Her well-documented condemnations and publicized confrontations with anti-mother propagandists provide an indispensable sounding board on which to explore and critique the holiday's multiple maternal meanings. Her personal and public critiques add both drama and theoretical depth to the larger narrative, because they were as outrageous and entertaining as they were clever and poignant. Throughout the history of her Mother's Day movement, Jarvis served as the requisite sentimental foil to the postsentimental celebrations of motherhood, since the only hypocrisies she failed to expose were her own.

Chapter 3 explores how the early twentieth-century emphasis on the domestic role of fathers encroached on the holiday's glorification of a mother's unrivaled influence over her children. An increased interest in the importance of fathers and children within the modern family challenged the domestic imagery of husbands and children beholden to the care only a mother could provide. Fathers and children became autonomous family members who served different and significant roles requiring specialized attention and praise. The call for fathers to play a larger domestic role naturally accompanied a call for a larger share of the recognition, including appropriate holiday tributes. Sentimental holidays venerating the values of domesticity, however, traditionally placed fathers on the periphery. Father was the parent honored for his economic contributions, the one who provided the means to pay for holiday feasts and gifts; it was Mother who received direct validation for her pivotal role in the celebration's success, whether through the preparation of the perfect Thanksgiving meal or the time spent selecting just the right Christmas gifts.[26] In a 1929 editorial, George Hecht, editor of *Parents Magazine*, pondered the apparent holiday marginalization of fathers and asked the provocative question of "Why not a Parents' Day?":

The father's contribution to the family life has too often been considered merely a financial one. But with a better understanding of the importance of family relationships has come the realization that the father exerts a strong influence on the lives of his children. Parents' Day would foster in children a proper recognition and appreciation of the unselfish devotion and self-sacrificing of both mothers and fathers.[27]

The editorial was Hecht's endorsement of the ongoing campaign led by a New York City radio personality to replace Mother's Day with a more generic Parents' Day. Other promoters, in contrast, did not wish to combine the commemoration of fatherhood with motherhood and strove instead to establish a separate Father's Day on the heels of the first Mother's Day observance.

Jarvis viewed the Father's Day and Parents' Day celebrations as, on the whole, blatant schemes concocted by infringers to circumvent her legal copyright for commercial gain. And her assessment was not completely wrong. On a deeper level, however, she recognized the power of the rival celebrations to diminish both the significance of the Mother's Day observance and its traditional veneration of motherhood. Since the national calendar was already full of days honoring American fathers, such as the annual commemoration of George Washington as the country's greatest "Founding Father," she did not see the need to further overshadow the nation's only feminine tribute with yet another memorial father's day.[28] She expressed even less tolerance for the Parents' Day observance:

When a son or daughter cannot endure the name "mother" for a single day of the year it would seem there is something wrong. One day out of all the ages, and one day out of all the year to bear the name "mother" is surely not too much for her.[29]

As with her commercial adversaries, Jarvis fought rival holiday promoters and campaigns on multiple personal, legal, and ideological levels.

Chapters 4 and 5 examine how the American War Mothers, the American Mothers Committee of the Golden Rule Foundation, and the Maternity Center Association used Mother's Day in their educational, promotional, and fund-raising efforts and, by during so, altered the meaning of its celebration. Through independent holiday campaigns, the organizations dramatically transformed motherhood from a private issue into one demanding public attention by portraying mothers as the entitled recipients of the country's respect, concern, and generosity. Moreover, they provided a larger opportunity for maternal activism in their social relief and welfare movements. Even when the organizations failed to completely escape the trappings of the holiday's sentimental rhetoric—after all, tragic stories of suffering mothers effectively tugs on the proverbial heart and purse strings of potential supporters—their Mother's Day campaigns promoted a richer model of American motherhood, one inclusive of both maternal vulnerability and empowerment, and one deserving of domestic praise and public deference. In an odd twist of fate, the same organizations that Jarvis derisively referenced as "charity charlatans" and the "expectant mother racket" were modern representations of her mother's original Mothers' Day vision.

Jarvis denounced their charitable abuse of Mother's Day as a callous intrusion on the sanctity of the home and the absolute praise of motherhood. What the American War Mothers, the American Mothers Committee, and the Maternity Center Association considered a maternal tribute smacked only of pity to Jarvis, who designed Mother's Day to honor the supremacy of a mother's domestic influence and not exploit her weaknesses for public sympathy. Her accusations of ingratitude and charges of exploitation, regardless of her personal agenda, reveal the underlying conflict between the sentimental and postsentimental portrayal of the maternal role. Jarvis's veneration of motherhood clearly clashed with the modern organizations' persistent depictions of mothers in need, whether it be in need of housing, medical care, or maternal training. Her Mother's Day celebration, in comparison, never questioned a mother's intrinsic worth or natural ability to care for her children. If a mother was victimized at all, it was only by her children's failure to pay tribute to her indispensable role in their lives. "There is ONE DAY in the year we do not talk of POOR MOTHERS and ask charity for them," affirmed Jarvis. "Your Mother can never be poor with your love."[30] Even the poorest mother was entitled to unconditional commemoration on Mother's Day; she did not deserve to be pitied for her apparent misfortunes, reminded of her maternal failures, or made a public source of social policy debates.

The historical narrative concludes with the decline of Jarvis's Mother's Day movement in the 1940s. Four decades as the self-proclaimed defender of Mother's

Figure I.2. Grafton Historical Marker. Courtesy of the West Virginia and Regional History Collection, West Virginia University.

Day took a heavy financial, physical, and emotional toll on Anna Jarvis. Nonetheless, she never relinquished her proprietorship of the sentimental holiday, which, in her mind, included the right to end its celebration. "We would rather have 100 persons celebrate Mother's Day in a true spirit, and for its perpetuation on its established lines, than we would prefer to have 1000 persons abuse it," Jarvis vowed on behalf of her movement and its supporters. "To us the Mother's Day work has been carried to wonderful success. It will not be a loss if it is never again celebrated." But, she warned, "when Mother's Day stops we will stop it, and in our way, if we so choose."[31]

THE FOREMOTHERS AND FOREFATHER OF MOTHER'S DAY

O n May 8, 1914, the U.S. Congress officially designated the second Sunday in May as Mother's Day:

> Whereas the service rendered the United States by the American mother is the greatest source of the country's strength and inspiration; and whereas we honor ourselves and the mothers of America when we do anything to give emphasis to the home as the fountain head of the State; and whereas the American mother is doing so much for the home, the moral uplift and religion, hence so much for good government and humanity; therefore be it resolved by the Senate and House of Representatives of the United States of America in Congress assembled, that the President of the United States is hereby authorized and requested to issue a proclamation . . . . as a public expression of our love and reverence for the mothers of our country.[1]

The following day, President Woodrow Wilson asked the American people to observe the holiday by displaying the national flag as a "public expression of our love and reverence for the mothers of our country."[2] The congressional resolution and presidential proclamation formally recognized a day already being observed in every U.S. state, as well as several foreign countries, courtesy of Anna Jarvis and six years of dedication to her Mother's Day movement.[3] Yet the origins of the American observance predate both the U.S. Congress and Anna Jarvis. Although popular history credits Jarvis as the official founder of Mother's Day, having led the successful campaign for its national recognition, others before her promoted the idea and succeeded in endorsing its annual celebration. Altogether, four women and one man advanced the idea of a Mother's Day before Anna Jarvis began her movement in 1908: Ann Reeves Jarvis in 1858, Julia Ward Howe in 1873, Juliet Calhoun Blakeley in 1877, Mary Towels Sasseen in 1887, and Frank Hering in 1904.

Whether formally acknowledged by Anna Jarvis or not, they helped inspire the modern holiday, not just with their words but also through their actions.[4]

Though each of the five Mother's Day figures envisioned a day honoring the roles of mothers in American society, the meaning behind the observance varied among them. The definitive difference was their perspective of motherhood, derived from the experience of mothering or from the experience of being mothered. As mothers, Ann Reeves Jarvis, Julia Ward Howe, and Juliet Calhoun Blakeley recognized the ability (if not the moral obligation) of women to expand their maternal role into the public sphere. Their maternal experiences indelibly shaped their visions of a day designed to celebrate and facilitate the social activism of women as mothers. Sasseen and Hering, in comparison, knew only the view of motherhood from the perspective of the child-mother relationship and therefore celebrated mothers within their traditional and private familial role; they envisioned a day reserved to honor the woman who reared you, either through emotional tributes or benevolent service done in her name.

The conflicted ideological history of Mother's Day at the center of this study begins with the contrasting maternal tributes of the holiday's five earliest inspirations. Throughout the early twentieth century, groups endorsing the day's observance debated the significance of the dueling legacies, weighing the cultural merits of a Mothers' Day (possessive plural) that acknowledged the self-awareness and collective power of mothers versus a Mother's Day (possessive singular) that honored a motherhood rooted in domesticity as seen—not through the nuanced perspective of mothers but through the naiveté of those most dependent on a mother's care.

MOTHERS' DAY

Ann Reeves Jarvis, Julia Ward Howe, and Juliet Calhoun Blakeley may have never enjoyed an equal sense of fulfillment from their maternal roles or mothered their children in identical ways, yet each incorporated social activism into their maternal identities and proposed Mothers' Day celebrations. For Reeves Jarvis, Howe, and Blakeley, a Mothers' Day was meant to honor and facilitate what Molly Ladd-Taylor best defines as a woman's "mother-work."[5] To identify the maternal tasks of reproduction and caregiving as work is to challenge the image of motherhood as purely a private endeavor performed out of love and benefiting only the individual family.[6] The draping of motherhood in sentimentality, as epitomized by the possessive singular model of Mother's Day, typically obscures, even devalues the public dynamic of women's maternal identities.

In its original possessive plural form, however, Mothers' Day was invested with a social and political significance. It was a vehicle for public reform, not just for the private celebration of a mother's singular devotion to her family. "Mother-work" was inclusive, laboring for the needs of individual children and the needs of future generations.[7] Reeves Jarvis, Howe, and Blakeley exemplified the potential reach of women's mother-work through their own social activism, which in turn served as their inspiration for a Mothers' Day. They envisioned a holiday rooted in a model of social or organized motherhood, a day that genuinely venerated the public dynamic of the maternal identity by offering mothers an active role in their own tribute.

At first glance, it is hard to discern a model of social motherhood amid the nineteenth-century "Cult of True Womanhood," which reserved for women a role described by Carroll Smith-Rosenberg as "bounded by kitchen and nursery, overlaid with piety and purity, and crowned with subservience."[8] No other era imbued the home and motherhood with more sentiment than the Victorian era and its defense of gendered spheres of influence. Child-rearing literature, directed for the first time primarily to mothers, valorized the sanctity of the home and the redemptive power of maternal love over the corruptive individualism and materialism of the outside world.[9] A mother's love was "eternal," "unquenchable," and "irrepressible."[10] It was not just the physical care she provided that bonded her children to her but also her role as the affectionate moral educator entrusted to instill the emotional fortitude needed for her children to one day prosper as adults in an industrializing society. Authors of maternal advice assured every woman that to preside over a loving and pious home with such skill that her family would "rise up and call her blessed" was "nobler than to rule an empire."[11]

Historians continue to debate the full ramifications of such maternal rhetoric on the actual lives of women in the nineteenth century. The grandiose notions of women's undeniable maternal destinies or the indestructibility of a mother's love did not, inevitably, translate into real power outside the domestic sphere. The era's highly sentimentalized model of motherhood was not designed to provide women a new sense of empowerment; rather, "it grew out of an ideology whose objective was to vanquish power with love, to replace selfishness with affection and virtue," according to historian Jan Lewis. "Thus, the doctrine of maternal influence was bound to take away with the same hand that which it gave. Mothers could be powerful only if they renounced power, loved only if they renounced self."[12] Yet even historians who classify the Victorian cult of motherhood as a meager substitute for genuine political justice and economic equality have also acknowledged the ideology's potential power to bolster women's self-respect. It offered them, if only on the domestic scale, "an innate, unassailable, untestable claim to charismatic authority and prestige, a sanction for subjectivity and self-love," notes Ann Douglas.[13] While the majority of American women chose to exercise that new charismatic authority and prestige only within the home, others sought to extend it beyond its domestic boundaries and thereby justify their role in a range of benevolent organizations and reform movements.[14] In other words, Reeves Jarvis, Howe, and Blakeley offered a model of social motherhood that encompassed the full range of the maternal role, viewing mothers as essential to the social cohesion of both family and community.

ANN REEVES JARVIS
AND THE MOTHERS' DAY WORK CLUBS

Anna Jarvis was Ann Reeves Jarvis's tenth child. According to legend, a young Anna first heard the special plea for a Mothers' Day during a "Mothers of the Bible" Sunday school lesson taught by her mother in 1876. She listened as her mother closed the morning class with a simple prayer that allegedly "burned" forever within the daughter's heart and soul. "I hope and pray that someone, sometime, will found a memorial mothers day [original spelling] commemorating her for the matchless service she renders to humanity in every field of life," Ann Reeves Jarvis wistfully told her students. "She is entitled to it."[15] When Reeves Jarvis died in May 1905, Anna Jarvis repeated the prayer at the burial and promised, "by the Grace of God," to fulfill her mother's greatest wish.[16] But the Mother's Day that Anna Jarvis established in the twentieth century differed fundamentally from the Mothers' Day envisioned by her mother in the nineteenth century, as represented by Ann Reeves Jarvis's lifetime of social activism. Reeves Jarvis imagined a day honoring a mother's service to "humanity in every field of life" and not just the service directly rendered to her immediate family. She saw a Mothers' Day that included community service—mothers working with and for other mothers and the immediate needs of neighboring families. Her model of social motherhood embraced the power of a woman's mother-work to extend well beyond the home and the sentimental image of motherhood ultimately promoted by her daughter.

Of the range of maternal experiences that can define a woman's maternal identity, none can compare with the loss of a child. With an estimated 15 to 30 percent of infants dying before their first birthday throughout the nineteenth and early twentieth century, few mothers were spared the experience of losing a child; thus, many women's maternal consciousness was inescapably shaped by the incessant anxiety that all their children would not survive.[17] Sadly, maternal grief dominated the expanse of Ann Reeves Jarvis's childbearing years. Over the course of seventeen years, she bore thirteen children to see only four live to adulthood. She buried her firstborn child in 1853. He was eighteen months old; she was twenty-one. Twenty years later, Reeves Jarvis buried her ninth child, her beloved seven-year-old son, Thomas. At the age of seventy-three, it was Thomas's picture that hung above her death bed and the handmade sailor suit he wore to church before his death remained one of her most treasured possessions; the suit pocket still contained Thomas's completed Sunday school lesson.[18]

Anna Jarvis described her mother's mementoes as sacred relics that wove the "story of a Mother's love and heart aches." Hers was a life of "care, anxiety, illness, sorrow, and self-sacrifice," her daughter recalled. "It was a life of births and deaths."[19] By the time of her daughter Anna's birth in May of 1864, Reeves Jarvis had already buried seven children, ranging in age from three months to six years old. In a cruel twist of fate, she lost her oldest daughter, Annie Elizabeth, on the same December day in 1856 that she gave birth to daughter Columbia. Annie Elizabeth died one hour before her baby sister's birth, according to family lore. The timing at first convinced Reeves Jarvis that God gave her Columbia to replace the daughter He took from her. Tragically Columbia, nicknamed "Little Lummie," succumbed to measles in February 1862. Columbia's older sister Clara, younger brother Ralph, and baby sister Mary also perished that same year.[20] When Reeves Jarvis died of heart failure in 1905, Anna Jarvis again looked back on the overwhelming losses her mother faced and remarked, "A life of sorrow and shocks as that, it is no wonder her heart should have proved her weakest organ."[21]

When Anna Jarvis recalled her mother's life, she stressed the unremitting tragedies and the solace her mother sought in her faith. Had it not been for her mother's Christian grace, Jarvis believed her mother would have surely "fallen by the way side in her sore distress."[22] What the daughter failed to recognize was the strength her mother found amid the tragedies, a strength that propelled her to seek solace in public action as well as private faith. The Jarvises were not the only family in Taylor County, (West) Virginia to lose children to the measles, typhoid, and diphtheria epidemics that swept through the communities.[23] The entire region experienced appalling infant and child mortality rates, fueled mainly by the poor sanitary conditions that allowed sickness to thrive. Issues of sanitation and hygiene practices would remain a leading concern for Appalachian communities well into the twentieth century. In the early nineteenth century, however, the limited availability of professional physicians in the mountains exacerbated issues of public health, increasing a community's vulnerability to the spread of communicable diseases.[24]

In 1858, pregnant with her sixth child, Reeves Jarvis organized Mothers' Day Work Clubs to combat the devastating health crisis that threatened every area family. Her proactive response to the identified threat challenges the broad characterization of nineteenth-century mothers in general, and Appalachian mothers in particular, as either fatalistic in regards to infant mortality or isolated by their private anxieties and grief.[25] Instead of passively accepting the continual loss of children as God's will and out of a mother's control, Reeves Jarvis inspired collective action by appealing to a mother's duty to safeguard her family; she aspired to unite women in the intertwining and mutually beneficial work of familial and community service.[26] With her call to action, Reeves Jarvis's mothers' clubs joined the ranks of a nascent public health movement prevalent in the larger urban areas of the Northeast and Midwest. Like other early public health advocates, Reeves Jarvis viewed infant mortality as combatable through the improvement of sanitary conditions and parental education addressing the care and feeding of young children.[27] Historian Norman Kendall, a former Sunday school pupil of Reeves Jarvis, describes her as the most magnetic personality he has ever known, explaining her ability to motivate the mothers around her to embrace a larger civic role and assume responsibility over the environmental factors that determined the health of their children. "In her organized 'Mothers' Work,'" Kendall recalls, "she always sought to secure goodwill community cooperation in order to obtain the best things for a modern progressive neighborhood."[28]

The Mothers' Day Work Club members began by gathering in local churches to listen to area physicians lecture on the health concerns facing each community and learn recommendations on how best to address them. Reeves Jarvis relied heavily on the advice of her brother Dr. James Reeves, who was already known for his work with typhoid fever epidemics in northwestern Virginia. After the Civil War, Dr. Reeves became both a national and international leader in the field of public health. He was a founder and early president of the American Public Health Association, and his medical research earned him an invitation by Queen Victoria to discuss the public health crisis in England.[29] As a professionally trained physician, he was instrumental in helping individual clubs design and implement health programs tailored to address the immediate needs of their respective neighborhoods. Eventually, all the clubs, organized in five area towns, sponsored households requiring assistance in improving their overall health conditions. Through regular visits, club members educated families on the importance of proper sanitation, reinforced the necessity of boiling drinking water, and inspected all milk fed to children for contamination. They worked to ensure that families received proper medical care by providing medicine and even employing women to help care for homes where mothers before had silently suffered alone from tuberculosis. When necessary, they quarantined households to prevent a countywide epidemic.[30]

The limits of established medical professionals in the region allowed the Mothers' Day Work Clubs a vital degree of autonomy in implementing their community programs. Although they sought medical advice in their initial planning and execution, the clubs were not under the direct control of area physicians and, consequently, did not face the same obstacles experienced by regional women's clubs in the twentieth century. Nineteenth-century physicians were more inclined to view the assistance of area women's clubs as a necessity in safeguarding community health instead of a bothersome interference or direct threat to their medical authority.[31] The clubs' motto, "Mothers work—for Better Mothers, Better Homes, Better Children, Better Men and Women," reflected the women's heightened self-awareness and maternal confidence.[32]

When Virginia joined the Confederacy in the spring of 1861, the state's western counties became the first front of the Civil War. The Mothers' Day Work Clubs were suddenly caught in the middle of communities torn by competing allegiances. Reeves Jarvis struggled to hold them together, convincing the various club branches to remain neutral and united in their work in the face of the wavering loyalties of each town. Her efforts to rise above the turmoil made her a local hero. According to legend, she illustrated her bravery to lead a divided community in the earliest days of the conflict. It began with her refusal to support the division of the Methodist Episcopal Church into northern and southern branches. She advised the southern minister who sought her assistance in the endeavor that he would best serve God by taking the next train home and praying for "Peace on earth and goodwill among men."[33] In May of 1861, she alone offered a prayer over the body of Thornsbury Bailey Brown, the first Union soldier of the war to be killed by a Confederate soldier, when others refused to publicly express their sympathies for fear of retribution by Confederate loyalists. "There was one person in the audience who had the courage to do so and that was Mrs. Ann Reeves Jarvis," remembered Colonel James K Smith. "She came forward and with bowed head over that soldier made the most beautiful prayer I ever listened to."[34]

Along with the escalating hostilities and the growing presence of Union and Confederate regiments encamped throughout the region came the increased threat of disease. Typhoid and measles epidemics spread through the encampments of both armies. Out of desperation, Union Colonel George R. Latham approached Reeves Jarvis to enlist the services of her Mothers' Day Work Clubs, warning her that soldiers were dying faster than they could be buried. She agreed to help but with the stipulation that all soldiers would receive the women's assistance regardless of the color of their uniforms. "We are composed of both the Blue and the Gray," she reminded the colonel. The legend, unfortunately, fails to detail the clubs' assistance in combating the epidemics. The account boasts only of the collective "gratitude and highest recommendations" they received from the many soldiers they tended.[35] Lost are the stories of the women's personal wartime experiences as often is the case in the chronicles of war. We can only imagine the physical and emotional burden Reeves Jarvis shouldered. In the midst of the war and the club work that earned her legendary accolades, she carried three pregnancies and buried five children. The same epidemics that took the lives of soldiers most likely took the lives of five of her children.[36]

The celebrated work of the women to heal the wounds of the Civil War did not end with the war itself. Feelings of distrust and bitterness ran deep among the veterans returning home to live beside those they once considered the enemy. The passage of time had done little to ease underlying hostilities, and communities worried about potential violent consequences. In 1868, the Mothers' Day Work Clubs agreed to meet yet another challenge. Reeves Jarvis rallied the women to bring their families and all the area soldiers to a meeting at the Pruntytown Courthouse, then the county seat, in order to begin the public healing process. She warned them to refer to the meeting simply as a "Mothers' Friendship Day" in hopes that the respect men held for their mothers, if not for each other, would bring them to the courthouse steps. An immense crowd of veterans gathered on the designated day, many of them allegedly armed. Wary town officials pleaded with Reeves Jarvis to cancel her plans, but she refused, declaring defiantly that she was no coward. Shrewdly, she had directed the women to separate the men upon arrival as a means to disarm their collective animosity and deter any violence. She knew that the day's success depended on the men's ability to stand as individuals, not as soldiers, so they could perhaps view each other as they once did before the war.[37]

Despite their initial suspicions, the men remained to listen to Reeves Jarvis. She stood before them, flanked by two teenage girls dressed in blue and gray, and keenly explained the gathering's message of forgiveness and unity. Eventually, more women dressed alternately in blue and gray came forward to link hands with Reeves Jarvis, and they led the crowd in choruses of "Dixie" and "The Star-Spangled Banner." Reeves Jarvis appealed to the men to offer their neighbors a hand in reconciliation as they sang their last song, "Auld Lang Syne," in a final gesture of peace and absolution. Witnesses recalled veterans weeping and shaking hands by the first chorus.[38] "It was a truly wonderful sight to see the boys in blue and the boys in gray meet, shake hands and say, 'God bless you, neighbor; let us be friends again,'" remembered Hon. J. Hop Woods who had witness the event as a teenager.[39] Reeves Jarvis and her Mothers' Day Work Clubs received full credit for the successful reunion. The "remarkable event," according to a local minister, was clear proof of "what a good woman can do."[40]

The history of Ann Reeves Jarvis and her Mothers' Day Work Clubs do not appear in the larger Civil War chronicles nor in the more focused accounts of the war in western Virginia—beyond the local lore of Taylor County. Mother's Day historian Howard Wolfe popularized the details of Reeves Jarvis's Civil War heroism in his book *Behold Thy Mother: Mother's Day and the Mother's Day Church*, published in 1962. Wolfe was not the first historian to introduce the story of Reeves Jarvis's community leadership and the role played by her Mothers' Day Work Clubs, however. Norman Kendall's 1937 history, for instance, praised her maternal activism.[41] But Kendall's history does not provide the same level of detail offered by Wolfe's account twenty-five years later.[42] Wolfe further complicated the situation with his exclusion of historical citations for the often theatrical elements he added to his accounting of events ; thus many of the historic details surrounding Reeves Jarvis's wartime activism have never been independently confirmed. Wolfe's renditions of the Mothers' Day Work Clubs and the Mothers' Friendship Day event, nonetheless, are popularly repeated as fact.

Fortunately, additional Jarvis family histories and secondary sources help provide a historical context for the legends surrounding Ann Reeves Jarvis.[43] In the spring of 1861, Granville and Ann Reeves Jarvis lived in Webster, (West) Virginia, with their five surviving children. The couple moved to Webster in 1852 after two years of marriage so that Granville Jarvis could establish a mercantile business separate from his father's in the neighboring town of Philippi.[44] Now located four miles south of the strategic Baltimore and Ohio Railroad junction at Grafton, the Jarvis family was caught in the middle of the Union and Confederate forces battling to control the western counties of Virginia. Though over forty western counties of Virginia voted to reject the southern state's ordinance of secession, the region's communities were far from unanimous in their support for the Union, ultimately resulting in a civil war within a civil war.[45] By May of 1861, Union troops to the north in Grafton and Confederate troops fifteen miles south in Philippi encircled the Jarvis family in Webster. The two armies clashed at the Battle of Philippi on June 3, marking the first official land battle of the Civil War.[46] Amid such political and social turmoil, Reeves Jarvis certainly would have struggled to command the attention of the area women now consumed by the war raging around them. Yet in a conflict where soldiers were more likely to die of disease than in battle, any service provided by the Mothers' Day Work Clubs would have been invaluable to the surrounding communities. Widespread outbreaks of contagious diseases such as mumps, measles, scarlet fever, smallpox, and typhoid were well documented throughout every theater of the Civil War. Most of the dreadful epidemics were preventable, originating as they did from the poor diet and sanitary conditions of army life. These same camp epidemics spread recurrently throughout the local communities, taking the lives of civilians caught in the wake of war.[47]

It is also plausible that lingering animosities continued to disrupt the social stability of Taylor County communities in 1868, three years after General Lee's surrender at Appomattox. Reflective of the region's divided loyalties during the Civil War, West Virginia furnished the Union with twenty-five thousand troops and the Confederacy with fifteen thousand. By 1863, the Union garrisoned over thirty-five thousand soldiers in West Virginia and the surrounding Shenandoah Valley to guard the Baltimore and Ohio Railroad line from Confederate raids and guerrilla bands.[48] Many cities and towns changed hands several times throughout the conflict, leaving civilians with rival sympathies vulnerable to economic retribution and physical violence. Every county recorded atrocities inflicted on civilians by both Union and Confederate troops by the end of the war.[49] A certificate of exemption from the Union draft corroborates the Jarvis family's depiction as loyal Unionists; in 1864, forty-one year old Granville Jarvis avoided military service by hiring an eighteen-year-old substitute, Robert Turner, for a single year of enlistment.[50] There is no evidence to suggest that the Jarvis family experienced any specific wartime harassment as a result of their Union sympathies. If the legend is accurate, Reeves Jarvis obviously retained a significant degree of community respect to keep her mothers' clubs relatively intact and functional.

After the war, the family lived among neighbors rightfully fearful of violent outbreaks fanned by the underlining acrimony. John Shaffer's detailed Civil War study of bordering Barbour County reveals the attempts of various communities to physically threaten, arrest, or forcibly expel former southern sympathizers and returning Confederate soldiers. The use of sanctioned loyalty oaths to disenfranchise ex-Confederates, and ensure Republican Party control of state politics, also triggered rioting in several West Virginian counties in the early years of Reconstruction.[51] Such situations undoubtedly warranted a bold community attempt at reconciliation like that sought by Reeves Jarvis through her 1868 Mothers' Friendship Day.

In 1864, the Jarvis family moved to Grafton where Granville Jarvis added inn keeping and land speculation to his mercantile business. Anna Jarvis described her parents' fifty-two-year marriage as one rooted in a deep love but filled with financial and emotional strife. Granville Jarvis frequently "relaxed his hold on success," according to his daughter, forcing his wife, ten years his junior, to bear "bravely the vicissitudes which came to her as such."[52] He also did not share his wife's Methodist faith. Although the Jarvis children were reared in the Methodist church, their father remained a Baptist his entire life. As her mother's closest confidant, Anna Jarvis believed only she knew the moral sacrifice demanded of Reeves Jarvis to sustain her faith amid the years of family and community turmoil, no doubt complicated by her husband's divergent religious views, questionable business acumen, and suspected alcoholism.[53] "I thought so much about you children yesterday I could not keep from crying," confessed the Reeves Jarvis to her daughter. "Sometimes if your father could treat me with any kindness or consideration, I would not miss you so much."[54] Despite any problems within the marriage, there is no evidence to suggest that Granville Jarvis actively interfered with his wife's church work and community activism.

Reeves Jarvis maintained her strong community presence while living in Grafton. She was instrumental, for example, in the construction of the Andrews Methodist Episcopal Church; upon its completion in 1873, it stood as the largest church building in the state.[55] She remained active within the church's administration, serving as superintendent of the Primary Sunday School Department for twenty-five years.[56] There is no historical record of Reeves Jarvis's Mothers' Day Work Clubs after 1868, despite the fact that public health crises continued to plague the area throughout the late nineteenth century. The same year, young Thomas Jarvis died of diphtheria, Grafton experienced a smallpox epidemic that required rigid quarantine procedures to subdue. Between 1880 and 1881, sixty more area children reportedly perished from infectious diseases.[57] Yet Howard Wolfe insists that Jarvis "never ceased to stress the importance of delegating a wider and more important role for women, in political, civic, social, and religious concerns of the community."[58]

Contemporary accounts of Grafton residents offer only tiny hints of Reeves Jarvis's community activism beyond her association with her early mothers' clubs. She was a coveted public speaker, able to lecture on a variety of religious, literary, and health topics. Leonidas Johnson, the son of a former Virginia governor, remembered her lecture, "Value of Literature as a Source of Culture and Refinement," as his personal favorite. She never fully lost her interest in public health issues either, including lectures on the "Great Value of Hygiene for Women and Children" and the "Importance of Supervised Recreational Centers for Boys and Girls" to her repertoire of speaking engagements.[59] As a middle-class woman (at least socially if not always economically), her involvement in the self-culture club movement of the period was not unusual. Nonetheless, she obviously commanded an active role within the movement. As a public speaker who addressed audiences of both men and women, Reeves Jarvis transcended the typical feminine role of passive listener.[60]

Throughout her adult life, Reeves Jarvis channeled her mother-work into community activism, exemplifying the collective social power of motherhood and the public scope of the maternal influence. "Mothers must have faith in God, faith in the church, faith in their country, faith in their community, faith in their family," she believed, all of which rested first on mothers' "large faith in themselves."[61] To honor motherhood was to affirm the full potential of the maternal role both within the home and community. Her experiences as a mother drove her model of social motherhood and gave her original prayer for a memorial Mothers' Day a depth of meaning lost to her single daughter who shared neither her mother's perspective on motherhood nor the maternal experience that bore it. Yet it was the daughter who made the graveside promise to fulfill her mother's greatest wish for a national day of tribute to mothers and who became the holiday's official designer.

JULIA WARD HOWE AND MOTHERS' PEACE DAY

As the famed author of "The Battle Hymn of the Republic," successful poet and suffragist Julia Ward Howe is the most notable figure linked with nineteenth century celebrations of a Mothers' Day. As a public figure, her designation of June 2 as a Mothers' Day earned a small degree of national attention with its inaugural celebration in 1873.[62] Yet, it was not until well after the 1914 federal designation of the holiday that Howe became popularly associated with the day's history. Many early twentieth-century reference periodicals did not include Howe's role in the holiday's founding, only modern founder Anna Jarvis.[63] Later reference guides that did include Howe's role in the observance's history credit her with proposing the Fourth of July as Mother's Day.[64] Nevertheless, several American cities, including Boston, New York, Philadelphia, and Chicago, as well as the European cities of London, Geneva, and Rome, held a Mothers' Day service between 1873 and 1913 on June 2.[65]

It is doubtful that Ann Reeves Jarvis and Julia Ward Howe, although contemporaries, knew of their shared Mothers' Day visions or influenced each other in any meaningful way. It is possible, of course, that Ann Reeves Jarvis read of Julia Howe and the June observances of the holiday that she promoted by the 1870s. But the establishment of the Mothers' Day Work Clubs in the 1850s and the 1868 Mothers' Friendship Day event that inspired Reeves Jarvis's memorable Sunday school prayer predated Howe's similar endorsement. As for Howe, she may have finally learned of Reeves Jarvis's history through the promotion of the daughter's Mother's Day movement in the early twentieth century, although Anna Jarvis rarely referenced her mother's maternal activism. Yet Howe possessed at least a peripheral awareness of the growing popularity of the new Mother's Day designation. The Universal Peace Union (UPU) in Philadelphia, for example, faithfully celebrated Howe's holiday for forty years. She often sent a greeting of appreciation to their annual service. In June 1909, a year after Philadelphia hosted one of the first official observances of Anna Jarvis's Mother's Day, Howe thanked her "friends of Peace" for observing *her* maternal holiday that year, although another party had instituted their own Mother's Day celebration with "much public commendation."[66]

Even if unknown to each other, Julia Ward Howe and Ann Reeves Jarvis shared similar experiences as women, wives, and especially mothers.[67] As women, both were well versed in scripture and classic literature and were active in the nineteenth-century club movement. They also witnessed and responded in their own ways to the horror of the Civil War: Reeves Jarvis turned to her mothers' clubs, and Howe penned "The Battle Hymn of the Republic." As wives, the women overcame comparable trials—being married to men whose careers, petty jealousies, and social vices tested the strength of their marriages and the stability of their families. And as mothers, each felt the intense grief of losing a child to disease. Howe's beloved youngest son, three-year-old Sam, succumbed to diphtheria in 1863. So shaken by his death, she confessed to having recurring dreams where she felt Sam's arms around her neck and his kisses on her cheek. Reeves Jarvis, too, spoke of dreams, even premonitions, involving the death of her children.[68] Each woman's maternal experiences strengthened her commitment to a model of social motherhood and its moral directive to take responsibility for the suffering of others. While addressing a meeting of the Association for the Advancement of Women, Howe reminded the privileged mothers in attendance of their shared social duty:

> Mothers, who lay your infants in a silken bed, or gather around you your well grown children, have a care for the mothers whose infants pine in unwhole-some dens, whose children, if left to themselves, will learn only the road to the gallows. Rise to the entertainment of this true thought: "The evil which we could prevent and do not, is in that degree our fault."[69]

Howe considered war a preventable evil. According to her autobiography, the barbarity of the Franco-Prussian War forced on her the question of women's responsibility in combating the evils of war, especially through their roles as mothers. "Why do not the mothers of mankind interfere in these matters, to prevent the waste of that human life of which they alone bear and know the cost?" she asked.[70] Her vision of a peace movement led by women inspired her Mothers' Peace Day Proclamation in September 1870 and subsequent annual celebration of a Mothers' Day. She had hoped to send a worldwide plea to women and awaken them to their "sacred right" to protect the lives of those they bore and nurtured.[71] Her proclamation, officially titled "Appeal to Womanhood Throughout the World," was a direct call to action:

> Woman need no longer be made a party to proceedings which fill the globe with grief and horror. Despite the assumptions of physical force, the mother has a scared and commanding word to say to the sons who owe their lives to her suffering. That word shall now be heard, and answered as never before. Arise, then, Christian women of this day! Arise, all women who have hearts, whether your baptism be that of water or of tears! Say firmly: We will not have great questions decided by irrelevant agencies. . . . As men have often forsaken the plow and the anvil at the summons of war, let woman now leave all that may be left of home for a great and earnest day of council. Let them meet first, as women, to bewail and commemorate the dead. Let them then solemnly take council with each other as to the means whereby the great human family can live in peace.[72]

Although popularly known as the Mothers' Day Peace Proclamation, Howe initially had hoped to inspire the formation of a women's international peace association that would assemble annually for a world's congress of women on behalf of international peace.[73] There was no specific mention of a Mothers' Day celebration. Only after her plans for an international peace congress "melted away like a dream" two years later did Howe propose the more informal idea of a Mothers' Day as the "easiest and pleasantest method of initiating anything like a general concert and action among women."[74] She called women to gather once a year in the parlors, churches, or social halls to listen to sermons, present essays, sing hymns, or pray if they wished. Regardless of the style of observance, she insisted the theme of the day be how to bring God's peace on earth.[75] Howe selected the second of June for her celebration so that the pleasant weather and abundance of flowers would allow for open-air meetings and easy decorations.[76]

The celebration's primary relevancy within the national and international peace movement may explain Howe's absence from the early histories of the holiday's founding. Since mainly peace organizations in the northeast endorsed Howe's Mothers' Day at the turn of the twentieth century, the celebration did not possess the same degree of "public commendation" as Anna Jarvis's later Mother's Day movement. The UPU in Philadelphia led the way in promoting Howe's day. The organization commemorated

Figure 1.1. Julia Ward Howe, ca 1898. From the Julia Ward Howe Papers, 1857–1961. Schlesinger Library, Radcliffe Institute, Harvard University.

Mothers' Day until its collapse in 1913, recording the annual celebrations in its official magazines, *The Voice of Peace* (1872–1882) and *The Peacemaker and Court of Arbitration* (1882–1913). At its peak, the UPU enjoyed a membership of three to four thousand; however, only a core group of four hundred members actively participated in and financed the organization. At no time did subscribers to UPU publications exceed a total of six hundred and fifty. The UPU's call for the complete eradication of war that required, among others things, the abolishment of the American military and the replacement of the War Department with a Peace Department, alienated it from other organizations within the larger peace movement.[77] Nonetheless, the UPU enthusiastically embraced Howe's day and easily tailored the observance to its radical pacifist ideology. In the process, though, the group's view of maternal activism drifted away from Howe's original hope for mothers to eventually command an equal voice in the international arbitration of peace.

Howe did not completely abandon her dream of an international women's peace congress after the failure of her initial attempt, but she conceded that women were not as yet prepared to assume a larger role in the peace movement due to a lack of confidence in their perceived capabilities.[78] On the eve of her first Mothers' Day observance, she held high hopes in the day's potential power to bring women together and nurture within them the necessary first step of self-awareness and self-confidence and that her Mothers' Day could carry women from the collective expression of their maternal anger and fears in the individual parlors and churches to a collective social and political action on a national scale. She understood that "much of the power and many of the opportunities of women are wasted, because what they can do seems so small, when compared with the great operations which men are able to institute and carry out."[79] In response, she called on women to "emulate, not only the industry, but also the harmony of the ant, the bee, and the coral insect" so that their efforts that once seemed so "insignificant in isolation, may build up institutions and sentiments which shall bless and protect the whole human race."[80] She thus envisioned her maternal observance reaching far beyond the peace movement, ultimately building on established networks of female associations and broadening the scope of their ambitions. Howe encouraged celebrants to record a copy of the day's events to be sent to a central committee where they could be published and circulated in an annual report for participating groups. For the first few years, she attempted to serve as that central committee, compiling and publishing the annual report at her own expense.[81]

The UPU appeared ideally suited to spread Howe's holiday message of maternal empowerment with the peace movement. It was among a handful of peace organizations that allowed female members a role in its leadership and steadfastly endorsed the women's rights movement. Belva Lockward was a prominent female figure within the group, for example, and both Lucretia Mott and Susan B. Anthony attended early UPU meetings. Even Elizabeth Cady Stanton grudgingly admitted in 1888 that she should best become an advocate for peace since Alfred Love, UPU founder and president, was "so warm a friend to woman."[82] The UPU believed war went against women's natural (or maternal) instincts and hoped for the day that a voting female populate would legislate war out of existence. Subsequently, it was common for Mothers' Peace Day celebrations to include the issue of women's rights. Participants at the UPU's third annual commemoration reasserted the importance of women's equality for achieving universal peace: "We are convinced that the love in woman's nature should be more thoroughly incorporated with our institutions, in which she should possess equal rights and opportunities, and thus be better able to contribute to her influence to the establishment of Peace."[83]

During that same meeting in 1875, the UPU also defended its decision to broadly refer to the June 2 gathering as the "Woman's Peace Festival" instead of Mothers' Day, as the organization felt the original name did not fully explain the primary objective of the observance.[84] (Both names were used interchangeably during its years of observance.) Howe did not object to the "Woman's Peace Festival" designation, but she did challenge attempts to erase the gendered distinction of the day by changing the name to the Universal Peace Festival and eroding the custom of electing only female officers to oversee the proceedings.[85] She especially feared the lessening emphasis on the significance of maternal empowerment so central to her original vision:

This was *our new power*, that mother as such should make their protest in their own sacred character ... [Women] must oppose existing abuses in their own way. They are not fighters, they are not legislators, *but they are mothers*, actual or possible, and this great office invests them with its own honor and dignity ... and while I welcome the men as fellow-laborers, even on *our* Mothers' Day, I yet feel that the opportunity it offers to women to make their protest, as such, is precious and not to be neglected.[86]

Over the expanse of its Mothers' Peace Day celebrations, the UPU emphasized a mother's individual duty to rear her children according to pacifist principles as the best way to protest the abuses of war over that of joining larger collective actions. Alfred Love preached the necessity of reaching the unsaturated minds of children in order to create a society void of violence in any form. This essential training of future generations began at home by implementing pacifistic child-rearing techniques, such as refraining from physical punishment and prohibiting war-like toys and violent games such as football. The ban on violent content included any Mother Goose rhymes that praised or encouraged aggressive and destructive behavior.[87] Rare was the holiday celebration that did not locate the power of motherhood within the primary realm of the family by affirming the maternal duty of preserving the home and instilling within children the qualities required to ensure universal peace: "The influence of woman is closely connected with her moral and educational influence over the children whom she trains. Here lies her chief power, and our chief hope for the world's peace."[88]

Beginning in the 1880s, the published accounts of the June gatherings hinted at the event's focus shifting away from the celebration of the maternal role to the central significance of a mother's offspring. Promotional advertisements for upcoming observances highlighted the special entertainment and treats promised for children who attended, and occasionally the magazine relegated its discussion of the day to its "Children's Hour" section.[89] Gradually, the UPU replaced Howe's original appeal for women to take counsel with each other and assert their voice in the arbitration of international peace with the singular instruction for mothers to not raise sons to be "food for powder"—as went the popular phrase.[90]

Internal and external influences minimized the role of Howe's Mothers' Day within the peace movement by the turn of the twentieth century. In 1893, Belva Lockwood and May Wright Sewell secured the formation of the International Congress of Women, first promoted by Howe twenty years earlier. Unlike Howe's model of a separate nurturing space for women to strengthen their awareness and confidence, Lockwood and Sewell encouraged women to cooperate with men, certain that greater success would come by working together rather than apart.[91] Eventually, the congress even ignored the celebration of the gender-specific Mothers' Day or Woman's Peace Festival and endorsed the observance of Universal Peace Day in mid-May, commemorating the anniversary of the First Hague Peace Conference. In 1906, the UPU began sponsoring the celebration of Peace Day in the Philadelphia school system.[92]

The popularity of Anna Jarvis's Mother's Day movement in Philadelphia inevitably encroached on Howe's Mothers' Peace Day as well. The superintendent of schools, for example, incorporated the wearing of the white carnation emblem of the new Mother's Day into the children's 1909 Peace Day celebration.[93] That same year, the UPU noted the success of the new maternal observance and reprinted an article endorsing the day's sentimental celebration of motherhood. Fatefully, the UPU now endorsed a Mother's Day celebration that bore little relationship to the original intent of Howe's day. Instead of venerating maternal empowerment and public activism, the May 1909 issue of *The Peacemaker and Court of Arbitration* equated womanhood with motherhood, itself synonymous with self-denial and sacrifice. "Pity the childless woman," it avowed:

> A woman without children is a woman meaningless. All the wealth of her maternal instinct is lost to her, a want of her nature unsatisfied, the purpose of her creation unfulfilled. . . . Until a woman has become acquainted with the joy of self-abnegation that children give birth to she is a spring dried at its source. It is her cross and her splendor that she was brought into the world to make sacrifices, and when she makes them for her children she is achieving her destiny.[94]

The Mother's Day promoted by Anna Jarvis, and subsequently praised by the UPU, celebrated a mother's primary sacrifice to her own offspring and not her mother-work on behalf of an entire generation, or even a local community, of children.

Julia Ward Howe died the following fall. In an editorial dedicated to her memory, Alfred Love took comfort in the UPU's role in promoting Howe's Mothers' Peace Day. "It is gratifying to be able to say we never missed this meeting for peace," he admitted.[95] The meetings ended in 1913, however, with the death of Alfred Love and the disbanding of the Universal Peace Union.[96]

JULIET CALHOUN BLAKELEY, "ALBION'S ORIGINAL MOTHER OF MOTHER'S DAY"

Few Americans outside of Albion, Michigan, recognize Juliet Calhoun Blakeley's name. She has received the least amount of popular attention out of all the early promoters of the holiday, perhaps because the details of Blakeley's life and her role in the day's history are sketchy. Even Albion historians concede that the local legend rests on a thin foundation of historical evidence.[97] Neither Blakeley nor her admirers launched a concerted campaign to publicize her role unlike the other noted founders. Anna Jarvis cultivated the historical legacy of her mother in her establishment of the national holiday, feminist historians have recently championed Howe's Mothers' Peace Day, and both Mary Towles Sasseen and Frank Hering had dedicated supporters willing to sign legal affidavits to authenticate their involvement in the holiday's history. Blakeley, in comparison, remains more a local heroine. Nonetheless, on May 13, 1877, Blakeley allegedly led the first Mother's Day service outside of the peace movement in American history.

The legend begins with Albion's role in the temperance movement of the late nineteenth century. As the Midwest remained the "heartland of prohibitionism" throughout the century, temperance crusaders by the 1870s had gained a foothold in Albion.[98] Opponents of the movement, the saloonists, quickly mobilized to defeat the growing temperance campaign and, in a rather desperate move, they concocted a plan to discredit the movement by scandalizing its prominent local leaders. On the night of May 11, 1877, the group lured three sons of temperance leaders into a local establishment where they encouraged the boys to heavily imbibe in liquor. The next morning, when the streets were crowded with Saturday shoppers, the obviously intoxicated boys were turned loose to parade about the town. Albion residents gathered at the First Methodist Episcopal Church Sunday morning still stunned by the previous day's event. No one was more stunned then Reverend Myron Daughterty, father of one of the drunken boys, who was unable to lead the morning's service due to his grief over the affair. This was when Juliet Calhoun Blakeley rose to fill the empty pulpit and called on the rest of the mothers in attendance to join her in encouraging the congregation to support the cause of temperance. As mothers, the Albion women were concerned about the social unrest that brewed around them. And as mothers, they led the church service that morning—hence its designation as the first Mother's Day service. That evening a few saloonists, angered and clearly threatened by the morning events, vandalized the Blakeley home.[99]

Figure 1.2. Juliet Calhoun Blakeley. Courtesy of the Albion Historical Society, Albion, Michigan.

The events of May 13, 1877, moved Blakeley's sons, Charles and Moses, to commemorate the actions of their mother by designating the second Sunday in May as a day to honor her and then later all mothers. The exact day was chosen to honor Blakeley's birthday. Their careers as traveling salesmen enabled Charles and Moses Blakeley to carry the message of honoring mothers beyond Albion. They convinced friends and business associates to pay tribute to their own mothers each May with letters, candy, and the wearing of red and white carnations: red carnations in honor of mothers still living and white carnations in memory of those deceased. Locally, the First Methodist Episcopal Church honored Blakeley every second Sunday in May until her death in 1920.[100] The city of Albion did not publicly designate Blakeley as the holiday's original founder until after the national acceptance of Anna Jarvis's Mother's Day in the twentieth century. Before 1914, the First Methodist Episcopal Church addressed Blakeley simply as the "Mother of Albion Methodism," as she was the oldest female member of the congregation.[101] It is, therefore, unlikely that the church actually referred to the annual May service as "Mother's Day" as it paid homage to "a mother" as opposed to motherhood in general.

Blakeley certainly deserved the annual personal tribute. Leading the first Mother's Day service was only one of her contributions to community life in Albion. Like Ann Reeves Jarvis and Julia Ward Howe, she believed in the moral obligation of mothers to ameliorate social ills and was active in reform movements throughout her life. Before the Civil War, the Blakeley family joined the cause of abolition by harboring fugitive slaves in their home as part of the Underground Railroad. Blakeley's eldest son, barely in his teens at the time, recounted helping his parents transport slaves to the next safe stop on their way to freedom in Canada. He often drove the wagon that hid escaping slaves beneath an artificial coop and bags of grain. Years later, when the First Methodist Episcopal Church formally recognized Blakeley's participation in the abolition movement (possibly during a Mother's Day service), two young African American boys were given the honor of ceremoniously unfurling a large American flag as tribute to her.[102]

Of all the nineteenth-century reform movements, none encouraged women to carry their mother-work into public service like the crusade against the sale and consumption of alcohol. The movement's indictment of alcohol as a source of numerous social evils, and thus a direct threat to American families, appealed to the nineteenth-century maternal mandate to protect the sanctity of the home and the children who resided there.[103] Members of the Woman's Christian Temperance Union (WCTU), founded in 1873, specifically identified themselves as mothers united against a common enemy through their "organized mother love."[104] As the union insisted, "save the children today and you have saved the nation tomorrow."[105] The WCTU became one of the most prolific women's organizations in the country, nicely illustrating the ability of a model of social motherhood to empower female activism.[106] Unfortunately, Charles Blakeley's twentieth-century recollections of his mother's life remain the primary source of Albion's Mother's Day story, and his account does not offer details about his mother's deeper participation in the temperance movement.[107]

Yet, the presence of the Prohibition Party lends credence to the holiday legend's showcasing of women's active involvement in the Albion temperance crusade. Organized in 1869, the national party not only called for a constitutional amendment favoring prohibition, but it also endorsed woman's suffrage and worked closely with the WCTU. The party's inaugural meeting marked the first time in American history that women sat with men at a political convention, a tradition continued by the Prohibition Party.[108] In 1887, after a failed gubernatorial campaign, local resident Samuel Dickie served as Prohibition National Committee chairman for thirteen years, thus moving the party's national headquarters to Albion. Later, the town elected Dickie as mayor on the Prohibition ticket.[109]

Blakeley's last recorded act of community service was the offering of her home as the town's first hospital at the turn of the twentieth century. She was in her early eighties at the time; she went on to live another twenty years in her beloved Albion, dying at the age of 102.[110] It is currently unknown whether or not the message of maternal activism remained the central theme of the city's annual Mother's Day tribute to Blakeley or if it became an element of the wider Mother's Day observance her sons promoted on their sales routes. Regardless, Blakeley's original 1877 Mother's Day service captured the same spirit of organized motherhood as did Reeves Jarvis's

Mothers' Day Work Clubs and Howe's Mothers' Peace Day. Unfortunately, even Albion residents are beginning to forget Blakeley's role in the history of Mother's Day, as illustrated by her neglected gravesite. "Few know of Juliet's historical significance as they pass by the marker," regrets local historian Frank Passic: "Perhaps some civic-minded group in town could take it upon themselves this [Mother's Day] week to see that a nice flower urn and a bouquet could be placed in the Blakeley family plot and annually maintained, in memory of this pioneer woman: Juliet Calhoun Blakeley, Albion's original Mother of Mother's Day.[111]

A SHARED SENTIMENTAL VISION

By promoting a sentimental celebration of Mother's Day, Mary Towles Sasseen and Frank Hering earned enough notoriety to be drawn into a direct confrontation with Anna Jarvis. Mitigating factors explain their popular recognition over that of the three earlier Mothers' Day promoters. Both Sasseen and Hering secured loyal followers to attest to their original commemoration of Mother's Day; these followers embarked on vocal campaigns to ensure that proper credit was given to their individual founder and not to Anna Jarvis. After Sasseen's death in 1906, the city leaders of Henderson, Kentucky, campaigned for her posthumous share of the glory. Hering carried the endorsement of two influential national organizations, the Fraternal Order of Eagles and the American War Mothers (AWM), and, unlike Sasseen, was personally able and very willing to publicly defend his title as the "Father of Mothers' Day." (The possessive plural spelling is original to Hering's promoted title.)

The sentimental similarities of Sasseen and Hering's proposed observances to Anna Jarvis's popular Mother's Day movement complicated the early twentieth-century debate over the identity of the holiday's true founder. Each endorsed a day designed for children of all ages to pay tribute to a mother's love and essential familial service. In their possessive singular vision of the day, children celebrated motherhood, not mothers. Their desire that school children lead literary tributes to mothers or defend the welfare of the home on mothers' behalf diminished the status of mothers as active agents of community reform. As with Reeves Jarvis, Howe, and Blakeley, Sasseen and Hering's vision of Mother's Day also reflected their personal relationship to motherhood. Neither of them ever became parents and therefore maintained as adults the "outsider" perspective of motherhood, a perspective they shared with Anna Jarvis.[112]

Subsequently, their Mother's Day celebrations focused on the private dynamic of motherhood, sentimentalizing the most visible and valued aspects of the maternal role as viewed by children, namely, the emotional and physical care a mother renders in a child's rearing.

For the residents of Henderson, Kentucky, local schoolteacher Mary Towles Sasseen was the original authoress of Mother's Day, and many were even willing to legally testify to that affect throughout the early twentieth century. In 1912, the popularity of Anna Jarvis's Mother's Day prompted historian J. J. Glenn to write a letter to the editor of the *Henderson Gleaner* to remind Kentuckians of their original founder. As a personal friend and colleague of Sasseen, he could not allow her role in the day's history to be forgotten:

> That Miss Sasseen was the author of "Mother's Day" I have no more doubt than I have that she once taught school in Henderson or that she once lived in that city. In the celebration of "Mother's Day" I hope that the name of the author of that beautiful custom shall have the reverence that is due one whose life is spent in noble works and noble thoughts.[113]

Members of Sasseen's family, most notably a cousin named Miss Susan S. Towles, soon joined Glenn's efforts to memorialize the Kentucky native. As the reference librarian at the Henderson Public library, Towles was in the position to historically verify her cousin's authorship of Mother's Day and was willing to provide "hundreds of affidavits" for anyone demanding unequivocal evidence that Mary Towles Sasseen designed and promoted the first celebration of Mother's Day in 1887.[114]

The story begins in the summer of 1886 when Sasseen sat next to J. J. Glenn, then a school superintendent of a neighboring county, on the train to Louisville to attend a meeting of the Kentucky Education Association. The pair shortly struck

Figure 1.3. Mary Towles Sasseen. Henderson County Public Library, Henderson, Kentucky.

up a conversation, and Sasseen spoke of her school system's plans to implement annual reception days as a means to strengthen the relationship between teachers and parents. She detailed her own idea of reserving a day for children to pay homage to their mothers by inviting them to school to enjoy a morning of songs, recitations, and other tributes. Glenn immediately agreed to help Sasseen introduce her idea at the association's meeting where, he claimed, it received unanimous approval. (It is unknown, however, exactly how many Kentucky school systems actually observed a Mother's Day after the association's initial endorsement.) Sasseen returned home from the meeting that summer confident in her plans, and the following spring, Henderson pupils celebrated their very first Mother's Day.[115]

In 1887, Sasseen was an independent twenty-four-year-old woman serving as the principal of the Intermediate Department of the Center Street School.[116] Despite the fulfillment gained from her teaching career, to Sasseen, nothing compared to the ultimate fulfillment achieved through the power and influence of a woman's maternal role within the home:

> Home! That name touches every fiber of the soul. Nothing but death can break
> its spell, and dearer than home is the mother who presides over it. . . . The
> home being the center of all civilization, the mother is the star around which
> all civilization resolves. Strengthen the ties of affection around that mother
> and home, and you strengthen the nation composed of the individual homes.
> I think of all [the] words I could say to mothers and for mothers, the first and
> last words be, Have A Home! Have A Home of Your Own! This would be the
> Alpha and Omega of my advice.[117]

When she offered the "Alpha and Omega" of her advice to mothers, she was not speaking from direct experience. Sasseen did not become a mother until late in life, and then only briefly, as she died in childbirth.[118] But she was a deeply devoted daughter. According to a former pupil and neighbor, "mother-love burned to almost divine height" in Miss Sasseen.[119] Knowing no other perspective of motherhood than that of a dedicated and dutiful daughter, she envisioned Mother's Day as a day of tribute from a daughter to her mother. The fundamental sentiment drove her campaign to establish the celebration in the schools of Kentucky and then in schools across the country. "Indeed, she constantly expressed the hope that this day would be observed over the entire world," swore fellow teacher Julia Alves Clore in a 1923 affidavit.[120]

In 1893, Sasseen published and copyrighted the instructional guide, *Mother's Day Celebration*, to encourage other school systems to adopt the annual observance. For forty cents a copy, she supplied a compilation of songs, readings, recitations, compositions and poems, "chosen more for the sentiment expressed than for rhythm," that were adaptable for school programs at all grade levels.[121] In the booklet's introduction, she admitted her fear that the youth of today lacked the same degree of reverence as past generations, being "apt to accept too much as a matter of course that boon of mother-love and care."[122] As a teacher, therefore, she hoped that Mother's Day and the exercises offered in her instructional guide would awakening within children a deeper appreciation of their mothers and thereby strengthen the family bonds, "making them more beautiful and tender."[123] As a daughter, Sasseen lovingly dedicated the booklet to her mother, in the hope that schools would annually designate her birthday, April 20, as Mother's Day.

Throughout the 1890s, Sasseen sought endorsements for her Mother's Day celebration outside of Henderson, taking every opportunity to press upon fellow educators the value of the annual observance in strengthening the bond between children and parents, as well as improving the relationship between parents and the schools. She allegedly traveled throughout the country lecturing on the subject of Mother's Day, and promoting her instructional booklet, but the extent and success of her nationwide campaign remains unclear.[124] Sasseen's name was popularly associated with the celebration of Mother's Day within her home state, at least, if nowhere else. Her campaign for Kentucky superintendent of public instruction in 1899, for example, showcased her authorship of Mother's Day as a notable qualification for the position. And even though Sasseen lost the election, her campaign nevertheless generated additional publicity for the day's observance. In 1901, Sasseen retired from teaching due to health problems and moved to Florida, where she married Judge William Marshall Wilson in 1904. Sasseen finally realized her dream of presiding over a home of her own, only to tragically die in childbirth eighteen months later. Her Mother's Day movement came to an untimely end as well. The Kentucky General Assembly did not acknowledge Sasseen as the "originator of the idea of the celebration of Mother's Day" until 1926.[125]

According to the Fraternal Order of Eagles (F.O.E.), it was Brother Frank E. Hering, and not the Kentucky schoolteacher, who was mainly responsible for the origination of Mother's Day. Affixed to the front of the English Opera House in Indianapolis, Indiana, is a bronze plaque commemorating Hering's first public plea for a nationwide observance of Mother's Day on February 7, 1904. The F.O.E. unveiled the plaque in 1931. The previous year, twenty-three men and women, who had personally witnessed Hering's noble plea, legally swore to the historic event and proudly signed an ornamented scroll, officially certifying that Hering's endorsement of a Mother's Day preceded Anna Jarvis's by four years. Although the F.O.E. eventually acknowledged Anna Jarvis's contribution to the day's celebrations, such as selecting the second Sunday in May as the official date and personally lobbying for a Congressional resolution, they maintained that the leadership of Hering and the national efforts of their fraternal order paved the way for Mother's Day federal designation in 1914.[126]

According to F.O.E. accounts, Frank Hering conceived of the idea of a Mother's Day while on faculty at the University of Notre Dame in the 1890s. During his tenure as head football coach and a professor of history and economics, Hering learned of a fellow faculty member who required his students to write a note to their mothers once a month; the professor reserved the time in class for the monthly "mother's day" and provided the penny postcards to each student.[127] The idea of reserving a day to honor mothers stayed with Hering, as the story goes, and his involvement with the F.O.E. offered him the perfect opportunity to endorse the national recognition of a Mother's Day. His historic plea at the Eagles' memorial service in Indianapolis in 1904 was just the beginning of his long career of sponsoring Mother's Day celebrations and advancing himself as the day's official founder.

Hering's two terms as Grand Worthy President of the F.O.E. (1909–1910, 1911–1912) and position as the first editor of *Eagle Magazine* enabled him to successfully promote Mother's Day observances in Eagle lodges (otherwise known as aeries) across the country in the years preceding the Mother's Day designation as a national holiday. Hering did not assign a specific date to the observance when he first proposed the idea beyond his preference for holding Mother's Day services on a Sunday. This initially allowed individual aeries a degree of flexibility in planning their celebrations.[128] During his second term as Grand Worthy President in 1912, however, Hering urged the Grand Aerie to officially adopt the second Sunday in May as the appointed date of the Eagle's Mother's Day observance to correspond (or perhaps better compete) with Anna Jarvis's already nationwide movement. Yet an early F.O.E. history identified only two states, Texas (1912) and Nebraska (1913), as ever specifically referencing their May observances as a "Eagles' Mother's Day." No doubt meant as evidence of Hering's and the Eagle's successful national influence, the historical account conveniently failed to acknowledge the parallel observances of Anna Jarvis's Mother's Day in the remaining states, as well as in several foreign countries by 1912.[129]

In the various accounts of the Mother's Day campaigns, it was not unusual for Hering and the F.O.E. to employ the holiday's possessive plural spelling, either intentionally or unintentionally. By the 1930s, Hering considered his originally intended use of the possessive plural spelling as clear evidence of his primary founding of the day and that he in no way violated any copyright claims Anna Jarvis asserted over the holiday's possessive singular spelling. (This left Anna Jarvis to contend how one could always key the imposters of Mother's Day through the use of the false spelling.)[130] Meanwhile, other early twentieth-century F.O.E. publications continued to use the possessive singular spelling.

Despite the apparent confusion in the spelling of the day, Hering and the Eagles indelibly grounded the significance of the maternal role within the domestic sphere, thereby celebrating a socially passive motherhood best reflective of the possessive singular Mother's Day legacy. Beginning in the 1920s, Hering directly tied Mother's Day commemorations to the Eagles' social service campaigns, believing that the best means in which to honor mothers was to protect the welfare and integrity of the home on their behalf. "The observance of Mother's Day is only a part of a logical and consistent social welfare philosophy that for a quarter of a century has been intelligently followed by the Eagles," explained Hering. "The fundamental proposition is: 'Protect the home.' . . . And the rallying cry is, 'For Mother and Home.'"[131]

The Fraternal Order of Eagles was a vocal advocate in the national campaigns for the social assistance of impoverished and elderly mothers in the early decades

Figure 1.4. English's Opera House in Indianapolis, Indiana. This was the location of Hering's call for the establishment of a Mother's Day in 1904. Courtesy of the Indiana Historical Society.

of the twentieth century. In 1911, an Eagle member sponsored and drafted the country's first mothers' pension legislation. The Missouri law authorized government assistance to widowed mothers to help in the care of dependent children and prevent their placement into foster homes or orphanages.[132] As chairman of the Eagles' Old Age Pension Commission, Hering made the passage of such legislation a primary objective of the organization's social and political programs in the 1920s and 1930s. President Franklin Roosevelt later expressed his appreciation for Hering's undaunted support of Social Security Act of 1935 by officially presenting him and the Eagles with a pen used to sign the legislation into law.[133]

The F.O.E.'s Mother's Day observance was an ideal vehicle in which to promote its political agenda, and Hering's political career, as social crusades in the name of motherhood:

Where others might be content to pay only lip service to motherhood, Eagles worked to protect living mothers from want. They saw around them destitute widows who didn't know where they could get the next meal for their hungry brood. *For them*, the Eagles worked to get mothers' pensions. They saw the aged women—whose children were gone or themselves pinched by poverty—facing the poorhouse. *For their sake*, Eagles worked long and hard to win old age pensions. . . . Consistently the Order has done more than voice an ideal. The F.O.E. has *acted on it*.[134]

In this scenario, the F.O.E. was the noble guardian of the home and the active agent of reform and social justice, not mothers. The Eagles' Mother's Day campaigns, with its rhetoric of maternal victimization and passivity, inverted the *Mothers' Day* message of maternal empowerment first offered by Reeves Jarvis, Howe, and Blakeley by asking society to serve and protect mothers and not the other way around.

ANNA JARVIS, THE ORIGINAL MOTHER'S DAY FOUNDER

Although Anna Jarvis's twentieth-century sentimental Mother's Day observance was plainly in accordance with Mary Towles Sasseen and Frank E. Hering's holiday model, she refused to acknowledge their legitimate role in the day's history. Instead, she spent years passionately asserting the original or distinctive nature of her Mother's Day movement, thereby disavowing Sasseen and Hering's dueling claims. Jarvis challenged the state of Kentucky's stake to her Mother's Day on the grounds that no one outside of the town of Henderson had ever heard of Sasseen. "If she failed thru an attempt of some quarter century ago," Jarvis argued, then "that is all the more reason why [Kentucky] should now recognize her complete disconnection with any work that may have succeeded."[135]

Between the two sentimental predecessors, however, Hering proved to be the stronger adversary. In the midst of the growing rivalry, another national organization entered into the dispute to defend the F.O.E. and Hering's original connection to the day's founding. The American War Mothers (AWM), an association created for mothers of World War I veterans, led an independent investigation of the Mother's Day controversy to confirm the holiday's true origins. As an "interested and dispassionate observer of the fray," the AWM presented evidence proving that Hering spoke publicly on the issue of a Mother's Day on at least ten different occasions in as many cities between 1904 and 1906, with the first Mother's Day plea in Indianapolis being four years "before anyone else had even thought of it."[136] In accordance with the evidence, the patriotic organization officially crowned Hering the "Father of Mothers' Day" in 1925 and invited him to speak at its inaugural Mother's Day service at the Tomb of the Unknown Soldier.[137] Four years later, the AWM publicly reaffirmed their commitment to Hering's founder status with the presentation of the Victory Medal, the organization's highest honor; he was the first civilian to receive the coveted distinction.[138] Hering graciously accepted the accolades he received from the war mothers and remained a close ally of theirs throughout the early twentieth century as the organization fought its own battles with Jarvis over the ownership of Mother's Day (detailed in chapter 4). Invariably, the AWM's endorsement of Hering further cemented his and the Eagles' association with the holiday's national observance.

Nonetheless, Anna Jarvis stressed the simple fact that Sasseen and Hering visibly failed where she had clearly triumphed. Despite their promotion of a Mother's Day celebration, neither of them successfully obtained the holiday's national and international designation. Consequently, they did not deserve to share in the glory of her Mother's Day movement. "Success belongs to those that accomplish," she insisted, "not to persons of a mere 'idea' of some variety never put into practice."[139] Her title as the legitimate founder of Mother's Day, coupled with the notoriety she both craved and earned through her holiday movement, eventually formed the core of her identity and measure of self-worth. As a means of self-preservation, Jarvis aggressively pursued any potential threat to her founder status, both past and present. Her single-minded devotion inevitably motivated her systematic dismantling of the Mothers' Day legacy established by the holiday's foremothers and the recasting of the commemoration's nineteenth-century origins as she built her twentieth-century Mother's Day movement.

ANNA JARVIS AND HER MOTHER'S DAY MOVEMENT

A strong parallel exists between the historical celebration of Thanksgiving and Mother's Day. Both are floating holidays in that each falls on a specific calendar day rather than a fixed date, the first on the last Thursday in November and the latter on the second Sunday in May. Although Protestant churches played a role in spreading the observance of Thanksgiving and Mother's Day, each was established primarily as a secular holiday with a president serving as a "midwife" in the national designation. Abraham Lincoln issued the first presidential proclamation in recognition of Thanksgiving in 1863. Woodrow Wilson issued the first Mother's Day Proclamation in 1914. Since then, presidents and governors have followed the annual tradition of issuing their own holiday proclamations, officially acknowledging each day's role in the national calendar.

In addition, the popular acceptance of both Thanksgiving and Mother's Day corresponded with a period of political and social instability in American history. Subsequently, advocates espoused the holidays as potential remedies to problems of national concerns. By reserving a day in honor of the country's Pilgrim forefathers, promoters hoped the holiday would inspire national unity after the Civil War. Thanksgiving also offered an old-fashioned holiday to a country experiencing rapid industrialization, urbanization, and increased immigration. By the turn of the twentieth century, changes in the nation's economic, political, and social landscape brought a new visibility to the public roles of women. The growing college enrollment of women, the agitation of a vocal women's rights movement, the attraction of women to social reform movements, the noticeable increase in divorce rates, and the decrease in birth rates among white middle-class women ushered in debates over the dire fate of the American family and, by extension, the country's future. With its national veneration of motherhood, Mother's Day promised to remind women of their primary roles as mothers and their unequaled influence within the home.[1]

Of all the similarities between Thanksgiving and Mother's Day, however, it is the vision and dedication of two women—Sarah Josepha Hale and Anna Jarvis—that truly link the holiday celebrations. Hale was not the first person to endorse the observance of a Thanksgiving in commemoration of the Pilgrims and their legendary feast. New England had celebrated a Thanksgiving or a Forefathers' Day since the end of the eighteenth century. When New Englanders migrated west in the early nineteenth century, they carried their Thanksgiving traditions with them, introducing the observance to a new population of Americans. By 1843, three years before Hale began her national campaign, the transplanted Yankees had convinced governors of seven Midwestern states to issue Thanksgiving proclamations.[2] Similarly, Anna Jarvis was not the first to promote the observance of a Mother's Day, as discussed in chapter 1.

Yet Hale and Jarvis promoted their sentimental celebrations of Thanksgiving and Mother's Day more effectively than anyone before them. After launching her Thanksgiving campaign in 1846, Hale wrote letters to national and state politicians seeking endorsements. And as the editor of the popular women's magazine, *Godey's Magazine and Lady's Book*, she wrote annual editorials, espousing the cultural meaning and value of the celebration to readers across the country wishing to join in the holiday festivities. By the end of the 1850s, thirty of the thirty-three existing states, plus two territories and the District of Columbia, observed Hale's Thanksgiving.[3] Sixty years later, Jarvis embarked on her own aggressive letter campaign, urging governors to issue Mother's Day proclamations and appealing to prominent economic, political, and religious figures for their national sponsorship; within three years, every state observed Jarvis's Mother's Day. Instead of a national magazine, Jarvis worked through her Mother's Day International Association to guide the holiday's annual observance for over thirty years.[4]

Through their holiday movements, Hale and Jarvis successfully domesticated and sentimentalized the observance of Thanksgiving and Mother's Day. Hale transformed the traditionally masculine observance of a Forefathers' Day, marked by strident public speeches and tributes, into a feminized national celebration of the home and family reunions.[5] Jarvis replaced a Mothers' Day observance originally designed as a vehicle for social action with a Mother's Day that exclusively venerated a mother's private service to her family. Although rarely linked in the popular imagination or in academic scholarship, Jarvis's twentieth-century observance of Mother's Day commemorated the same Victorian ideals of domesticity and femininity that Hale's celebration of Thanksgiving popularized. Like Hale, Jarvis depicted her holiday as ultimately a "Home Day." It was to be a "day of family reunions; of home-comings; a day of gladness and of beautiful memories; a day of uplift and inspiration."[6] And through their sentimental domestic tributes, Hale and Jarvis honored women as the moral guardians of the home and reaffirmed their power within the traditional private sphere. "Should not the women of America have one festival in whose rejoicings they can fully participate?" asked Hale in 1876.[7] Jarvis echoed Hale's concern in 1908: "Is it not time that a more magnanimous reward be given these splendid women and that they, too, be praised and honored one special day of the whole year?"[8]

Anna Jarvis's self-proclaimed Mother's Day movement evolved over forty years as she dedicated her life to fulfilling a daughter's interpretation of a mother's wishful prayer. "I hope and pray that someone, sometime, will found a memorial mothers' day,"

41

her mother, Ann Reeves Jarvis, had implored, a day designed to commemorate mothers for the service they render to "humanity in every field of life."[9] After her mother's death, Jarvis swore to answer the maternal prayer she had first heard as a young girl. "I felt I wanted to carry on in some way her 'mother spirit'" Jarvis explained, "and I thought this could best be done by having a day set apart to honor all mothers, and through them all womanhood."[10]

Yet Jarvis transformed her mother's legacy of celebrating the full potential of women's maternal roles and identities. Ann Reeves Jarvis believed the universality of women's maternal experiences could unite them in community activism, hence her wish of a day praising women for their influence in every field of life, not just their singular devotion to the private family. As a single woman living with a bachelor brother and dependent younger sister, however, Anna Jarvis did not share her mother's perspective on motherhood, instead viewing motherhood solely through the eyes of a daughter. She described Mother's Day as a day for all to become children again and show gratitude to the mother who had tenderly watched over them.[11]

To ensure the holiday's national observance, as well as protect the ideological integrity of its domestic celebration, Jarvis defended her movement from anyone and anything she perceived as a threat, beginning with those who promoted the maternal holiday before her, including her mother. "We celebrate Mother's Day as sons and

Figure 2.1. Anna Jarvis, 1912. Courtesy of the International Mother's Day Shrine, Grafton, West Virginia.

42

daughters and not as mothers," she emphasized. "Therefore, perhaps, it is right that a mother's daughter should be its leader."[12] Jarvis soon discovered, however, that it was easier to posthumously reinvent her mother's legacy to fit the designs of her movement than it was to fight the "Mother's Day Imposters"—the label she gave those claiming original authorship of the holiday. Moreover, Jarvis struggled to protect the integrity of her holiday observance from the public taint and intrusion of commercialization, an experience that Hale and her Thanksgiving celebration did not share. Because the tradition of presenting gifts never became a formal part of the Thanksgiving observance, the commercial forces shaping its celebration have remained relatively hidden or secondary to its sentimental message. Until recently, the official commercial countdown to Christmas did not begin until the day after Thanksgiving.[13]

Ultimately, the story of Anna Jarvis and her Mother's Day movement is a story of a woman completely invested in the idea of reserving one day out of the year to honor mothers' familial duties and the belief that only she could successfully design and lead such a commemorative day:

When I thought of the daily work that countless millions of mothers are performing every day, quietly, unobtrusively, unheralded, I felt that a day set apart in their honor would be the most inspiring and expressive recognition that could be afforded them. I wanted this day dedicated to mothers as women, citizens, patriots, to stand for the family, and to represent its unity. You can't imagine how hard it was to make people take it seriously at first, or how rude and scoffing they were. But I was determined and my plan was simple.[14]

Jarvis certainly possessed the determination to lead the national and international observance of Mother's Day. Yet the plan was not as simple as she implied.

HER MOTHER'S LEGACY

It is impossible to fully understand Jarvis's Mother's Day movement separate from her relationship with her mother, both before and after Ann Reeves Jarvis's death. The few scholars who have seriously explored the history of Mother's Day have attempted to reconstruct Jarvis's relationship with her mother based on the few personal correspondences, written recollections, and local lore that still exist. But they all remark on Jarvis's ambiguous relationship with her mother.[15] While sifting through the limited historical evidence, however, it is often difficult to separate legend from fact and extremely tempting to resort to psychological speculation to uncover the motives that drove Jarvis's holiday movement.

Previous studies portray Ann Reeves Jarvis as a controlling figure who purposely restrained her daughter's ambitions to fit the boundaries of proper womanhood; they locate the psychological roots of Jarvis's Mother's Day movement in either her need to seek an outlet for the ambitions once denied to her or as a form of "pathological mourning" in order to reconcile her grief with the resentment she felt toward her mother while she was alive.[16] Those authors' interpretation of the women's turbulent relationship meshes well with the common perception of female intergenerational conflict associated with the late nineteenth and early twentieth centuries. The fear of a growing generational gap was a popular theme in the periodical literature during that era. Articles warned of acrimonious mother-daughter relationships caused by an apparent incompatibility between an older generation of matrons and a younger generation of women coming to age at the turn of the early twentieth century. This generation of New Women, as they were popularly known, willingly challenged the traditional restraints of womanhood that had helped to contain their mothers' generation in the domestic sphere. As best described by *Good Housekeeping* in 1915, "The mothers of these modern girls are very much like hens that have hatched out ducks."[17]

Yet Jarvis never publicly spoke of a mother-daughter relationship based on anything but absolute love and mutual esteem. Mother's Day, after all, was meant to serve as a testimony of a child's love for her mother and the home she governed. Jarvis based the celebratory design of Mother's Day on personal tributes to her mother as evidence of her love. She chose the second Sunday in May to mark the anniversary of her mother's death and selected her mother's favorite flower, the white carnation, as the day's official emblem. Her request for children to visit or write letters home on Mother's Day reflected the significance she placed on her correspondence with her mother during the years they lived apart.

In the absence of definitive evidence, the local lore detailing a mother-daughter relationship fraught with personal conflict has earned unfair significance over the years. Like the scholarly accounts, hometown legend portrays Ann Reeves Jarvis as a woman of great presence who ruled the lives of her children—particularly Anna, her only daughter to survive to adulthood and live independently.[18] The youngest Jarvis child and last surviving daughter, Elsinore Lillian, struggled with impaired vision due to a childhood bout with scarlet fever. She remained semi-dependent on her mother and then sister's care her entire life. Unlike the two daughters, the surviving Jarvis sons, Josiah and Claude, left West Virginia early to strike out on their own and build successful careers. Josiah Jarvis went on to practice medicine in Baltimore, while Claude Jarvis established a thriving taxicab service in Philadelphia.[19]

The popular assumption is that Anna Jarvis longed to follow the same independent path as her brothers, free from the continual interference of their mother. And without hard evidence to the contrary, the interpretation of *escape* to explain the Jarvises move from West Virginia is as plausible as any other. The only photograph of the Jarvis matriarch hanging in the International Mother's Day Shrine certainly corroborates the image of her as a formidable maternal figure, for there is little hint of maternal indulgence in the focused grey eyes. But local gossip and one fading black and white photograph is not overpowering proof of the allegedly troubled mother-daughter relationship that drove Jarvis's Mother's Day movement. Besides, the historical evidence better lends itself to an interpretation of the women's relationship as one of mutual support and companionship, therefore making it harder to simply categorize Jarvis as an adult daughter unable to psychologically break free from an irrational attachment to her mother.

Born on May 1, 1864, in Webster, West Virginia, Anna Jarvis was one of the thirteen children of Granville and Ann Reeves Jarvis. As noted in the introduction, seven of Jarvis's siblings died before she was even born. When Anna Jarvis was four year old, her mother bore the last child, Ellen, who was probably stillborn. The only sibling death that Jarvis vividly remembered was the death of her younger brother, Thomas, who died when she was nine years old. "His death robbed my mother's life of something she never regained," she recalled.[20] Considering the repeated tragedies experienced by Ann Reeves Jarvis, a deep attachment to her four surviving adult children that bordered on direct interference in their lives was certainly an understandable, if not a typical, reaction of a mother who witnessed the death of nine of her children. Few nineteenth-century mothers were spared the experience of losing a child in an era where as many as one out of four infants died before their first birthday. Thus countless mother-child relationships were unavoidably shaped by a mother's incessant anxiety over the health and welfare of her children. Nor was it uncommon in the nineteenth century for a mother to rely heavily on the eldest unmarried daughter for companionship.[21] "She always seemed so proud of you all. But Anna I think she found a great deal of comfort in you," reminisced a family friend. "Of course, as the eldest daughter you were a companion for her. She seemed to depend on you."[22]

Historical research reveals that conflict and animosity did not plague mother-daughter relationships as much as popular women's magazines and advice literature stressed at the time. Maternal support of daughter's choices appeared the norm, even when daughters chose the newly available, but still untraditional, life paths. Indeed, daughters who succeeded in leading particularly untraditional lives may have owed their success to their mother's encouragement.[23] In relation to the Jarvis women, Ann Reeves Jarvis encouraged her daughter to attend college, an opportunity that she regretted never having as a young woman.[24] In 1883, Jarvis earned a diploma of completion for two years of course work at the Augusta Female Seminary in Staunton, Virginia, now Mary Baldwin College. Classmates remembered Jarvis as a "quiet, studious girl," well-liked by students and teachers for her pleasant disposition and "kind word for everyone."[25] After graduation, Jarvis worked as a teacher in the Grafton public school system and joined her mother as an active member of their church.[26]

A handful of letters between both the Jarvis women and Reeves Jarvis's brother Dr. James Edmund Reeves suggests that Anna Jarvis's close relationship with her mother may have impeded her willingness to leave home. In 1891, Reeves urged his niece to resign her teaching position and come live with him in his adoptive home of Chattanooga, Tennessee: "If you commence school then you are 'done for' for sometime. Don't think of such timid steps but come right along."[27] He promised her that, in Chattanooga, a city ten times the size of Grafton, a single woman of twenty-seven years of age could surely begin a life "worth living."[28] Reeves suspected the unwelcomed influence of his sister when his niece hesitated to take his advice. He warned Reeves

Jarvis not to interfere further with her daughter's decision. "So, please dry up," he scolded, "and send your child off on her triumphal march with gladness, not in sorrow, and tears."[29] Jarvis finally heeded her uncle's advice and moved to Chattanooga, taking a position as a bank teller that he helped secure for her.[30]

The next year, however, she left her uncle's home to live with her bachelor brother in Philadelphia. If Jarvis's mother had disapproved of her life in Chattanooga and prodded her to return home, it is apparent that she resisted such prodding. The only evidence indicating differently is a letter to Jarvis concerning a possible teaching position at West Virginia Conference Seminary, present-day West Virginia Wesleyan College in Buckhannon, West Virginia. For whatever reason, Jarvis declined the offer to instruct classes in English and shorthand at the seminary.[31] The fact that she originally inquired about a possible position reveals her contemplation of returning home, yet even if she had accepted the seminary's offer, she would have still lived and worked over thirty miles away from her parents in Grafton.

Jarvis decided instead to remain in Philadelphia with her brother, where she found outlets for her ambition and obvious talents. After a brief stint as the personal stenographer for the president of the Edison Electric Light Company, Jarvis took a position with the Fidelity Mutual Life Insurance Company, eventually becoming the firm's first female literary and advertising editor.[32] She also became a shareholder in her brother's successful business, the Quaker City Cab Company, and an active participant in her brother's business affairs. In 1914, a Philadelphia newspaper credited her for settling a labor dispute between management, namely her brother, and 140 striking drivers.[33]

Despite Jarvis's refusal to return to West Virginia, the surviving correspondence between mother and daughter while separated offer little evidence of a tumultuous relationship. Nothing indicates that Reeves Jarvis disapproved of her daughter's independent life. On the contrary, she must have admired her daughter's courage and accomplishments, since the youngest daughter, Lillian, accused her sister of monopolizing their mother's affection even while miles away. "Over the past five years it has been your aim to render me virtually Motherless," she swore. "Nothing would help me and encourage me like your death, for you are the one barrier between me and all I deserve."[34] Lillian's emotional outbursts, especially after Jarvis assumed financial control of their ailing father's business assets, strengthened the bond between Jarvis and her mother. Jarvis was well aware of her sister's jealousy and attempted to counsel her mother on how to deal with Lillian's hurt feelings. "Of course she is mad at me, I have the burden of all the disagreeable things you all want me to assume," she wrote.[35] Nonetheless, she urged her mother to show her youngest child more attention and affection: "For I know you have love enough for us all to have our share." She reminded her mother to give her "the best of all and everything, for she has so little and can enjoy so much less."[36] This frequent correspondence between mother and daughter served as an important physical and emotional connection for them. It is not surprising that the call to write home or visit your mother on Mother's Day became a cornerstone of Jarvis's observance.[37]

Figure 2.2. Although identified as Anna Jarvis by the Library of Congress, this may actually be a photograph of her younger sister Lillian Jarvis. Francis Benjamin Johnston Portrait Collection, Library of Congress Prints and Photographs Division, Washington, DC.

When their father died in 1902, both Jarvis and her brother begged their mother to join them in Philadelphia. They feared for her health, believing that she had sacrificed her vitality in the last years caring for her ailing husband (who reportedly became a bad-tempered alcoholic) and the emotionally volatile Lillian. Relatives wrote to Jarvis fearing that Lillian's erratic behavior was contributing to her mother's failing health. "Anna, surely that poor child is crazy, nothing could make me think otherwise," they cautioned.[38] In 1904, when heart problems finally prevented the Jarvis matriarch from remaining on her own with Lillian, both women moved into Claude Jarvis's Philadelphia home.

Finally Reeves Jarvis was united with at least three of her surviving children, and her eldest daughter spent the next year diligently caring for her mother as her health steadily declined. Jarvis tried to attend to her mother's every need by building a sun parlor for her convalescence and bringing her mother's doctor from Grafton to confirm or reject the diagnoses of the ten different Philadelphia doctors she had consulted. Jarvis resented the physicians' arrogant dismissal of her mother's approaching death as inevitable due to her age and questioned the qualifications of the entire profession. "It is with bitterest feelings that I revert to my dear Mother's medical attention," she wrote just after her mother's passing. "I do not know the cause of her death, one said her heart, another her liver, another her kidneys, another her stomach, others that she was old enough to die. Of course she died of heart failure, as everyone does," she retorted.[39] After weeks of anxious vigils, her mother died on May 9, 1905, surrounded by all the Jarvis children, including eldest brother Josiah from Baltimore. Reeves

Figure 2.3. Top: Andrews Methodist Episcopal Church, location of the first official Mother's Day service on the morning of May 10, 1908.
Bottom: An interior picture of the church's second floor sanctuary taken in the 1950s.
Courtesy of the International Mother's Day Shrine, Grafton, West Virginia.

Figure 2.4. Ann Reeves Jarvis, taken shortly before her death.
Courtesy of the International Mother's Day Shrine, Grafton, West Virginia.

Jarvis's last words, however, were reserved only for her eldest daughter in a promise to one day return for her. Jarvis described her mother's room at the moment of her death as filled with a "light like a heavenly benediction on a blessed soul, that the angels did come and bear away their 'snow wings' this precious mother to her 'immortal home.'"[40]

ANNA JARVIS'S MOTHER'S DAY MOVEMENT

Although Jarvis claimed to have begun her plans for Mother's Day on the very day of her mother's funeral, her formal efforts to promote a national observance of Mother's Day did not begin until two years later.[41] She appealed to any local and national figure she believed could advance her plans, including such influential men as John Wanamaker, Henry J. Heinz, Edward Bok, Theodore Roosevelt, and even Mark Twain. Her initial letter-writing campaign paid off in a relatively short time, for, on May 10, 1908, Jarvis organized the first official observance of Mother's Day at her mother's home church in Grafton. Although Jarvis did not personally attend the morning service, she sent a telegram detailing to the congregation of the Andrew Methodist Episcopal Church the purpose of the day as one to "revive the dormant love and filial

49

gratitude we owe to those who gave us birth" and donated five hundred white carnations for those in attendance. That afternoon in Philadelphia, fifteen thousand people attended a Mother's Day service at the Wanamaker Store Auditorium courtesy of John Wanamaker, who relinquished his usual advertising space in the local newspapers to publicize the event. Jarvis spoke for over an hour at the afternoon service. So moved by her oration, the acclaimed minister Russell Conwell reportedly told Jarvis that her Mother's Day idea would honor her "through the ages to come."[42]

Jarvis renewed her letter-writing campaign every spring to remind politicians, church groups, and national fraternal organizations to reserve the second Sunday in May in honor of Mother's Day. The enormity of this task led her to resign her position at Fidelity Mutual and incorporate the Mother's Day International Association (MDIA) in 1912 to serve as a driving force behind the day's national and international recognition. Her efforts included an extended promotional tour of Western Europe in the summer of 1913, concluding with an invitation to address the World's Sunday School Association in Zurich, Switzerland, about her movement work. After countless letters, trips to Washington, and years of patience, Jarvis sat proudly in the gallery to witness the U.S. Congress's formal designation of Mother's Day in 1914. The next day, she graciously accepted the pen President Woodrow Wilson used to sign the first Presidential Mother's Day Proclamation.[43]

The official placement of Mother's Day on the national calendar did not mark the end of Jarvis's movement. She welcomed the designation as a public validation of the previous seven years of dedication, but she never considered Mother's Day as residing in the public domain like other calendar holidays and therefore refused to relinquish leadership of the day's observance. She tenaciously held to her view of Mother's Day, especially its sentimental design, as her special province, down to the smallest detail.

Figure 2.5. Mother's Day Seal. Courtesy of LancasterHistory.org, Lancaster, Pennsylvania.

ANNA JARVIS AND HER MOTHER'S DAY MOVEMENT

Religious and community organizers could request fully prepared and authorized Mother's Day programs from the MDIA, for example, complete with selected readings, recommended music, and a personal message from Jarvis. The association also published circulars reaffirming the true meaning of the Mother's Day observance:

> Mother's Day is a personal, family and memorial day. Mother's Day is a celebration for sons and daughters. It is a thank-offering of them and the nation, for the blessing of good homes. . . . This is not a celebration of maudlin sentiment. It is one of practical benefit and patriotism, emphasizing the home as the highest inspiration of our individual and national lives.[44]

Jarvis regularly evoked her mother's memory throughout the years of her Mother's Day movement. She contended that she carried on her work, not on account of her great love for her mother, but on the account of her mother's great love for her, which naturally added to the day's emotional appeal.[45] Ultimately, the heart of Jarvis's Mother's Day design was the portrayal of her mother as the quintessential symbol of true motherhood and womanhood, a woman who found true fulfillment only in motherhood and carved her identity from her selfless dedication and service to her family, friends, and faith. Based on that maternal portrait, Jarvis saw no better memorial than a day that promised a mother her greatest joy—praise from "the loved ones she lived for."[46]

Yet when Jarvis memorialized her mother, she minimized the complexity of Ann Reeves Jarvis's maternal identity and Mothers' Day legacy. Details of her mother's life and work that fell outside Anna Jarvis's idealized perspective of motherhood were conveniently excluded from the historical account of Mother's Day, especially Reeves Jarvis's advocacy of a mother-centered, not child-centered, commemoration. Regardless of Anna Jarvis's insistence that Mother's Day was more than just maudlin sentiment, she rarely portrayed the power of motherhood beyond its traditional boundaries and thus never directly acknowledged the aspects of her mother's life that celebrated a public facet of motherhood.

Jarvis's exclusion of her mother's maternal activism may not have reflected disapproval of Reeves Jarvis's community service nor resentment of her controlling influence in Jarvis's life, as proposed by other historians. In many ways, it appears this exclusion was Jarvis's conscious effort to secure her credibility, as a childless woman, to lead a movement designed to celebrate motherhood. During this same era, many challenged the ability of single female social reformers to council mothers on how best to rear their children. Political opponents of progressive reforms targeting issues of child care, for example, frequently cited precisely the young women's lack of maternal experience as clear evidence of their poor qualifications, insisting that the true wisdom gained from actual motherhood could not be replicated in the pages of a college textbook.[47]

Jarvis no doubt recognized a similar dilemma in the public perception of a single woman extolling a Mothers' Day celebration based on a model of empowered motherhood or a shared maternal craft. In contrast, however, all women shared the experience of once being mothered. "The common possession of the living world is a mother," clarified Jarvis. "Everyone has—or has had—a mother."[48] The restriction of Reeves Jarvis's maternal persona to the prescribed boundaries of a domestic ideal, therefore, best suited the daughter's design of a familial or child-centered celebration of motherhood and furthered reinforced the legitimacy of her holiday leadership.

The recurring themes of duty, love, faith, sacrifice, and domestic harmony that composed the sentimental model of motherhood subsequently provided the framework for Jarvis's reconfiguration of her mother's life and Mothers' Day legacy. Buried among Jarvis's surviving papers is an unfinished biography titled, "Recollections of Ann M. Jarvis 1833–1905." Jarvis began the account of her mother's life and final illness in response to the many condolences sent to the family in the wake of the funeral.[49] For unknown reasons, she never completed the biography, and it remained among her personal documents until her own death. Clearly evident within this manuscript's several drafts and hand-scribbled rewrites is the sentimental maternal model that later served as the foundation of Jarvis's Mother's Day celebration. It is, in essence, the original draft of her mother's simplified maternal persona and the first step in dismantling her Mothers' Day legacy.

From the beginning, Jarvis admitted that she was not an objective biographer of her mother's life. She confessed to having loved her mother more than anyone else and believed Reeves Jarvis represented only the "highest type of motherhood." [50] She exposed her skewed perspective throughout the entire narrative by refusing to portray her mother as anything other than the embodiment of the highest type of motherhood. [51] Even in the description of her mother as a child, Jarvis identified her as a "little mother" who helped raise her younger siblings:

The discipline that came with these responsibilities, that made duty her every-day religion, that made her life one of loving sacrifice and self-denial to all around her, and deprived her of so many of the pleasures that came to each and all of the other members of her family, [molded] her life throughout its course. She joyfully pushed aside self-gratification, and gave comfort to those around her.[52]

Jarvis repeated this imagery continually throughout the manuscript. Her mother was a "mother to all," "a living sacrifice," a woman who "filled her place in the household with remarkable tenacity of purpose" and whose "immeasurable" maternal love was surpassed only by the Christian faith that sustained her through the tragic loss of nine children. Ultimately, Jarvis believed it was lives like her mother's that made the "earth wholesome."[53]

The Ann Reeves Jarvis of historical record is barely recognizable beneath the mawkish prose. Without explanation, the daughter chose to exclude her mother's famous public roles in the Mothers' Day Work Clubs and Mothers' Friendship Day and instead relegate her activism to the proper feminine confines of only home and church. Her mother's life reads as if it ended at the front door of the Jarvis home or on the steps of the Andrews Methodist Episcopal Church. Jarvis praised her mother's refined and discriminating tastes, her love of reading, and her "faculty of absorbing it in a way that she could apply it."[54] Yet she failed to expound on her mother's public invitations to lecture on subjects ranging from classical literature to children's health issues, often before substantial crowds of both men and women.[55] She described her mother's pride in preventing the Civil War from dividing her church into northern and southern denominations but not of the gratification she must have felt after reuniting an entire community through her Mothers' Friendship Day.[56] Jarvis also ignored her mother's direct involvement in the governing of church business, beginning with its construction, to highlight instead only her twenty-five years of dedication as a Sunday school teacher and the love for her students.[57] Jarvis effectively minimized her mother's active roles by either disregarding evidence of her assertive leadership or by reducing them to passive acts of sacrifice and service to others. "In her struggle to get nearer to God," she explained, "she got nearer to her fellow beings."[58]

Only once in the narrative did Jarvis hint at her mother's ambivalent feelings about her life of familial and maternal sacrifices. At the age of seventy-two, Reeves Jarvis shared with her daughter one of her biggest disappointments as they passed the Girls Normal School of Philadelphia while out for a drive one morning. "How I wish I could go to college," she ruminated. "I would make such good use of my opportunities."[59] Jarvis recorded her reaction to the tangible regret and sincerity that mingled within her mother's words:

If this mother of [13] children, whose ambitions had been restrained by the ties of motherhood, homemaking, years of frail health, and finally the financial losses of my father, had led a selfish life and devoted herself as faithfully to her own pleasures and ambitions as she did to those of others her achievements would [no] doubtedly have brought her unusual honors, and made her a woman of prominence in her undertakings.[60]

It is a startling revelation on Jarvis's part, considering her selective exclusion of the very acts that earned her mother unusual honors during her life and made her a woman of prominence within her local community. Jarvis never explicitly address the irony within her own life either; as an independent single woman, she found an outlet for her own ambitions by personally rejecting the maternal role she strove to commemorate with her Mother's Day movement. Yet just as quickly as she acknowledged her mother's regret over opportunities lost, she dismissed them as irrelevant, writing, "But after all, was she not a masterpiece as a Mother and gentlewoman. We who love her best as life's most precious gift to us, think so?"[61]

Jarvis always gave her mother formal credit as the original inspiration for Mother's Day, referencing that legendary 1876 Sunday school prayer, but she never discussed her mother in ways that contradicted the image first cultivated in that unfinished biography. Her deception is difficult to detect by those unfamiliar with the original history of Ann Reeves Jarvis or her Mothers' Day vision. Although too young to have directly witnessed the events that made her mother a respected public figure, Jarvis most certainly heard the stories while growing up. She was twelve years old when she first overheard her mother's wish for a maternal memorial day and, by then, would have known the famed events in her mother's life that inspired her Mothers' Day model. In contrast, Jarvis's childhood friend Norman Kendall eagerly recorded the stories of Reeves Jarvis's courageous acts of community leadership in his published history of Mother's Day.[62] What Jarvis failed to grasp as a girl, she also failed to understand as a woman of forty-one, her age when her mother died.

Since no one challenged the daughter's exclusion of her mother's activist legacy, she was not forced to deny it directly on record. A closer examination of her MDIA letterhead, however, reveals provocative evidence of the false persona Jarvis created for her mother. For over thirty years, Jarvis purposely confused her name with her mother's, referring to her mother in all public documents as Mrs. Anna M. Jarvis. When questioned about the frequent confusions with their names, Jarvis swore she was named for her mother, and they both shared the same middle initial. But to distinguish between them, she often dropped the "M" from her full name in public records as she felt it properly belonged to her mother—"its original owner thru baptism."[63] Her mother's middle name was Marie, but her birth name definitely was not Anna—as her daughter clearly knew. According to birth records and the family bible, Anna Jarvis did not have a legal middle name and was most likely named for the older sister who died in 1854. Still, the true motivation behind Jarvis's deliberate distortion of their names is open to speculation.

Jarvis family biographer and Mother's Day historian Howard Wolfe viewed the name confusion as the daughter's selfless attempt to make her mother famous posthumously. Due to the difficulty in carrying forth a movement in someone else's name, she claimed the identical name as her mother in order to share the credit for founding Mother's Day.[64] That certainly is a noble and even reasonable justification

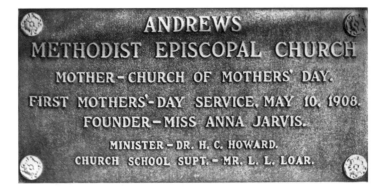

Figure 2.6. Commemorative plaque at the entrance of the Andrews Methodist Episcopal Church added in the 1960s. Ironically, note the possessive plural spelling of the holiday. Courtesy of the West Virginia and Regional History Collection, West Virginia University.

for her actions. In the beginning, perhaps, that may have been Jarvis's true intention, as she often declared. But if it was Jarvis's honest goal to equally share the spotlight as Mother's Day founder, why not reveal her mother's full history and Mothers' Day vision? Why not embrace those who celebrated motherhood in the same spirit originally intended by her mother? On the contrary, she repackaged Ann Reeves Jarvis's legacy, name and all, and condemned all attempts to use the possessive plural spelling of Mother's Day. "You may always key the impostor thru this false spelling," she warned.[65]

Ultimately, Wolfe's defense of Jarvis is too generous when one considers the full scope of her career as Mother's Day advocate and self-proclaimed defender. It was not unusual for Jarvis's public speeches and personal statements to be riddled with contradictions that revealed how acutely she invested her personal identity in her Mother's Day movement, as opposed to just her mother's memory. Her address to the Associated Fraternities of America in 1911 is a classic example. At the start of the address, she reminded her audience that she was not the true founder of the Mother's Day, but her own good mother, whose death placed the work in her hands. It was never her intention to be connected with the day, she insisted. She even confessed to not judging herself worthy of leading such a movement: "I felt its guiding spirit should be a good, true, noble "motherly" mother—such as you feel you had and I feel I had."[66] That being said, she quickly went on the defensive to set straight the critics who denied the potency of her movement work and all she had sacrificed to make Mother's Day a global observance. Had it not been for her "untiring, earnest personal effort," she knew there would be no annual celebration. And not only did her efforts risk her own economic stability as "limited funds melt away like snow under a summer sun," but she risked her very reputation:

Previous to this time, Mother's Day had been ridiculed all over the country. I was pointed out as, "the woman with the 'silly' or 'foolish' Mother's Day idea," and "friends" did not hesitate to make it a personal humiliation and misfortune. So acute was this criticism and antagonism, that, had Mother's Day been a failure, it would always have been a personal stigma.[67]

Despite her humble acknowledgment of her mother, there was no doubt whom she believed really deserved recognition for the day's existence and respect for all she risked in the name of honoring American mothers.

Throughout the twentieth century, Jarvis gained national and international notoriety as the holiday's founder. Never was she identified (positively or negatively) in the press without "The Founder of Mother's Day" title, regardless of the article's relevance to the actual holiday. The *Washington Post*'s inclusion of her on its list of "Women Who Count" in 1911 certainly offered her the praise she relished, and the *Chicago Tribune* gushed of her commanding skill as a public promoter of Mother's Day in 1913, specifically her ability to touch the "most tender spots in the hearts" of any audience.[68] In 1924, Boston Mayor James Curley presented Jarvis with a gold key to the city and a grand public reception. The *Boston Globe* described the events as "the greatest honor the city ever accorded a woman personal achievement."[69] And rare was the governor who did not praise her accomplishments in the traditional Mother's Day Proclamation that she personally requested from each state every year.[70]

Her determination to retain control over the observance rose along with her celebrity-style recognition and publicity. After dedicating years to promote the observance of Mother's Day and defend the day's integrity from exploitation in any guise, Jarvis was not about to share the notoriety with any other alleged Mother's Day founder, aside from the crafted persona of her mother. Beginning in the 1920s, however, national organizations and individual promoters contested Jarvis's designation as the sole authoress of the maternal holiday. She adamantly denied the validity of such claims, denouncing them as "far-fetched," "foreign," "pitiful," "a brazen deception," even outright "evil." [71] *She* was the only legitimate founder of Mother's Day and no other alleged Mother's Day observances compared to hers—any more than "a brick would compare with the Washington Monument."[72]

THE MOTHER'S DAY IMPOSTERS

In reality, none of the other claimants vying for the title of Mother's Day founder were real threats to Jarvis's official status. Despite their vocal supporters or regional appeal, neither Julia Ward Howe, Juliet Calhoun Blakeley, Mary Towles Sasseen, nor Frank Hering succeeded as Jarvis did in the creation of a national holiday. Their initial contributions, though significant to the ideological history of Mother's Day, played only a minor role in the holiday's popularity at the turn of the twentieth century.

Moreover, the organizations that campaigned for the proper recognition of rival founders were willing, at first, to concede to their figure's secondary status in the day's history and formally acknowledge the significant accomplishment of Jarvis's national movement. In sponsoring their hometown founder, Mary Towles Sasseen, Henderson, Kentucky, residents were simply asking for a portion of the holiday's spotlight, not its full focus; therefore Jarvis's blatant disdain genuinely perplexed them. "Her peculiarly abusive language in many letters to our Chamber of Commerce and to us, has diminished our enthusiasm for her personally," admitted the secretary of the Henderson County Historical Society. "However, we shall always be glad to aid in the establishment of the facts of what she did—so much in the name of true history."[73] Jarvis was not as gracious in her treatment of rival Mother's Day founders or their supporters. Through her Mother's Day International Association, she declared any person questioning her status as the legitimate founder of Mother's Day as legally liable as if they questioned the legitimacy of her parentage. [74]

The motives behind Jarvis's firm stance against rival claims were more complex than they initially appeared to her contemporary and modern critics. Jarvis's ego

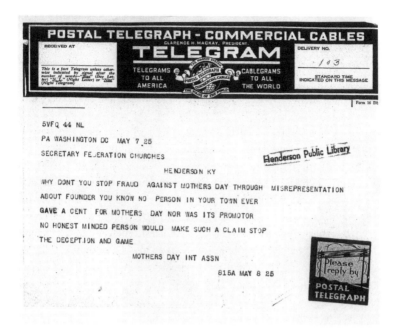

Figure 2.7. Telegram sent to the Chamber of Commerce of Henderson, Kentucky, from the Mother's Day International Association in 1925. Henderson County Public Library, Henderson, Kentucky.

certainly explains her actions in part. Over the course of her Mother's Day movement, she undeniably invested the whole of her personal and professional identity in her status as official founder. Yet the ferocity and audacity of her public accusations and behavior has historically overshadowed the validity of her allegations against her holiday rivals. Her shocking actions and stinging indictments made it easy to dismiss her claims as the baseless ranting of an eccentric or bitter spinster. Nonetheless, Jarvis viewed the attacks against her founder status as more than personal affronts; they violated her legal copyrights and represented an ideological threat to the day's celebratory message of home and valorized mother-love—one untainted by commercial profit or political aggrandizement.

Her unending battle against the holiday's commercialization, especially with the floral industry, made her suspicious of hidden agendas. This was evident in her automatic questioning of the sincerity of those requesting a share of the credit for the holiday's existence. She identified greed, personal ambition, and "trying to get something for nothing" as the primary incentives of all those attempting to possess the day.[75] The timing of the rival claims, emerging as they did after Mother's Day's designation as a national holiday, further fueled her suspicions. She clearly grasped their eagerness to share in the glory without having contributed to the years of work and financial commitment originally required to establish the day's national and international recognition:

It is not supposed in these materialistic times that even the most obtuse person would expect volunteer, unpaid workers, such as Mother's Day leaders have always been, to turn over the fruits of their labor, the benefits of their sacrifices, their arduous work, their expenditures to some person or firm or concern that has never shown interest in, nor loyalty for the Mother's Day Cause, nor sustained it in any manner. Who knows of such a case?[76]

That was not an irrational contention for a woman who deemed Mother's Day the legal and intellectual property of her incorporated association.

Jarvis typically defended her status as sole founder through the simple omission or denial of historical evidence, public denunciation of individual claimants, and threats of legal action. In her primary struggle to maintain complete legal and ideological control over the day, she failed (or refused) to appreciate the connections between her Mother's Day vision and the conceptual legacy of those who conceived the idea before her. Jarvis's denial of Julia Ward Howe's Mothers' Peace Day first observed in 1873 is a perfect illustration. As discussed in chapter 1, American peace organizations sponsored Mothers' Day celebrations each June in several major northeastern cities until the turn of the twentieth century. Of those peace organizations, the Philadelphia-based Universal Peace Union led the way in endorsing and observing Howe's Mother's Peace Day until 1913. Jarvis lived in Philadelphia for over fifty years after joining her brother there in the early 1890s. It seems extremely unlikely that she would not have had at least a peripheral knowledge of the UPU's observance of a Mothers' Peace Day. In her support of the League of Nations after World War I, Jarvis echoed many of the same pacifistic principles the UPU previously popularized for ensuring world peace. She too viewed war as contrary to the maternal instinct, seeing peace best expressed by the security a child felt when clutched to his or her mother's breast, and she believed in the duty of all mothers to rear children to embrace values of peace over the glories of war.[77] Despite the similar views on achieving world peace, Jarvis never directly named Howe or the Universal Peace Union's use of Mothers' Peace Day to emphasize women's duty to rear the next generation of pacifists.[78]

In Philadelphia, the two celebrations initially overlapped but Jarvis's Mother's Day quickly eclipsed Howe's in the interwar years. Only when escalating fears of America's involvement in another world war triggered a resurgence of Mother's Peace Day celebrations in the 1930s was Jarvis compelled to address the day's legacy. In May 1938, Jarvis refused to issue her traditional international Mother's Day greetings due to the war conditions in Europe. Regardless of the hostilities abroad, she predicted that the American celebration of Mother's Day would be one of the most peaceful ones seen in years.[79] Later that same month, however, Jarvis reportedly denounced a Mother's Peace Day.[80] The peace paraders made the fateful mistake of holding their festivities on the second Sunday in May and not on Howe's designated date of June 2 or on the national Peace Day observed at the end of May. Jarvis's support of world peace obviously did not extend to sharing her day with the larger cause.

She regarded the observance of a Mother's Peace Day as a camouflaged exploitation of her Mother's Day, another crass attempt to skirt her legal copyrights.[81] But "nobody," she allegedly told *Time*, "pays any attention to law anymore."[82]

Jarvis subjected the other claimants of the founder title to the same public accusations of fraud and infringement, with the exception of Juliet Calhoun Blakeley. Presumably, Jarvis was never aware of the annual Mother's Day celebration in Blakeley's honor. The only significant publicity Albion, Michigan, gave Blakeley's role in the holiday's history was with the 1934 issuance of the Mother's Day stamp. The Albion Business and Professional Women's Club published a special cachet (first-day issue envelope) hand stamped with the words, "Commemorating the Birthday Anniversary of the Founder of Mother's Day, Juliet Calhoun Blakeley. May 13, 1819–Nov. 29, 1920. Albion, Michigan."[83] Although treasured by Albion residents, the cachets did not have a wide circulation and therefore did not draw Jarvis's attention. Plus, Albion residents did not make the same fatal miscalculation as those of Henderson, Kentucky, of personally requesting Jarvis's help in promoting their founder.

Ironically, Anna Jarvis and Mary Towles Sasseen shared a great deal in common and, had they known each other under different situations, might have become friends. They were of the same generation, with only a four-year difference in their ages. Both were educated and socially independent women who worked as public school teachers. They also harbored larger ambitions not common among the majority of women of their generation. Jarvis moved from teaching to become the first female literary and advertising editor in an insurance company and then later built a national career through the Mother's Day International Association. Had Sasseen won her 1899 bid for the office of Kentucky Superintendent of Public Instruction, she would have become the one of the earliest elected female officials in the state.[84] Above all, neither woman became a mother. Accordingly, each viewed motherhood through the perspective of an eldest daughter and devoted companion to a mother whose death deeply affected her; they even built similar floral shrines in their homes in memory of their respective mothers and as testaments to their individual grief.[85]

Both women envisioned a Mother's Day that glorified the home and the centrality of the maternal role despite their lives as independent career women. The true power of mother-love for these daughters remained within the private sphere and was expressed through a mother's relationship with her children. Their respective Mother's Day mottos reflected that sentiment and even complimented each other's holiday designs. Sasseen selected "Home, a world of woe shut out; A world of love shut in" for her Mother's Day observance.[86] For Jarvis, Mother's Day honored the primary source of a home's security and love: "The Best Mother Who Ever Lived— The Mother of Your Heart."

In 1923, the Henderson Chamber of Commerce launched a nationwide project to build a memorial monument to Sasseen to commemorate her authorship of Mother's Day. Jarvis ignored the community's earlier attempts to inform her of Sasseen's history and request for the Mother's Day International Association's endorsement.[87] She initially did not find Henderson's claim any real threat until a representative of the town traveled to Philadelphia in 1924 to make an appeal in person for Jarvis's assistance in their plans. A Philadelphia newspaper reported Jarvis as unfriendly to the suggestion.[88] Over the next twenty years, Jarvis led her own counterassault against Henderson organizations and individual residents through personal correspondence, publicized statements issued through the MDIA, and threats of legal action, all demanding that they "stop the deception and game."[89] Jarvis resented what she saw as them casting her as a fraud and trying to extort money for their monument scheme through a Mother's Day movement to which they had never contributed a single hour or dime in support. As she explained to the president of the Henderson Women's Club, "Any person of intelligence and justice will readily understand the impossibility of a dead woman developing such a movement as that of Mother's Day while she slept for a quarter of a century."[90] In a letter to the Henderson Chamber of Commerce, she wondered if the committee would be willing to stand by its claims to Mother's Day by obligating itself to pay the total expenses of the Mother's Day International Association's preparations for the day's national and international observance that year.[91]

Her nemesis, however, remained Frank Hering of the Fraternal Order of Eagles and his efforts to canonize himself as the founder of Mother's Day based on his 1904 public plea for a national day of maternal tribute.[92] No other single person gave her more aggravation. For nearly twenty years, Jarvis rarely missed an opportunity to challenge Hering's claims and correct anyone who mistakenly gave him or the F.O.E. any credit for the holiday's founding. "It has taken great courage to stave off his possession of Mother's Day as he has money, publicity and influence which I could not command," she confessed.[93] Not only did Hering have the full backing of the Eagles, but he also received the endorsement of the American War Mothers who formally crowned him the "Father of Mothers' Day" and awarded him its highest medal of honor. Jarvis went as far as accusing the Eagles of buying the title and "tin medal" with a $5,000 donation to the American War Mothers: "Anyone can buy a medal and give it to any person they please, but it is a joke on its wearer if his vanity and lack of truthful honor will ever permit him to show it."[94]

Jarvis felt briefly vindicated when the U.S. Justice Department indicted Hering for violating a federal lottery law in 1932. Hering, along with two other men, led a lottery ticket sale for the F.O.E. that earned over $1,750,000. An estimated $500,000 of the collected funds ultimately lined the pockets of Hering and his associates instead of entering the Eagles' treasuries to be dispersed to charitable organizations as publicized.[95] Jarvis cringed at the repeated identification of Hering as Mother's Day founder in the media's trial coverage, hating to see her movement and her "sainted mother's name" linked to the entire scandal. But she took comfort in the federal court judge's ruling not to permit the mention of Hering's association with Mother's Day over the course of the trial.[96]

Jarvis was in the courtroom when Hering received a guilty verdict, a sentence of four months in prison, and a $2,000 fine. To her chagrin, President Franklin Roosevelt extended Hering executive clemency in November of 1933.[97] (Roosevelt had joined the Eagles while governor of New York)[98] Hering's role in the lottery scandal only reinforced Jarvis's opinion of him as the ultimate imposter. She had hoped the ordeal would put an end to his Mother's Day claims, yet that was not the case. Not only did Hering continue his self-promotion as the "Father of Mothers' Day," but he also allegedly sought credit for President Roosevelt's New Deal policies. "Hering claims never knowing until other persons never knowing of him, ACHIEVE," Jarvis scoffed.[99] It continually amazed her that Hering maintained his political reputation while she was dismissed or ridiculed by the media, commercial interests, and political pundits. If they had only seen him as she did, she believed, nonchalantly chewing gum in court during the federal trial, then they "would not feel respect for his type."[100]

Her growing resentment and desperation to maintain control of her Mother's Day became obvious in the public statements she issued throughout the 1920s and 1930s. Gradually, Jarvis blurred the lines between herself and Mother's Day, eventually refusing to distinguish herself from the day's observance—as if one could not exist without the other. In a statement titled "Kidnapping Mother's Day: Will You Be an Accomplice?" she pleaded for the assistance of all the country's loyal sons and daughters to defend Mother's Day by defending her from Hering:

> Every basic feature, name, emblem, dates and slogan established by me in connection with this day has been appropriated by him. You are not asked to take sides in this matter but to do me the justice of refraining from furthering the selfish interests of this claimant, who is making a desperate effort to snatch from me the rightful title of originator and founder of Mother's Day, established by me after decades of untold labor, time, and expense. This day and movement originated by my "sainted mother" and myself, will be defended to the limit.[101]

In her worthy efforts, she asked for everyone's cooperation as a simple "matter of sheer justice."[102]

"HOLY DAY" VERSUS HOLIDAY: ANNA JARVIS AND THE COMMERCIALIZATION OF MOTHER'S DAY

Jarvis had greater success rewriting her mother's Mothers' Day legacy than fighting the rival founders who shared her sentimental celebration of motherhood. The same was true with her battle against a variety of organizations drawn to the holiday's sentimental appeal and popularity. Some social and political groups that first ridiculed Jarvis's proposed day as silly, rejecting its maudlin depiction of motherhood, quickly overcame their initial reluctance by 1914. With the obvious success of Jarvis's Mother's Day movement, they discovered a use for the holiday's sentimentality in promoting their agendas. That was the "bitter part about it" for Jarvis, having those who once scorned her and refused to aid in the day's inception eventually seek to benefit from it.[103] Just like the Mother's Day imposters, they wished to gain "something for nothing" by taking their piece of a movement to which they never before contributed.[104]

The floral, confection, and greeting card industries that eagerly embraced Jarvis's idea for a Mother's Day did not fall into the same category as those who initially rejected the observance, only to embrace it later. These commercial industries recognized the marketability of the holiday's sentiment from the start. The maternal model that Jarvis constructed through her movement lent itself beautifully to commercial exploitation; the themes central to her work became central themes in the holiday advertising campaigns. The call to pay tribute to mothers by writing letters home fueled the greeting card industry. The selection of the white carnation as the emblem of a mother's love provided the floral industry with a generous opportunity to command the day. Moreover, Jarvis's own story as a daughter dedicated to fulfilling her dead mother's greatest wish was better than anything a copywriter could invent. The sentiment of home, faith, and maternal devotion practically sold itself, and it was that precious sentiment that helped conceal the crass commercialization brewing beneath it. "Let everyone boost Mothers' Day [original spelling]—talk it up, make a fuss about it, believe in it, get enthusiastic over it," rallied the *American Florist*. "The Sentiment is here; it is only waiting to be awakened. Get together, boys, and arouse it."[105] When all is told, the commercial industries that Jarvis grew to despise deserve a large degree of the credit for the holiday's success and, in turn, the cultural acceptance of the sentimental, child-centered, view of motherhood that she designed the day to commemorate.

Jarvis selected the second Sunday in May as Mother's Day for two primary reasons. The main reason, as noted previously, was to mark the anniversary of her mother's death on May 9, 1905. Instead of designating the exact date of her mother's death as Mother's Day, however, she selected the closest Sunday—which points to Jarvis's second reason. It was essential to Jarvis that the observance always fall on the Sabbath, as she wanted Mother's Day to be a "holy day," representing nothing but the expression of noble and memorial sentiments toward American mothers. In the winter of 1908, she wrote to John Wanamaker, "Our busy, selfish lives crowd out so many of our noble impulses that we need such a Sabbath day as this to remind us of our loving neglect of the mother of quiet grace, who through self-denials, devotion and patience gave us a better chance than our parents ever knew."[106]

Designating a Sunday for the celebration of Mother's Day served several strategic purposes. First of all, it enabled churches to become important vehicles in promoting the nationwide observance and its conservative emphasis on women's essential familial service. Historian Kathleen Jones, for example, contends that the holiday's popular acceptance owed more to the Protestant-led American Sunday school movement than to any other contributing factor.[107] Jarvis nurtured the relationship between her Mother's Day movement and the Protestant church from the beginning. Her mother's home church, Andrews Methodist Episcopal Church, in West Virginia organized memorial services in 1906 and 1907 for Ann Reeves Jarvis at her daughter's request before hosting the first official Mother's Day observance in 1908. And when she initially proposed her idea to John Wanamaker, she ostensibly appealed to him as the superintendent of the Bethany Church Sunday School and member of the Pennsylvania Sunday School Association, not as the influential merchandiser. In her first written request to Wanamaker, she stressed the educational and spiritual uplift promised by such a special day for each member of a congregation. She explained, "An address to the Sabbath-school and a sermon from the pulpit on the gratitude we owe, and our duty toward this parent; the bringing of mothers to the church by children, the distribution of the white carnations to wear as a pledge of love and greater loyalty, would certainly be of benefit to all."[108]

Above all, her persistent description of Mother's Day as a holy day reflected her growing discomfort with the modern commercialized holiday celebrations.[109] Mother's Day was to always be a Sabbath day, she insisted, not a market day. Despite her best efforts, however, Jarvis could not prevent the invasion of commercial forces on Mother's Day. After 1910, most holidays experienced the same market encroachment; rare was the holiday devoid of at least one of the trade elements that plagued Mother's Day: gifts, flowers, cards, and candy.[110] Yet a closer look into the formation of her Mother's Day movement proves that Jarvis was not exactly the innocent victim of exploitation that she consistently claimed after 1914. In addition, the enormous profits generated by the commercial marketing of Mother's Day were not the main source of her denouncement of them as trade vandals.

By 1908, Jarvis had left her position as literary and advertising editor at Fidelity Mutual to devote herself full time to her Mother's Day movement, no doubt taking her advertising experience with her. She illustrated that experience and mastery of the "sell" when she first courted the influential religious, political, media, and commercial figures she believed could assist her cause. Surviving copies of her letters to *Ladies Home Journal* editor Edward E. Bok and former President Theodore Roosevelt reveal the tailoring of her argument to appeal to each man. Although similar in their wording and phrasing, they are not exact copies, which make the subtle changes in the letters evidence of Jarvis's calculated appeal to the individual recipients.

To the socially conservative Bok, who championed his view of women as essentially domestic creatures in the pages of the popular magazine, Jarvis stressed the opportunity that a Mother's Day would offer a modern generation to honor their often-neglected mothers. "It would afford us all an opportunity to pay deserving tribute to that type of womanhood and motherhood that we all love to honor," she wrote; "[It] would call to mind the deep gratitude we owe the mother who gave us life and would no doubt be the means of many of us resolving to make amends for the loving neglect our busy, selfish lives often impose."[111] Coincidently, the lack of deference shown by young women to their mothers was an issue Bok addressed in his own editorials.[112] For Roosevelt, the man who equated the reproductive duty of women to the military duty of men, Jarvis reminded him of the country's duty to honor its patriotic mothers: "They not only have gone into the jaws of death to give life to this nation's sons, but they have also offered them in sacrifice for our country's welfare and honor in time of war." [113] She reminded him of how mothers of every generation have "bravely met the perils of war that came to them in their unprotected homes with little children to rear and feed."[114]

For all practical purposes, Jarvis *was* the Mother's Day International Association. She primarily financed and, with the help of only one positively identified assistant, operated all association business from its headquarters in her Philadelphia home. She understood, nonetheless, the importance of having influential names tied (even if only superficially) to her movement work; it underestimates Jarvis's intelligence and vision to suggest that she appealed to such powerful men as Wannamaker, Heinz, Conwell, Bok, and Roosevelt purely because they shared her sentimental view of motherhood. These men, whom she described as "busy," "successful," and "reverent" in her letters to them, offered essential avenues to the legitimacy, notoriety, and above all, publicity her movement required to succeed. In 1913, for example, Jarvis wrote Speaker of the House Champ Clark asking him to serve as the MDIA's honorary vice president for his state of Missouri. "No duty will be required," she promised, "simply the influence of your name."[115] Association letterhead that year included Honorary President William Taft, Honorary Vice President Theodore Roosevelt, and a total of fifty-three honorary state vice presidents. It also included the name of the thirty-nine total members of three other honorary committees.

In the early years of her movement, Jarvis capitalized on her relationship with commercial magnate John Wanamaker as well. Not only did the Wannamaker Auditorium host one of the first official Mother's Day services in 1908, but the department store was also the first to use the observance in its advertisements and profit from its celebration as a public relations gimmick. Wanamaker hosted a Mother's Day program each May, which included speakers, music, and gifts of flowers to customers. Struck by the quality of the department store's 1913 Mother's Day campaign, an enamored customer wrote to Wanamaker to complement him on his advertising man: "Whoever wrote that Mother's Day stuff is 'it'—with caps. By golly, that's more than advertising. That's literature."[116] In response, Wanamaker thanked the admirer and proudly admitted that he had been the father of those Mother's Day words. "My idea of advertising is much higher than merely selling goods," he insisted, "It is to educate our own people and, to some extent, whoever reads what is upon our page."[117] Wanamaker and his store thus served as an essential partner in educating the public on the sentimental ideal of Jarvis's Mother's Day observance.

Jarvis also understood the importance of the media in publicizing her movement. She initially accorded the media a degree of the credit for the day's national popularity. In 1911, she publicly thanked the popular press for its help spreading the message of Mother's Day in the first year of her movement. During a time when the different women's organizations and religious leaders she approached dismissed her idea as foolish and she feared her own humiliation and disgrace at the thought of failure, the media rallied to save her movement. When the major Philadelphia and New York papers "caught the spirit of the Mother's Day idea" their publicity generated a "tender enthusiasm" for her observance and support spread throughout the country.[118] (She subsequently invited the editor of the *Philadelphia Inquirer* to join her movement).[119] Jarvis even earned the early endorsement of *Good Housekeeping*, which described the observance to its readers as a day meant to "make us better children by getting us closer to the hearts of our good mothers" in May 1909.[120]

As for the floral industry, Jarvis initially embraced florists as vital suppliers of the holiday's white carnation emblem. In 1910, the Philadelphia Rapid Transit Company distributed 10,000 white carnations to its employees and passengers. In the Grand Court of Wanamaker's department store, management presented 29,000 carnations, 19,000 roses, and 1,000 peonies to its Mother's Day customers in 1913. In addition, Jarvis purchased an estimated 8,000 white carnations between 1908 and 1912 for the annual Mother's Day services held at Andrews Methodist Episcopal Church at a personal expense of roughly $700. Such grand gestures relied on a cooperative and well-organized floral industry. Perhaps the best evidence of Jarvis's once amicable relationship with the floral trade was her willingness to personally prepare and provide Mother's Day placards for florists to display in their shop windows.[121]

Jarvis's relationship with the commercial industries associated with the holiday did not deteriorate until after 1912. That year marked the formal incorporation of her Mother's Day International Association and her copyrighting of the white carnation emblem and the words "Mother's Day"; the phrase, "Second Sunday in May"; and her own photograph. The first three appeared on the association's official letterhead. Two years later, she filed the same trademark in Canada.[122] She frequently issued public statements through the MDIA warning of her copyrights:

WARNING: Any charity, institution, hospital, organization, or business using Mother's Day names, work, emblem, or celebration for getting money, making sales or on printed forms should be held as imposters by proper authorities, and reported to this Association.[123]

From 1912 until her death in 1948, Jarvis was unwilling to relinquish control and accept the status of her day as a public holiday and, therefore, cultural property. Repeatedly, she threatened to sue those who designed their own Mother's Day celebrations (whether merchant, minister, or mayor) without her express permission, especially if she recognized the celebration as a blatant act of commercial gain. At the peak of her battle against the commercialization of Mother's Day, she allegedly had thirty-three pending lawsuits.[124]

It is crucial to emphasize that Jarvis's anger toward her identified anti-mothers propagandists was never just a matter of jealousy over their economic success in comparison to her own failure to profit from her movement. She insisted from the beginning that the MDIA never financially benefited from its work, and surviving financial records verify that she was not exaggerating her selflessness for dramatic effect. Basically, Jarvis funded the bulk of her work with the personal inheritance from her parents and later her brother, Claude. Although she sought supporters for her association in all realms of public life, she never requested explicitly financial support. No records exist of Jarvis's soliciting money for Mother's Day beyond the annual MDIA membership dues that ranged from two dollars to a life-time membership of one hundred dollars and the request for a minimal fee to cover the printing and shipping costs of official Mother's Day programs and paraphernalia. It is also true that no records exist to clearly determine the receipt and expenditure of any funding or financial sponsorship the association received from those Jarvis regarded as friends of Mother's Day.[125]

As with her criticism of Mother's Day imposters, Jarvis's primary objection to the commercial exploitation of Mother's Day was likely one of principle. Since she considered the observance her intellectual and legal property, Jarvis sincerely felt the injustice of having her ownership rights openly violated, as well as the distortion of her Mother's Day sentiment and the belittlement of her recognized role as official founder. She expected celebrants to consider the welfare of Mother's Day and be vigilant in protecting it from unauthorized profiteers, believing that it was not too much to ask of them. "If you are a friend of Mother's Day, if Mother's Day is helpful to you in any way, it is indeed a very small thing for you to use the Official Mother's Day supplies," she beseeched, instead of fueling the profiteering of rival holiday sponsors or commercial interests.[126] If unable or unwilling to use the association's official Mother's Day supplies, she requested that one refrain from even observing the day: "All that is asked of you is to forget Mother's Day entirely, just as you forget its welfare."[127]

Jarvis let few slights go unnoticed when individuals or organizations declined to go through her for approval of their Mother's Day observances or promotional campaigns, including her one-time benefactor John Wanamaker. A former personal assistant recounted in a newspaper interview that Jarvis ordered a salad while dining at the Wanamaker Tea Room only to dump it onto the floor. She disapproved of the salad's designation as a Mother's Day Salad.[128] For her, the smallest, seemingly insignificant violations threatened to open the floodgates of further exploitation; thus the most innocent of lunch salads were not safe from her disdain. In 1922, she denounced Wanamaker's endorsement of the International Sunday School Association's "Mother and Daughter Week" program meant to correspond with (or encroach on) the observance of Mother's Day. Jarvis accused Wanamaker of trying to split Mother's Day and subsequently crush her movement work. She threatened to sue all five of the Sunday school associations involved in the scheme and openly ridiculed its male leadership as men of "puny types of manhood" for their eagerness to hide "behind the petticoats of women and girls for their unrighteous work."[129]

So attuned was Jarvis to the arguments used to commercially assail Mother's Day that she refused to grant President Woodrow Wilson excessive credit for his role in its national establishment. She railed against any public statements accrediting Wilson's 1914 presidential proclamation as the beginning of the holiday observance, understanding how such a claim bolstered the classification of Mother's Day as a public holiday. She astutely reminded people that as governor of New Jersey, Wilson never issued a Mother's Day proclamation as governors of other states did. Nor did he play any role in the passage of the congressional Mother's Day Resolution "beyond affixing his signature in a perfunctory way." [130] As both a governor and president, he was simply not a sentimental man, according to Jarvis. Moreover, she insisted that the congressional resolution was strictly a "Flag Resolution" and nothing more. Its objective was not to establish Mother's Day, as it was already being celebrating throughout the country. In fact, it was exclusively her success in establishing the national and international observance of Mother's Day during the seven years prior that made such a resolution even possible.[131]

In the popular histories and annual media coverage of Mother's Day, Jarvis's infamous assault on the floral industry has overshadowed her equally combative relationships with other noncommercial organizations. Her battle with the commercial floral industry, however, does epitomize her entire fight to protect the legal and ideological integrity of her "holy day." Throughout the early twentieth century, this influential commercial adversary aggressively repudiated Jarvis's ownership of Mother's Day through every imaginable means. Changing the holiday's name to its possessive plural spelling was one popular strategy. Like the acclaimed "Father

Figure 2.8. "Say It With Flowers," Saturday Evening Post, *4 May 1918, 52.*

of Mothers' Day," florists argued that their use of the alternative spelling in their advertisements avoided copyright infringement.[132]

Yet even before 1914, Jarvis faced a floral industry that adamantly declared its entitlement to the holiday. Just one year earlier, the *Florists' Review* bragged of the industry's primary role in the day's popularity: "For the success of the 'day,' we are to credit ourselves, us, we, the members of the trade who know a good thing when they see it and who are sufficiently progressive to push it along—Mothers' Day is ours; we made it; we made it practically unaided and alone." [133] Ironically, the industry quickly became as proprietary of Mother's Day as Jarvis, defending the holiday as exclusively a floral event when rival merchandisers, such as confectioners, sought their share of the day's marketability.[134]

Again, Jarvis did not resent the floral industry's profit margins per se. She once allegedly rejected the Florists Telegraph Delivery Association's (FTD) offer of a holiday commission on carnation sales.[135] Her resentment focused on the manner in which the trade sought those profits, all of which culminated in defaming her founder status, dismissing her movement's work, and abusing the sentimental design of the white carnation emblem that she worked so hard to cultivate. She originally selected the floral emblem as a tribute to her mother's love for the flower, one with the added benefit of being relatively inexpensive. In the wake of her movement's success, she embellished the emblem's backstory with the assertion that she selected the flower only after a careful study of its history revealed the flower's lack of connection with any state or national floral emblems. Eventually, she imbued the white carnation with the maternal imagery of purity, fidelity, beauty, charity, and love:

> Its whiteness is to symbolize the truth, purity and broad charity of mother love; its fragrance, her memory, and her prayers. The carnation does not drop its petals, but hugs them to its heart as it dies, and so, too, mothers hug their children to their hearts, their mother love never dying. [136]

The symbolism woven around the holiday's white carnation emblem was an excellent illustration of her artful engineering of a sentimental celebration of motherhood.

Only after the floral industry began to exploit and dilute the symbolism of the white carnation did Jarvis wish to sever its ties to the holiday. It started with the noticeable increase in the price of white carnations. Based on Jarvis's personal sale receipts, the price of a carnation jumped from one-half a cent in 1908 to fifteen cents each by 1912. By the early 1920s, she mocked florists for hiking the price of a single carnation to the exorbitant expense of one dollar when, at one time, they were "tickled to death" to get rid of their stock for pennies.[137] When the demand for white carnations surpassed the supply, the industry initiated an ingenious campaign to introduce the red carnation in the holiday's repertoire, marketing the purchase of a red carnation in honor of living mothers and a white carnation in memory of

Figure 2.9. Jarvis attempted to undercut the floral industry's holiday sales by designing an official floral badge as a lasting alternative to fresh flowers. Courtesy of the International Mother's Day Shrine, Grafton, West Virginia.

deceased mothers. It was never intended that the "honor badge of Mother's Day be a mourning badge through any such distinction," Jarvis retorted.[138]

She endeavored to undercut the floral industry's holiday sales by offering celebrants an official floral badge featuring the Mother's Day emblem as a lasting alternative to fresh flowers. She had originally hoped to distribute the badges for free through her association but, out of necessity, requested a minimum fee to cover only the cost of materials. She was even willing to abandon the floral emblem completely to stop the profiteering. Jarvis encouraged the public to recall the original intent of the congressional Mother's Day resolution and display the American flag on their homes instead of purchasing flowers.[139]

Since Jarvis's fight to defend her movement was based on perceived principles of justice and fairness and not economics, not even the social and economic crisis of the Great Depression slowed her efforts. Her tenacity led her to send a telegram to

Figure 2.10. Despite Anna Jarvis's dislike of pre-made Mother's Day cards, she occasionally did purchase and send greeting cards to friends as evidenced by this card sent to a Mrs. Reist in 1935. Courtesy of LancasterHistory.org, Lancaster, Pennsylvania.

Figure 2.11. Anna Jarvis. Courtesy of the International Mother's Day Shrine, Grafton, West Virginia.

President Franklin Roosevelt in 1933, urging him to prevent the National Industrial Recovery Act from assisting the observance's commercial vandalism:

> Please omit Mother's Day name from greeting cards, floral, confectioners and every code. Don't list Mother's Day as holiday. Infringing industries facing legal penalties for unfair trade practices and profiteering and intolerable methods seek estate through codes, your protection is earnestly solicited. Mother's Day, Inc. Anna Jarvis, Founder.[140]

The telegram was one of many appeals Jarvis sent to President Roosevelt seeking his intervention on her behalf, and in turn, on the behalf of Mother's Day. The tone of her numerous telegrams and letters ranged from righteous indignation for not being worthy of the president and first lady's consideration to courteous offers to relieve the president of the added burden of responding to Mother's Day matters with which he was not familiar; in one telegram, she politely requested that the White House forward any persons or organizations inquiring about Mother's Day directly to the MDIA.[141]

In a sad twist of fate, Jarvis beseeched the one president willing to deliberately exploit the marketability of holidays in order to stimulate a struggling economy. In the summer of 1939, President Roosevelt announced his plans to advance the

71

celebration of Thanksgiving by one week in order to prolong the holiday shopping season. He had apparently been under pressure from retail associations to make such a bold move since 1933. As eloquently captured by the *New York Times* headline, "Roosevelt to Move Thanksgiving: Retailers For It; Plymouth Not," Americans overwhelmingly disapproved of the president's tampering with the holiday's traditional calendar space for obvious commercial gain, regardless of the economy's fragile state. Yet, Roosevelt issued the same "Franksgiving" proclamation for the following year, despite a reported 62 percent of Americans disagreeing with his decision and the motives behind it. Congress finally ended Roosevelt's holiday experiment in 1941. Whether it stood as a testimony to the lack of Americans' discretionary income or their conscious refusal to be part of such commercial manipulation, the extra week of Christmas shopping did not translate into significant gains for retailers as expected.[142] Unfortunately for Jarvis, Americans were not as quick to defend Mother's Day from the same commercial encroachment, despite its ideological commonalities with the Thanksgiving observance.

Her failure to protect the integrity of the day's sentimental celebration from commercial contamination tainted her relationship with noncommercial interests as well, including philanthropic groups hoping to benefit from the holiday's observance. She was so battle-weary from her war with the floral industry that she could not help but reference it when criticizing the infringement of other organizations:

Would you feel friendly toward them, if just because they thought your flowers displayed were beautiful, that they should clip to take them for their own use, leaving you only with bare stalks? When if the stalks would grow another crop in a year, would not your time, patience, money and thought have been taken from you by trespassers, and would it not dishearten you to feel your work must be done all over another year?[143]

In the midst of her disappointment and feelings of betrayal, she ultimately questioned not the worth of her Mother's Day but the worthiness of Americans to share in its observance. Jarvis threatened to destroy her own beloved creation rather than watch its slow desecration. If the American people were not willing to protect Mother's Day from the hordes of money schemers that overwhelmed the observance, she vowed on behalf of the Mother's Day International Association to cease the annually celebration completely.[144] She offered no specific details on how she expected to commit such an act of matricide.

Even if she was mainly posturing for the media, the repeated threats to destroy the holiday movement to which she dedicated the sum of her adult life reveals Jarvis's intimate investment in the day's, as well as her own, cultural legacy. Today, scholars may continue to debate the holiday's cultural context, analyzing its significance from a variety of angles, but from Jarvis's perspective, there were no other legitimate interpretations of Mother's Day, regardless of the economic, political, or social guise in which they appeared.

"HONOR THY FATHER AND THY MOTHER": THE RIVALRY OF FATHER'S DAY AND PARENTS' DAY

O n May 8, 1908, Senator Elmer J. Burkett of Nebraska introduced a resolution requesting that Sunday, May 10, be recognized as Mother's Day and for Senate members, officers, and employees to observe the day by wearing a white flower. He introduced the resolution on the behest of the Young Men's Christian Association (YMCA), who felt a day reserved to encourage young men to think of their mothers and the maternal lessons of their boyhood would provide a wonderful service for such impressionable youths. Burkett had expected unanimous consent for the resolution but was instead startled when an objection ended its further consideration that day. The following morning, the resolution sparked a twenty-minute debate over the merits and relevancy of setting aside a day to honor mothers in such a manner. Baffled by the apparent confusion of his colleagues, Burkett assured them his intentions were not to declare a special holiday or make the observance perpetual but only to show the Senate's symbolic support for the noble work of the YMCA: "I think the Senators will admit that there is no sentiment which would bring home to the boys a sweeter and better thought than to devote one day in honor of their mothers."[1]

Most of the senators, however, were neither convinced by Burkett's argument nor moved by the resolution's sentiment. Senator Gallinger of New Hampshire denied such a movement for a "mother's day" existed, having never heard of it from the YMCA in his state. Besides, he found the entire notion of men requiring a special day to be reminded of their mothers' love and influence as both unnecessary and insulting: "I should feel it was almost a reproach to lay a burden upon me even by way of suggestion that [my mother's] memory could only be kept green by some outward demonstration."[2] But national holidays, countered Senator Augustus Bacon of Georgia, are not designed to guard people against forgetting why the day is revered, nor is the wearing of a flower meant to guard a son against forgetting for whom the

73

symbol is worn; it is for the gratification that comes with an "outward expression and manifestation of an inward sentiment and emotion that does honor to the man who conceives its use, and who wears it, and is proud of it."[3]

If such was the case, queried other senators, then why only single out a mother's love and influence for special recognition? Senator John Kean of New Jersey proposed amending the resolution to commemorate the fifth commandment, "Honor thy father and thy mother," to which Senator Henry Teller of Colorado readily agreed, believing it was unfair to have a mothers' day and not a fathers' day. As dear as his mother was to him, he admitted, she was no dearer to him than his father. But then again, debated the men, why stop with just mothers and fathers? Senator Fulton of Oregon saw no reason to make such "invidious distinctions" in the allocation of familial reverence and defended the inclusion of grandfathers, aunts, uncles, and cousins for special consideration. His flippant insinuation of a Senate-endorsed "mother-in-law day" generated a round of laughter among his colleagues.[4]

Poor befuddled Burkett, who believed his resolution a simple gesture of recognition to mothers and the YMCA, found himself accused of wasting the Senate's time with such a childish matter and on a Saturday morning no less. The Senate voted 33 to 14 to have the resolution referred to the Committee on the Judiciary, where it was "permitted to sleep peacefully," reported the *New York Times*.[5] Despite the resolution's failure, Burkett refused to apologize for his senatorial transgression and rejected his colleagues' primary argument that a mother's day was not a topic for federal legislation. He retorted, "I have seen the Senate spend hours and hours and spend money in building a monument to some particular man in recognition of some particular service, not to celebrate what he had done, but to inculcate in the minds and to burn in the memories of the young people of this land the things which that man had done for the glory and welfare of this country."[6] He was therefore openly disappointed in a Senate that refused to endorse the sentiment that the "mothers who gave us birth" deserved this country's tribute.[7] Six years later, Congress finally recognized Mother's Day as a topic worthy of federal legislation, and since then, it has designated days, weeks, months, and even years in homage to a wide array of topics once considered outside the purview of federal legislation; at times, as high as one-third of all bills passed during a congressional session have entailed the establishment of such commemorative periods.[8]

Nonetheless, the senators' lively debate about the merits of a mother's day over a commemorative day for fathers reveals an honest questioning of the sentimental supremacy of the maternal role. The men easily challenged the assumption that their fathers had little influence on their childhood and were somehow undeserving of individual praise, despite their rearing under the Victorian glorification of motherhood. That Sunday, May 10, 1908, an estimated twenty thousand people obviously disagreed and attended the inaugural celebration of Mother's Day in West Virginia and Pennsylvania. Even so, the failure of the first congressional Mother's Day resolution, and the heated debate it provoked, foreshadowed the new cultural interest in fatherhood during the early twentieth century. What began with a gentle encouragement for fathers to spend quality time with their wives and children grew in intensity throughout the 1920s and 1930s. By World War II, an array of medical, political, and social authorities urgently warned of the potential dangers of a mother's prevailing authority over her children if not checked by a physically and emotionally invested paternal figure.[9]

Coinciding with the changing expectations of fatherhood were movements to establish a holiday celebrating a father's role as an active partner (even if still a junior partner) in the rearing of children. Initially, the only dilemma promoters foresaw was whether to celebrate fathers jointly with mothers by replacing Mother's Day with a Parents' Day or by supplementing the maternal holiday with a separate Father's Day. Both holidays, however, struggled to find a broad appeal throughout the early twentieth century, seemingly caught in a sort of no man's land between their promotions as sincere days of paternal tribute and their derisive classification as crass marketing ploys.[10] The observance of Mother's Day was inevitably drawn into the Father's Day and Parents' Day campaigns to find a legitimate place on the American calendar. The eventual success of Father's Day and the ultimate failure of Parents' Day to replace the Mother's Day observance reveals just as much about the history of motherhood as it does the history of fatherhood. Thus the cultural significance of Father's Day and Parents' Day is best showcased by the holiday rivalry with Mother's Day, one that was more than a clash of personal egos and commercial interests. The holiday rivalry, at its heart, was a cultural dispute over the shifting ideological boundaries of fatherhood and motherhood within the modern American family.[11]

Anna Jarvis identified the rival holidays as serious threats to her Mother's Day movement. Ostensibly, she dismissed them as commercial gimmicks designed by unscrupulous men hoping to capitalize on the sentimental success of Mother's Day. But with the growing popularity of both holidays in the late 1920s and early 1930s, Jarvis recognized the power of the Father's Day and Parents' Day campaigns to diminish the influence of her movement work and its celebration of a mother's preeminent status within the home. Her Mother's Day celebrated mothers as the center of the domestic sphere and as the preserver of the home for all who resided there. Honoring motherhood honored the home and united the family that mothers served; therefore, a threat to Mother's Day was an affront to motherhood and, in turn, the harmony of the home. A mother's influence was simply irreplaceable, according to Jarvis, and any equating of the maternal and paternal role in status and reverence was not only erroneous but also dishonorable. "I cannot think in naming this honor day of the home after 'Mother,' that I have overestimated the chivalry and lofty-mindedness of American men," she challenged.[12]

"A MOTHER'S LOVE" VERSUS "A FATHER'S CARE"

In 1850, William Hudson wrote to his wife of his admiration for her maternal devotion to their children. "If there be anything I anxiously covet of our dear children," he wrote, "it is that next to love and devotion to their maker, they may appreciate your great care and love for them and make you the best return in their power by doing everything on their part that will please and gratify you."[13] Hudson's unmitigated respect for his wife's maternal authority reflected a common conceptualization of nineteenth-century fatherhood. Advice literature described a "good father" as a husband who provided his wife with both the material and emotional support she required to perform her essential maternal duties. A husband's deference to his wife's maternal authority was an essential component of his paternal role; apparently nothing threatened family harmony more than an interfering father who continually second-guessed a mother's management of the children.[14]

Historians, however, warn against the exaggerated image of the physically and emotionally distant Victorian father. Increasingly, scholars have challenged the historical accuracy of the paternal models depicted in traditional prescriptive literature, such as religious texts, childcare manuals, and popular magazines. There is a difference, they contend, between the reality of the paternal experience inside the home and the perception of fatherhood in popular culture.[15] Ignoring the class and racial distinctions in how men raised their children has also provided a distorted image of Victorian fatherhood. Nonetheless, most scholars agree that varying political, religious, economic, and legal changes did conspire to push fathers to the periphery of family life by mid-nineteenth century, especially for the middleclass.[16] Historically, it was a new position for them.

In late-seventeenth- and early-eighteenth-century America, religious beliefs, legal doctrines, and the structure of the agrarian economy awarded fathers the predominant role in the rearing of children. The Calvinist view of children's inherent sinful nature called for the family patriarch's moral supervision, instruction, and discipline to ensure a child's proper obedience to God, parents, and work. Women, prone to emotional weakness and a natural maternal indulgence, were considered incapable of the rational and emotional self-control required to follow the religious "spare the rod and spoil the child" philosophy of training children. Colonial society revered mothers instead for their willingness to face death in childbirth, their general physical care of children, and the domestic training of daughters, but it left the other parental responsibilities to the domain of fathers. Besides religious beliefs, the reproductive perception of the male as the active force of fertilization, the literal giver of life and the supplier of both reason and soul, reinforced a father's primary parental status, as did the legal sanctioning of near unlimited paternal authority over legitimate children. Above all, the foundation of colonial fatherhood rested on the realities of a preindustrial economy. The home-based economy facilitated a father's ability to incorporate his responsibilities as provider and spiritual role model within the daily routine of domestic life.[17]

By the late eighteenth century, the same republican ideology that exposed political tyrants as threats to American liberty also warned of the unyielding patriarch and his tyranny over the family. Post-revolutionary childcare literature, for the first time being written specifically for women, reflected American society's new democratic spirit: "It is with families as it is with states: they have been too busy with laws and too remiss in education. They contrive methods to punish, not to prevent crimes." [18] The dominant religious depiction of children as innocent redeemers complemented the political tempering of patriarchal authority. Nineteenth- century ministers valorized the moral persuasion of a mother's love in the rearing of children over a father's stern physical discipline characteristic of seventeenth- and eighteenth-century fatherhood. Finally, as the center of production left the home for the offices and factories, so did the family patriarch. The breadwinner role justified a father's regular absence from domestic life, effectively trusting an expanding maternal authority to fill the parental void.[19]

This is not to say that nineteenth-century childcare literature completely ignored the role of fathers within domestic life. Many authors cautioned fathers against neglecting their other fatherly duties in their pursuit of a career. The significance of the maternal role over that of the paternal one in rearing children, however, was reflected in the popular Victorian notion of a "father's care," as defined by a man's social role as breadwinner, versus a "mother's love," which was inherent in a woman's very nature. Fatherhood was not believed to complete a man's nature in the same way that motherhood completed a woman's. A man's paternal role merely complemented and further validated his separate economic and political roles and therefore was not deemed his primary source of fulfillment.[20] Thus, the glorification of motherhood was a double-edged sword for women; it explicitly anchored their identities to the domestic sphere as it served to free men from it. But the glorification of the maternal role as natural, superior, and irreplaceable, invested a degree of confidence and social trust in a woman's ability to rear children with minimal assistance. "The reproduction of the species—their nurture in the womb, and their support and culture during infancy and childhood—is the grand prerogative of woman," proclaimed an 1866 home health manual. "It is noble and a holy office, to which she is appointed by God; and the duty is both pure and sacred."[21]

By the end of the century, the Victorian sentimental faith in women's natural ability to rear children began to wane, courtesy of a new interest in a scientific worldview that included the study of child development and childcare techniques. Professionalism gradually replaced sentimentality in regards to motherhood and child rearing. Physician-authored advice literature publicly challenged the traditional notion that a mother's instinct and love were enough to raise children unsupervised; without the guidance of scientific knowledge and its experts, women were essentially ignorant of the proper techniques of childcare and thus put the next generation of children at terrible risk.[22] Rejecting motherhood as a natural panacea mirrored the larger cultural ambivalence over the status of the traditional family and its ability to keep pace with a rapidly changing American society.[23]

Leading medical, psychological, and public health experts promoted a view of children as exceptionally vulnerable to the physical, emotional, and psychological threats of modern life and called for a modern makeover of fatherhood and motherhood in order to address the new perils of childhood.[24] Debates over the exact rendering of the new parental models consumed the promulgators of childcare advice and dominated the pages of popular women's magazines. When modern experts stripped mothers of their instinctual knowledge of child rearing, they essentially demoted the maternal role to the level of a learned social skill, akin to the paternal role. If the ability to rear children did not spring from a natural instinct, but required serious study of the latest scientific advice, then, in theory, child rearing need not be gender specific. The advocates of what was popularly described as "trained motherhood," "scientific motherhood," or "mothercraft" had to acknowledge the existence of a paternal equivalent, thereby providing an impetus for the revaluation of modern fatherhood.[25]

In the midst of the twentieth-century makeover of fatherhood and motherhood, Americans observed Mother's Day, Father's Day, and Parents' Day with the same enthusiasm and skepticism that they approached modern childcare advice. As historians of both motherhood and fatherhood can attest, parents did not blindly follow all the dictates of modern experts. They accepted or rejected the advice as it fit their general and immediate concerns regarding the physical health and emotional development of their children. They were quite willing to both talk with and talk back to the leading experts.[26] In comparison, to celebrate Mother's Day, Father's Day or Parents' Day was to join the twentieth-century discourse over modern parenthood and talk back to the changing meanings of motherhood and fatherhood.

MOTHER'S DAY VERSUS FATHER'S DAY

In 1915, Anna Jarvis took a minute to reflect on the progress of her Mother's Day movement, scribbling her racing thoughts down on a memo pad: "Back of Mother's Day has been three years of unceasing hard work and effort. I feel appalled as I look forward and see the work required for next year and other years."[27] Contemplating the work yet to be done drew her thoughts to the topic of Father's Day. "A short time ago a man wrote and asked me how to start a Father's Day. He seemed to think a prescription might be sent on a post card," she mused. "He had the usual idea that no work would be necessary—simply the suggestion."[28] She could not help but mock the idea. "I think 'Fathers' would rather have a night. He can wear a night-blooming cereus or a sweet William, or a sunflower," she teased, "he might wear a 'poppy,'. . . Indeed all the flora of the country—like all the holidays seemed to be named after 'Father.' But to be more serious—Mother's Day is Father's Day."[29]

True to the Victorian image of fatherhood as the ultimate champion of mother-hood, Jarvis believed men honored their roles as fathers when they taught their children to revere their mothers. Thus her holiday's veneration of mothers and the home inexorably included a tribute to the domestic role of fathers, whose economic and emotional support facilitated the strength of a mother's influence. Jarvis even credited the ultimate success of her Mother's Day movement in part to the early and loyal support of men and their fraternal organizations, men who "found Mother's

Day a very ennobling Father's Day."[30] Yet, just like the senators who questioned the first Mother's Day resolution in 1908, Americans could not help but ask "what about a day for fathers?"

Less than two months and thirty miles separated the first official observances of Mother's Day and Father's Day. Although typically forgotten in the national story of Father's Day, the Central United Methodist Church in Fairmont, West Virginia, held the first recorded Father's Day service on July 5, 1908. According to local history, an overwhelming mixture of personal and community grief inspired Grace Golden Clayton to promote a special day of remembrance for fathers. She wished not only to honor the memory of her own father but to also pay tribute to the 250 fathers killed in a coal mining disaster six months earlier, a tragedy that left over one thousand children fatherless. Unfortunately, Clayton's decision to hold the service on the Sunday closest to her father's birthday guaranteed its quick descent into obscurity, as the day's significance was easily eclipsed by the weekend's celebration of Independence Day. Nonetheless, the state of West Virginia still lays public claim to the birthplace of both Father's Day and Mother's Day.[31]

In the following spring of 1909, Sonora Louise Smart Dodd attended a Mother's Day service in her hometown of Spokane, Washington. The special day of tribute naturally inspired members of the congregation of the Central Methodist Episcopal Church to remember the beloved parent who raised them. But instead of the fleeting memories of her mother, Dodd remembered her father, William Smart, a Civil War veteran who had been left alone to raise six children after the death of his wife in childbirth. Dodd decided to approach her minister about the idea for a Father's Day to be held on June 5, the anniversary of her father's birthday. By the following summer, Dodd had gained the endorsement of the local YMCA and the final approval of the Spokane Ministerial Association, with one small concession. The Spokane ministers requested the day be pushed to the third Sunday in June as not to interfere with the denomination's traditional celebration of Children's Day on the second Sunday of the month. Thus, Spokane hosted the first "official" Father's Day service on June 19, 1910.[32]

It only took one year, under Jarvis's keen leadership, for the observance of Mother's Day to reach Spokane, Washington, from its birthplace in the Appalachian Mountains. The strategy employed so efficiently by Jarvis, however, did not bring Dodd's Father's Day movement the same degree of success.[33] It was Mother's Day, and not Dodd, that inspired independent Father's Day observances across the country. It was hardly an ideological leap to imagine a paternal holiday comparable to Mother's Day; consequently, a handful of individuals led campaigns to establish a Father's Day on both local and national levels throughout the next thirty years—each supposedly unaware of the efforts of the other proclaimed founders.

Jane Addams and Harry C. Meek, both from Chicago, were the most notable promoters. Addams, the famous Progressive reform leader, lent her support for the holiday's adoption in 1911, but city leaders were less than enthusiastic about the idea and officially dismissed the issue. Once again, Addams lamented, "Poor father has been left out in the cold."[34] Lions Club president, Harry Meek, resurrected the holiday within his fraternal organization in 1915. Five year later, Chicago residents finally observed a Father's Day on the same day as the Spokane celebration; the Lions Club organization allegedly selected the third Sunday of June due to its proximity to Meek's birthday.[35]

Meek also hoped to follow the path that Jarvis first blazed and gain national recognition for Father's Day. Yet his efforts, like Dodd's, met with limited success throughout the 1910s and 1920s. Both Congress and a succession of U.S. presidents declined to formally endorse the paternal holiday despite the precedent set by the 1914 Mother's Day Flag Resolution and presidential proclamation. Nonetheless, presidents Woodrow Wilson, Warren Harding, and Calvin Coolidge at least agreed with the sentiment behind the commemoration and informally recognized the Father's Day observance. Wilson pressed a button in the oval office that unfurled a flag in Spokane, Washington, in honor of the town's Father's Day celebration. In 1924, Coolidge praised the day's noble intent to "establish more intimate relations between fathers and their children, and also to impress upon fathers the full measure of their obligations."[36] But the presidents' shared uneasiness over the day's exploitative commercial potential prevented their official endorsement.[37]

The presidents were right to have reservations over the holiday's irresistible marketing appeal, especially for commercial retailers who catered to male consumers. By 1925, the National Board of Tobacco Salesmen had already distributed 85,000 placards to promote the holiday. Four years later, the total climbed to 200,000. The holiday's transparent relationship with commercial interests was an important aspect of its founding. Unlike Jarvis, Dodd (who is generally recognized as Father's Day official founder) actively courted the commercial backing of Father's Day, preferring their endorsement over those of churches and social organizations. As a business school graduate with an interest in fashion design, she understood the power of advertising and sought to channel it toward her own holiday vision. Despite Dodd's formation of a committee to promote Father's Day and her open acceptance of help from all sectors of the Spokane community, the holiday movement stalled throughout the 1920s. Even Dodd briefly lost interest in her own creation, leaving Spokane and temporally abandoning her Father's Day movement for other pursuits.[38]

Father's Day campaigns in other parts of the country struggled to find a popular audience during the 1920s as well. In New York City, the residents found little initial interest in, and some confusion over, the paternal holiday. In their zeal to promote Father's Day, the National Board of Tobacco Salesmen mistakenly proclaimed the second Sunday in June as Father's Day, and not the third.[39] Such blunders added to the holiday's reputation as a marketing gimmick. Many Americans joined with Jarvis in ridiculing the Father's Day observance and shared in the joke over the dandelion being suggested as the holiday's official flower—in 1924, a Bible class in Pennsylvania had presumably selected the dandelion for its resiliency, since "the more it is trampled on the better it grows."[40] Ten years after the holiday's inaugural celebration, some fathers still described the day as "a lot of hooey" and "bunk," as reported in the New York Times.[41] The men's opinion fit the paper's characteristically irreverent coverage of the holiday: "Today is Father's Day. For 364 days of the year he is a poor, downtrodden, in-considered (though very necessary) nonentity, but today he will get a little respect and courtesy. That is, he will if he's lucky. Not like father wants a day set aside for himself."[42]

Why was it so easy to mock the idea of a special day of recognition for fathers? During the 1920s and 1930s, social conditions reshaped the father's primary roles as economic provider, companion, and male role model, into the revered image of modern fatherhood—creating what historians and social scientists define as a model of "New Fatherhood." The modern measures of fatherhood were not completely new to American society but were fashioned from the same repertoire of paternal roles that existed in the eighteenth and nineteenth centuries. What distinguished the early-twentieth-century paternal model as modern was its reconfiguration of the three roles and the degree in which they competed to define the meaning of fatherhood.[43] By the 1920s, for example, childcare literature included a larger discussion of a father's role in their children's lives, one beyond the primary role of breadwinner that defined nineteenth-century fatherhood.

As the call for a strong masculine presence in the family joined the medical consensus that a mother needed scientific assistance in rearing children, confusion erupted over whose masculine influence childcare experts were really referring to, their own or the influence of actual fathers. The predominantly male pediatricians and psychologists leading the modern makeover of the parent-child relationship added a distinct masculine tone to a previously feminized domain. "Thus in theory, at least, they opened [child rearing] to men as it had not been for more than a century, serving as role models of male interest and lending it rigorous prestige," explains historian Ann Hulbert. "On the other hand, in making [child rearing] a vocation, not an avocation, they in practice reduced the father, the wage earner, to newly amateur status on the sidelines while they usurped his place."[44] Adding to the confusion were the ambivalent feelings of mothers over the shifting boundaries of the paternal role. "What Is the Role of the Father?" was a frequent topic of women's child study groups in the 1920s. Women doubted their ability to meet the higher parental standards that experts endorsed without their husbands' help, yet they had little confidence in the level of direct assistance husbands were capable of providing.[45]

In the early decades of the twentieth century, then, it was unclear exactly where the modern father fit into the family beyond the role of economic provider. This opened discussion of alternative aspects of the paternal character as a means to broaden a father's influence. Childcare professionals, government pamphlets, and popular magazines encouraged fathers to cultivate a relationship with their children as a companion or "pal" to combat the traditional image of fathers as the absent authority figure.[46] The suggestion that fathers play with their children was drawn from the paternal repertoire of the nineteenth century. The Victorian model of fatherhood encouraged men to develop intimate and playful relationships with their children. It was a social perk of their newly redesigned economic authority and diminished domestic responsibilities. Relieved of the primary duty of raising moral children, and encouraged to view the domestic sphere as a haven of leisure and spiritual renewal, fathers could delight in their role as playmate or companion to their children. Victorian fathers had cultural permission to frolic with the children and cater to their whimsical nature in a manner once denounced as morally corrupting by their paternal counterparts in past centuries. The playmate role actively engaged fathers in domestic life (even if still sporadically) and reinforced the child-centered design of the middleclass family. Prescriptive literature continually stressed the mutual benefit derived from the playful father-child bonding, even though the role of playmate placed minimal demands on Victorian fathers, perhaps for only Sunday afternoons.[47]

It was easy for a father not responsible for the physical care of children to see them as a pure source of amusement or relaxation. The paternal roles of breadwinner and cherished playmate compared with the era's invention of Santa Claus. According to historian Stephen Frank, Santa Claus was the consummate father figure in the quintessential child-centered holiday:

A protean figure (successful factory owner, philanthropist, and secular saint), Santa Claus absorbed the dual aspects of modern fatherhood. Demanding goodness but seldom chastising children, he was the embodiment of nurturant male love, an ideal Victorian parent. At the same time, he reflected the work-centered life of American fathers, a man whose business—the preparation and annual delivery of toys to children in other families—seemed much more important than his own home life.[48]

In comparison, the twentieth-century father lacked the same air of confidence and admiration in the role of playmate. Children were no longer a simple source of his amusement and leisure. Play needed to fit scheduled times and fulfill defined purposes in a child's development. Psychologist John Watson, whose model of behaviorism dominated popular childcare advice in the 1920s, found that a good time for father's scheduled half hour with the children was close to bedtime. "I find that children, when allowed to romp, are loath to leave exciting play. They whine, and bad discipline results," he concluded. The quiet half hour spent with father was a nice solution. "It keeps the children used to male society. They have a chance to ply him with questions."[49] Experts considered fathers to be important in the establishment and reinforcement of good habits in children through regularity and restrained affections, which were hallmarks of behaviorist techniques. But the degree to which the father played a role in child rearing was often left vague.[50] He was essentially third in line in regard to authority over his children's management, after the experts and his wife, who had the time to make child rearing a vocation and read up on all the latest advice.

The Victorian father had earned his children's respect by making time in his busy work schedule. But in the 1920s, the modern Dad who strove to become closer to his children became harder to take seriously. When the popular press portrayed a father in a familial position outside the breadwinner role, it typically ended with him looking foolish.[51] Not even on Father's Day was Dad guaranteed respect. Sonora Dodd often expressed her hope that the observance of Father's Day would rectify the patronizing image of fathers as inept in the arena of childcare.[52] Her widowed father, after all, raised her and her five brothers. Apparently, it was easier to have fun at father's expense then grant him due reverence, mirroring a cultural ambivalence over the transitioning views of modern parenting.

Americans felt just as awkward about celebrating Father's Day as fathers themselves may have felt about stepping outside the clearly defined breadwinner role into a more ambiguous one. In his study of the holiday's commercial marketing, historian Leigh Eric Schmidt draws the connection between the social awkwardness surrounding the Father's Day observance and the tradition of buying gag gifts for fathers, epitomized, for instance, by the ugly neck tie:

> Father's Day was comical in part because fathers seemed so out of place or uncomfortable in this holiday world of sentimental gifts and domestic flattery.... Dad was bewildered by the attention or even somehow duped by these tokens of affection some of which were clearly purchased more with the giver than the receiver in mind.[53]

And in the end, it was the father who actually paid the bills for the gadgets and trinkets he received, which only added to the joke.

Despite the hopes of the commercial industries, they had to admit that Father's Day did not have the same sentimental appeal as Mother's Day. In 1934, Jarvis described the Father's Day movement that followed hers as "a fizzle and joke." They simply failed to understand that Mother's Day was for the whole family, just as was every other observance. "Did you ever hear of a 'Father's Day Christmas?'" she asked.54 But tobacconists and men's clothiers were not about to declare defeat in 1934. That year, the Associated Men's Wear Retailers in New York took the lead in advertising the observance and endorsing its recognition as a national holiday. What began as a Father's Day Committee within their association grew to include the interests of the National Retail Dry Goods Association, the National Association of Retail Clothiers and Furnishers, and the National Association of Tobacco Distributors. Renamed the National Council for the Promotion of Father's Day in 1938, the council aspired to build Father's Day into a second Christmas; a task made easier under the leadership of powerful New York businessmen and advertising executives who systematically streamlined the holiday's commercial campaign while simultaneously promoting the Father's Day Council as a nonprofit organization. Even Dodd rededicated herself to the Father's Day movement in the 1930s, throwing her full support behind the Father's Day Council's annual "Gifts-for-Father" campaigns.[55] In stark contrast with Jarvis, who threatened to permanently end the observance of Mother's Day in order to stop its commercial exploitation, Dodd never regretted her holiday's obvious marketability: "I like it, and I love it. I love seeing fathers get gifts."[56]

By the late 1930s, the *New York Times* reported the paternal celebration as a resounding commercial success. "Father's Day, according to the merchants, has finally become established," it announced. Even in the midst of the Great Depression, Father's Day continued its steady growth, gaining added legitimacy with the official endorsement of several state governors and respected fraternal organizations, such as the Rotary and Kiwanis Clubs. The outbreak of World War II inevitably boosted the holiday's sentimental appeal, as it did Mother's Day, by linking it to themes of patriotism. By midcentury, the Father's Day Council had come a long way from its original slogan of "Give Dad Something to Wear" in 1934, to the wartime call to "Salute Dad the American Way," to the 1949 slogan "Remember Father, Molder of Our Children's Future—For a Safe World Tomorrow Teach Democracy Today," which resulted in $106 million in holiday sales.[57]

Full credit for Father's Day popularity cannot go to the work of the Father's Day Council, however, despite its claim that the holiday would "die a miserable death" without its central leadership.[58] Commercial marketing alone could not create the necessary sentiment to ensure the holiday's longevity. Instead, the day's growing appeal corresponded with a maturing image of modern fatherhood. The childcare literature that marginalized the paternal role at the turn of twentieth century, for instance, began to speak directly to the importance of a father's involvement with his children's development. In 1914, the U.S. Children's Bureau published the first edition of its tremendously popular child-rearing manual, *Infant Care*, which provided detailed instructions on all aspects of childcare based on the latest principles of scientific research. The bureau sent the pamphlet free of charge to anyone who requested a copy, and congressmen often supplied the pamphlet to their constituents. The bureau distributed over 60,000 copies of *Infant Care* within the first six months of publication: that number climbed to 1.5 million by 1921, to 12 million by 1940, and then to 17 million by 1945.[59]

Throughout that time, the pamphlet underwent five revisions, reflecting the changes in scientific advice and noticeably charting the evolution of the modern paternal role. Slowly, the manual brought the father closer into the daily routine of childcare, moving him from a more supportive role (specifically one that did not purposely interfere with the children's schedule) to one of active partner in child rearing. The 1929 edition insisted that both parents needed to work together to teach the baby good habits and set him on the best path of development from the start. It included an illustration of a father and mother smiling down on their baby lying in a bassinet. By 1938, the manual encouraged fathers to be more active in the daily aspects of the baby's physical care. Even if a father did not participate on a regular basis, the advice stressed the importance for him to learn the skills of feeding and diapering a baby, especially if the mother became temporarily indisposed. The

1942 edition of *Infant Care* was the first edition to clearly identify both fathers and mothers as the manual's intended audience. To further promote this new model of proactive fatherhood, the bureau replaced the single illustration featuring a smiling, but still relatively passive, father standing over a bassinette with images of a father holding, playing, and bathing the baby.[60]

By 1950, one could finally flush out from within the prevailing childcare advice and popular magazine articles the distinct boundaries of the new paternal role in the modern American family. More importantly, it was a role that required serious respect and attention, as it was a position only a father could fill—specifically that of male role model. Experts and popular culture encouraged fathers to view their deeper familial involvement as a badge of masculinity.[61] "Being a real father is not 'sissy' business," insisted one male psychiatrist, "It is an occupation . . . the most important occupation in the world."[62]

Experts voiced their concern about the destructive nature of a mother's influence over a child's emotional and psychological development during World War II. A family required a strong intervening male presence to keep a mother's affections balanced between the two extremes of maternal rejection and maternal overprotection. Experts held American mothers accountable for their failure to maintain a proper balance of maternal affections, thereby raising emotionally stunted and overly dependent children.[63] Although the experts did not ignore a father's culpability in the rearing of maladjusted children, they tended to stress a father's involvement as a possible solution to the problem rather than a root cause. Fathers, moreover, were praised as key male figures in the gender socialization of their children, especially boys. Experts questioned women's capability to appropriately raise sons and accused mothers of the unforgivable crime of raising "sissies" or worse, homosexuals, by failing to reinforce normal masculine identities. With fathers serving as appropriate male role models, along with the assistance of masculine youth organizations such as the Cub Scouts and Boy Scouts, it was possible to raise sons to be "real boys" in spite of any misguided maternal tendency to overprotect them.[64]

The celebration of Father's Day gained popularity during the same decades in which parenting advice granted fathers an essential masculine role (other than economic provider) within the American family by increasing their domestic status.[65] A father was less likely by midcentury to be characterized as the "poor, downtrodden, in-considered (though very necessary) nonentity" that the *New York Times* described in 1927. In other words, as fathers were taken more seriously, so was the day dedicated in their honor. The postwar fear of "Momism"—the belief that domineering mothers were rearing weak children unable to meet the new national threat of Communism—explains that 1949 Father's Day slogan: "Remember Father, Molder of Our Children's Future—For a Safe World Tomorrow Teach Democracy Today."[66]

The overlap between Father's Day and the twentieth-century makeover of fatherhood was not accidental. Father's Day gave the new model of fatherhood a popular appeal and, in return, the new respect for American fathers enhanced the support for a day set aside for their tribute.[67] Of course, Father's Day earned its acceptance over

Jarvis's ardent pleas to not allow "anti-mother racketeers" to splinter the Mother's Day celebration into one for each family member. Americans, as evident by their increasing participation in the holiday's observance, did not agree with Jarvis that fathers were already included in the Mother's Day celebration and did not need special recognition. They did not share her alarm that a Father's Day would marginalize Mother's Day on the American calendar by adding yet another paternal day of tribute to the several that already existed: New Year's Day for Old Father Time, Memorial Day for Departed Fathers, Independence Day for Patriot Fathers, Labor Day for Laboring Fathers, and Thanksgiving for Pilgrim Fathers.[68]

Yet, there is evidence to suggest that Americans shared, at least partly, Jarvis's anxiety over the marginalization of motherhood. Important questions remain over the rivalry between Mother's Day, Father's Day, *and* Parents' Day. For instance, why did Father's Day find popular acceptance over that of Parents' Day first observed in 1924? If both fathers and mothers were indispensable parts of the traditional American family and jointly responsible for the health and happiness of their children, why not celebrate their parental partnership? Why insist on two separate observances? Moreover, what does the ultimate rejection of a national Parents' Day in place of Mother's Day imply about the cultural acceptance of the transitioning models of fatherhood and motherhood, especially when it threatened the "parental ranking" of men and women within the family?

MOTHER'S DAY VERSUS PARENTS' DAY

In its 1938 coverage of Mother's Day, *Time* highlighted a few of the sensational public exploits of Jarvis, the identified "60-year-old Philadelphia spinster who invented Mother's Day." The article recounted her disgust with the floral, confection, and telegraph industries over their persistent infringement of her copyright. It included her arrest for disorderly conduct after crashing an American War Mothers convention in protest of their Mother's Day carnation sales, and it mentioned her refusal to allow Postmaster General James Aloysius Farley to print "Mother's Day" on a 1934 commemorative stamp. The article also noted her denunciation of the Parents' Day celebration in New York's Central Park that year and her current Mother's Day International Association's slogan of "Don't Kick Mother out of Mother's Day."[69]

Jarvis had been critical of the New York City Parents' Day rallies, held annually *on* Mother's Day, since its inception; the holiday's founder Robert Spero held top ranking on her list of anti-mother propagandists from 1923 to 1941. Compared to Father's Day, Parents' Day was the larger symbolic and personal threat to Mother's Day and Jarvis, but it has left less of a historical record. Currently, only two primary sources reveal any details about the little known Parents' Day campaign in the early twentieth century: the *New York Times* and the personal accounts of Anna Jarvis.[70]

Ironically, Jarvis directly triggered the events that led to the creation of Parents' Day. No historian who has studied Jarvis and her Mother's Day movement in any detail has failed to mention her threat to sue New York Governor Al Smith over his plans for a gigantic Mother's Day celebration in 1923. Authors typically include this event in Jarvis's history to illustrate her obsession with protecting her day from political and commercial exploitation. The historical context behind her threat is secondary to the showcasing of her eccentric personality. Robert Spero, however, was at the center of that 1923 dispute. Since 1919, accounts of Spero's philanthropic work with poor and disabled children had been reported in the *New York Times*. The paper especially took note of the entertainment and gifts that "Uncle Robert," as he was commonly known, bestowed on the city's needy children during the Christmas season. It was an annual tradition for Spero to host a Christmas party for underprivileged children at his home in Long Branch, New Jersey. The tradition began in 1916 with fifteen children, and by 1921, he played Santa Claus to two thousand invited guests.[71]

In 1923, Spero organized the New York Mother's Day Committee with the full endorsement of Governor Al Smith and Mayor John Hylan. The committee quickly began plans for a large Mother's Day celebration to be held in the stadium of City College, complete with a parade of marching bands and singing troops of Boy Scouts and Girl Scouts. Jarvis, however, would not permit it, claiming that the New York committee had no legal right to celebrate Mother's Day according to their own design and threatened to sue the committee (which included Al Smith) for infringement. She apparently had evidence of Spero's misrepresentation of his committee as an authorized affiliate of her Mother's Day International Association by using its official letterhead on New York Mother's Day Committee correspondences. In response, Governor Smith pressured Spero to cancel his grand plans. Instead of celebrating Mother's Day in a large stadium rally, Spero spent the holiday with nine hundred women from the Home for Aged on Welfare Island and an assembly of two hundred children who were permitted an excursion away from the city's hospital wards. "Spero distributed 2,000 packages of animal crackers, 2,000 lollypops and 1,000 flags," reported the *New York Times*:

> Afterwards all the women were marched to the lawn to have their pictures taken by four or five motion picture companies. Spero promised the women he would get one of the reels for their own use in the big hall of the home.[72]

He had originally hired the motion picture company to make a newsreel of the previous planned Mother's Day rally.[73]

Spero credited that afternoon spent with the neglected men and women in the poorhouse on Welfare Island as the original inspiration for a Parents' Day celebration. He recalled, "Seeing those forgotten parents, those broken lives bent with age, the stories of bitter disappointment written on their careworn faces, made me realize that there still appeared among them a will be to be happy. If they only could feel that it was the island of welfare and not one of farewell."[74] Although one can see the ideological connection between that experience and Spero's desire to create a Parents' Day, it does not fully explain his motives for wanting to replace

Mother's Day. If he wished only to include recognition for fathers as active parents in the rearing of children, he could have easily endorsed the observance of Father's Day.[75] Instead, he insisted on the second Sunday of May for the observance of a Parents' Day. Jarvis believed she knew the true motivation behind Spero's Parents' Day campaign, citing mainly his greed and craving for publicity.[76] "If he were merely seeking a changed name—and not seeking to seize the decades of cumulative work, time and origination of Mother's Day—he could have his special Day some other season of the year—say October, or November or July," she argued.[77]

Spero's background further confuses the issue of his desire to replace Mother's Day with Parents' Day. According to the New York Times, Spero refused to reveal the source of the personal wealth that supported his generous tributes to disadvantaged children and the charitable work of his Uncle Robert Foundation. Over the span of forty years, however, the newspaper accounts of his activities tied him to a Brooklyn clothing house business in 1900 and then later to the Charles Zinn & Company of New York, a willow ware and basket manufacturer. Spero was also well known for his radio troop of child entertainers and private broadcasting studio; in his public work with children and Parents' Day, he preferred to go by "Uncle Robert."[78]

Jarvis's personal accounts of Parents' Day and her relationship with Spero provide additional insight into his history. Unlike the New York Times, Jarvis never referred to Spero as a philanthropist without the requisite quotations around the word, as she believed his hidden business connections with the floral industry tainted his reputation. Her confrontation with Spero in 1923 was apparently not her first run-in with him. She claimed to have first discovered him as a traveling salesman of florists' supplies in Omaha, Nebraska, who recognized early on the profitability of exploiting her observance. She accused him of trying to change the Mother's Day emblem of a white carnation to an insignia of valentine hearts with some "maudlin slogan" to boost his floral sales.[79] When his efforts failed, he settled for marketing his inventory of artificial carnations as a meaningful floral tribute to mothers on her special day. Throughout the same years he promoted Parents' Day, Spero allegedly continued his annual cross-country "salesmanship tour," filling floral supply orders for Mother's Day. "He has been much of an annoyance in this way," Jarvis claimed.[80] She viewed his Parents' Day observance as simply his latest scheme to profit off her life's work: "Spero realizes it will be illegal for him to use Mother's Day under its own name, and a change of name is his method of assuming ownership versus protests, and escaping legal pressures."[81]

The personal and commercial aspects of the holiday rivalry did not completely overshadow the cultural significance of Parents' Day. Like Father's Day, Parents' Day was a cultural product of the new debates over the role of modern fathers in the American family. The rhetoric associated with its annual promotions and observances illustrated its link to the new fatherhood model. "We want fathers to feel that they are more than breadwinners," Spero explained in 1926, "that when they go off to work they have some responsibility for what goes on in the home."[82]

That year, an audience of four thousand attended the Parents' Day celebration held at the City College stadium in the Bronx. The event included musical performances by local school children and the presentation of medals to children with the best essays on Parents' Day.

Above all, attendees listened to speakers, such as School Board President George Ryan, stress the essential familial duties of both parents:

> The Home is, as always, the foundation stone of the State, the great school of character, the nursery for moral stature, sturdy or dwarfed. . . . Among the contributions to the solidarity of the home, parental instruction, perhaps, makes the most permanent offering. Enforcing discipline, curbing selfishness and teaching self-control, incline the twig in the right direction. Excellent though the aim of parental instruction may be, it is really valueless if offset by a bad parental example.[83]

Language associated with the behavioral model of child rearing, so popular during the decade, was woven throughout the school administrator's address, including the important role that both parents needed to play in instilling the discipline and self-control required for children to thrive in a modern industrial society. His reference to the eighteenth-century proverb, "as the twig is bent, the tree's inclined," displayed the popular tenet of Watsonian behaviorism that stressed children's special malleability, especially in the first three years of life.[84]

Initially, Parents' Day garnered a greater public interest in New York City than Father's Day. A variety of factors shaped Parents' Day's larger popularity. The celebration's origin in New York City and its endorsement by well-known city and state public figures offer the most obvious explanation. Meanwhile, its shared date with the more popular Mother's Day observance ensured its exposure alongside the variety of maternal tributes throughout the city. But the overall tone of the holidays' respective media coverage deserves comparison, as well. As noted, the popular press considered Father's Day an easy target of ridicule during the 1920s. Eight of the fifteen *New York Times* articles written on Father's Day between 1920 and 1929, for example, focused on the holiday's commercialization, reinforcing its reputations as a marketing ploy designed to sell ugly neckties.[85] In contrast, Parents' Day did not have the same commercial taint, thanks to the public relations work of Spero and the charitable work of his Uncle Robert Foundation.

Spero took special care to dissociate Parents' Day from the commercialization of Mother's Day, to the point where he suggested Parents' Day as a possible antidote to the commercial cheapening of familial sentiment:

> At present, Mother's Day means little more than the purchase of flowers, a detail that has been made a mere business matter. If children save their pennies to purchase something jointly for fathers and mothers we can extend the idea of paternal regard over the whole year instead of the single day.[86]

Instead of depicting fathers as foolish or nonentities in the serious domestic arena of childcare, the accounts of Parents' Day celebrations presented fathers as respected partners in the modern parenting of their children.

The holiday's momentum continued throughout the early twentieth century as Spero worked toward a national recognition of Parents' Day. His efforts secured the official endorsement of publisher George Hecht, the editor of *Parents Magazine*, in 1929. This was a significant achievement. Throughout the Great Depression, *Parents Magazine* was the only commercial periodical to experience a steady gain in circulation and advertising revenues. Both childcare professionals and lay readers alike regarded the magazine as the leading popular educational periodical in the country under Hecht's leadership.[87] His personal appeals for Parents Day carried the merits of the new holiday to a significant national audience. Like Spero, Hecht praised the holiday as an ideal weapon to combat the saccharine sentimentality and commercialization of Mother's Day. He recognized the tangible social benefits in redirecting the power of a day commemorating the parental role toward nobler aspirations. "We have no quarrel with the fine sentiment that creates a Mother's Day but we feel that the significance of that day would will be immeasurably greater if Mother's Day becomes Parents' Day," Hecht wrote in a 1929 editorial, "its dual purpose, the honoring of parents on the part of children and the dedication of fathers and mothers to be the great ideal of creating throughout the country an enlightened parenthood."[88]

Meanwhile, Spero sought to replace New York State's official designation of Mother's Day on the second Sunday in May with Parents' Day as part of his expanded campaign. In 1930, Assemblyman Julius Berg introduced a bill in Albany to legally place Parents' Day on the holiday calendar in lieu of the traditional observance of Mother's Day. He was confident in the merits of his proposed bill, believing there was nothing to lose but much to gain by celebrating mothers and fathers together. "It may be that many who have been accustomed to honoring mother on that date will be jealous of having any part of the day devoted to anyone but mother," he admitted. "I believe, however, that the mothers of the State will not complain."[89] He assured potential skeptics that his bill had already obtained approval within all levels of government, naming President Herbert Hoover, Governor Franklin D. Roosevelt, and New York City Mayor Jimmy Walker as early supporters.[90]

Spero also embarked on his own letter-writing campaign to promote the holiday and even adopted an official Parents' Day motto: "A Kiss for Mother and a Hug for Dad." The holiday rallies in New York City became more elaborate in design as Spero's holiday campaign grew in intensity. In addition to the addresses of respected city and state officials and parades of children (including one in 1938 that showcased twenty-eight children dressed to represent the city's racial and ethnic diversity), Spero introduced a parents-of-the-year award. In 1933, the award went to a couple raising sixteen children. A couple married for seventy years won the honor in 1936. The following year, Spero presented the award to a couple who lost a child in World War I. By the late 1930s, Spero reported receiving letters from school officials and politicians across the country pledging their support for Parents' Day. Even Postmaster General James Farley, who commissioned the Mother's Day commemorative stamp in 1934, was scheduled to attend the Parents' Day rally in 1936.[91]

Spero was sure Parents' Day sat on the verge of becoming a full-fledged national movement by the 1930s. The day's message certainly fit the decade's reconfiguration of parenthood, as supporters praised Spero for his work to save the next generation of children from the perils of modern society through his holiday celebration.[92] Moreover, the Parents' Day movement could not have found a better spokesman than Hecht and his magazine for promoting the importance of fathers in the fight against modern threats. Indeed, *Parents Magazine* had a significant effect on modern perceptions of parenthood, especially the meaning of fatherhood. Between 1926 and 1942, *Parents Magazine* published seventy-five articles with fatherhood as the primary focus; overall, that constituted 47 percent of all fatherhood articles published in popular magazines addressing childcare issues.[93] That was an impressive percentage, considering that a 1931 survey estimated that as high as 96 percent of women and 55 percent of men depended on popular magazines for the latest child-rearing advice. Fathers interested in answers to particular problems or simply wishing to improve their general knowledge of childcare techniques could even read a column in *Parents Magazine* specifically designed for them, one that encouraged a father's interaction with his children independent from his wife's supervision. Titled "For Fathers Only," the featured column ran between 1932 and 1937, the same period during which Spero anticipated the imminent national success of his Parents' Day.[94]

The national success that Spero predicted never materialized, despite the apparent strengths of the Parents' Day movement. The *New York Times* coverage of the annual Parents' Day rallies revealed significant discrepancies between the predicted crowd attendance suggested by Spero's promotional buildup to the rally and the actual tally of the crowd. Spero may have expected crowds of forty to fifty thousand celebrants, but the newspaper's post-holiday estimations never exceeded twenty thousand.[95] In addition, Assemblyman Berg's bill to officially replace the legislative recognition of Mother's Day with Parents' Day failed in 1930, as did all subsequent attempts to legally kick mother out of Mother's Day in New York State.[96] Occasionally, the *New York Times* expressed the confusion that the dueling holidays created within the city, reporting that many residents had doubts over which day to actually celebrate. In 1933, an article addressing the celebration of both holidays identified the notable absence of any references to fathers or parents in President Franklin Roosevelt's holiday proclamation, in which he called for the national display of the American flag and the bestowing of gifts—in other words, his Mother's Day proclamation.[97]

Spero announced his retirement as leader of the Parents' Day campaign in April of 1940. He passed the reins to his friend, George Hecht, who tried but failed to hold that year's Parents' Day services at the World's Fair in Queens, New York. (The World's Fair did host a Mother's Day service, however).[98] In retrospect, Spero's selection of Hecht as his successor was a mistake. In 1941, Hecht abandoned the Parents' Day movement altogether to chair the newly incorporated National Committee on the Observance of Mother's Day, yet another group with no official connection to Jarvis's Mother's Day International Association. Its inaugural slogan for Mother's Day was "Remember mother! She never forgets!"[99]

Hecht's shifted loyalties reveal one significant reason for the parental holiday's demise. Despite his early work in Progressive reform efforts and later political advocacy for children, the publishing business was his true love.[100] With the publication of *Parents Magazine*, Hecht saw an opportunity to combine his interests in social reform and business, but they were not balanced interests. "I won't permit going into anything that doesn't have the prospect of being profitable," he confessed. "They don't have to make much money but they have to have good prospects. But I wouldn't go into any moneymaking project which I cannot be proud of."[101] During

Figure 3.1. By the 1940s, publisher George Hecht abandoned his campaign to replace Mother's Day with Parents' day. Author's Private Collection.

the magazine's first years in circulation, Hecht surely wished to appeal to the largest possible audience. That was motive enough to follow, or even exaggerate, any new trends in childcare advice, including the focus on fatherhood. His endorsement of Parents' Day reflected that new trend. By 1941, however, it was clear to Hecht that mothers, not fathers, were the primary readers of *Parents Magazine*.[102]

Jarvis and the sentimental popularity of Mother's Day were also formidable obstacles for the Parents' Day campaign to overcome. There was a fierce personal rivalry between the two holiday founders. Jarvis was Spero's leading critic during the entire Parents' Day movement, denouncing him and his associates as charlatans and profiteers to any public official she believed could assist her efforts to stop him; in her lowest moments, she derisively referred to Spero as "the New York Jew" or "the Hebrew."[103] Her assault on the Parents' Day observance escalated in the 1930s with Assemblyman Berg's efforts in Albany. Not only did she consider Berg's actions as a personal attack on her movement work, she deemed the bill as a patent insult to the mothers of New York:

> Of all the freak and amazing attacks on the home and respected woman-hood of New York State, surely this Anti-mother bill sponsored by a little clique of anti-mother sons is a humiliating one. It is inconceivable that any mother's son or daughter would try to knock even the name of 'mother' out of Mother's Day.[104]

Jarvis mobilized each year to stop the New York State legislature's adoption of the bill. Since the 1920s, she had cultivated connections with New York politicians, and she sought to use those connections throughout the 1930s.[105] Jarvis even appealed to Governor Franklin Roosevelt in 1932 to ignore any legislative attempts pertaining to the second Sunday in May, insisting that her Mother's Day movement was not a matter for New York Assembly legislation.[106] The following year, she bragged to her cousin of her success in blocking the bill thanks to her influence with the New York County Bar Association.[107] She also wanted the last word on the Parents' Day's inclusion in the 1940 World's Fair. This time, she beseeched Franklin Roosevelt for help in his capacity as president to stop the efforts of Spero and Hecht.[108]

Jarvis was never alone in her defense of Mother's Day and its sentimental celebration of motherhood. Americans illustrated their lack of interest in the Parent's Day movement through varying degrees of action or inaction. When considering New York City's ranking as the largest city in the country, twenty thousand Parents' Day observers out of an early twentieth-century population of five to seven million does not carry a strong impression. Furthermore, there is no significant evidence to suggest the holiday's greater success outside the city of New York, other than Spero's word.[109] Jarvis believed the Parents' Day movement was destined to fail because its leaders could never capture the true source of Mother's Day popularity. "They little realize the secret, enduring source of Mother's Day origin and achievement; they only know their failure to create any semblance of it," she observed.[110]

And what was that secret, enduring source of the holiday's achievement? It was the knowledge, sentimental or otherwise, that mothers were the primary rearers of children. Ironically, Works Progress Administration administrator Victor Ridder agreed with Jarvis's veneration of motherhood and asserted as much in his address at the 1936 Parents' Day rally:

> I want to speak to the children today and I want to express my appreciation to the mothers. Uncle Robert wants me to make this Parents' Day, but it will always be Mother's Day with me. You will never know how grateful to her you ought to be until you find out what she does for you. You mean more to your mothers than any of the men gathered here today, and that is as it ought to be.

Spero immediately attempted to diffuse Ridder's comments: "Now remember, pals, this is Parents' Day, no one-sided event. We want fathers to be more than just a meal-ticket."[111] Apparently, as Ridder's sentiment suggests, Americans believed that fathers deserved regard beyond that of "meal-ticket," but they debated whether or not fathers deserved the same regard as mothers.

TRIUMPHANT MOTHER'S DAY

In 1927, two years before George Hecht publicly endorsed the creation of Parents' Day, his magazine sponsored an essay contest on the topic of Mother's Day. As mentioned in the introduction, the magazine asked readers to share "frank expressions of opinion" on the merits of the holiday observance. The magazine received 116 essay entries, of which sixty-eight favored the continued celebration of Mother's Day and forty-eight did not. Although certainly not a representative sample of the population, it does hint at Mother's Day emotional appeal and sentimental edge over its holiday rivals. In one prize-winning essay, a mother admittedly defended the holiday's value in teaching children an important lesson. "Too often our little ones are not taught to think of Mother as other than giver of good things, to be loved, of course, but not to be rewarded in any way," she wrote. "Surely Mother's Day should be set apart to teach from the youngest to the oldest, that on that one day, Mother is first; that is her one day in the whole year when all should do her reverence."[112] In the end, early-twentieth-century Americans were not prepared to take away the one day in the whole year where "Mother is first." Despite the modern makeover of motherhood that questioned women's fitness to raise children unsupervised, Mother's Day emerged triumphant in its rivalry with Father's Day and Parents' Day.

When given the choice to recognize the importance of fatherhood through the observance of a Father's Day or a Parents' Day, celebrants opted to pay reverence to Father in a way that did not threaten the status of Mother or marginalize her role as the primary caretaker of children.[113] In understanding the ultimate failure of Parents' Day, therefore, we cannot ignore the symbolism behind the holiday's rejection. Perhaps the holiday's lack of broad appeal reflected the larger cultural understanding of the gendered hierarchy within the family, especially in regard to childcare. Its rebuff can stand as a social commentary on the unequal division of childcare labor shielded behind the gender-neutral term *parent*—an acknowledgement, in other words, that when childcare experts addressed parents, they were really addressing mothers. As for Father's Day, it took over sixty years for the day to achieve federal recognition, courtesy of President Richard Nixon.[114] Its spot on the American calendar *after* Mother's Day mirrors its secondary status in American culture. Today, Father's Day consistently falls second to Mother's Day in commercial sales and volume of long distance phone calls. Only in one category does Father's Day rival Mother's Day: more collect calls are made on Father's Day than any other day of the year.[115]

Like her beloved creation, Anna Jarvis also emerged triumphant in her rivalry with the promoters of Father's Day and Parents' Day. Her name is certainly more recognizable in the popular knowledge surrounding American holidays. For most holiday celebrants, Jarvis's reputation, for better or worse, will always eclipse the historic significance of Father's Day founder Sonora Dodd and Parent's Day founder Robert Spero.[116]

THE AMERICAN WAR MOTHERS AND A MEMOIR OF MOTHERS' DAY

O n Mother's Day, May 12, 1918, American mothers with sons serving in France received a special tribute courtesy of General John Pershing, commander and chief of the American Expeditionary Forces (AEF). He urged all soldiers and officers of the AEF to take a moment to write a letter home to their mothers in observance of the holiday. This small gesture from each man would mean everything for mothers at home, the general assured: "these letters will carry back our courage and our affection to the patriotic women whose love and prayers inspire us and cheer us onto victory."[1] In the army posts scattered across France, from the Young Men's Christian Association huts and Salvation Army cabins to the muddy battlefield trenches and dugouts, American soldiers followed their general's orders and wrote home. Postmaster General Albert Burleson pledged that envelopes marked "mother's letter" would receive preference over all other mail business to guarantee the fastest possible delivery.[2]

The *New York Times* reported the arrival of 475 sacks of mail for American mothers, the largest single assignment of mail received from France since the start of the war. Over a million mothers across the country received treasured letters from the war front. Some had been without word from their sons for months, in some cases, years. These letters sought only to lighten their mothers' hearts and ease their fears. Sons promised their mothers what they undoubtedly wanted to hear, that they were safe and in want of nothing, short of being home to share the day with them. "You can rest assured that no regiment could be in better spirits or have higher aspirations," wrote one soldier. "We are ready for whatever is in store for us. So don't worry; everything will be O.K."[3] The sample of letters published in newspapers across the country expressed how proud the men were to be serving their country and their mothers. Readers of the *Alma Signal* in Kansas were perhaps as filled with pride as Herman Arndt's dear mother when they read the hometown boy's touching words. "I am dissatisfied to be so far away from you, yet I am contented and happy to think that I can have my part, tho [*sic*] small it may be in this cruel war," he wrote. "Little would we have to fight for if it were not for all the dear mothers back home."[4]

Both Congress and President Woodrow Wilson reinforced the military tribute by applauding the inimitable role of mothers in the nation's war effort at home. In his fourth official Mother's Day Proclamation, Wilson asked for special attention to the patriotic sacrifices of American mothers selfishly offering their sons to fight and die in the defense of liberty and justice.[5] Across the country, communities repeated the president's sentiment and linked their Mother's Day observances and maternal tributes directly to the war. Churches asked parishioners to keep in their thoughts the mothers who gave up their most cherished possessions for the cause of worldwide democracy. Women's groups promoted a day of international prayer to ask God to grant mothers the "Spartan heart" required to send their sons to war. Anna Jarvis followed suit by presiding over a military observance at Camp Sherman in Chillicothe, Ohio. At one point, the forty-two thousand soldiers stood at attention for one minute and recited the Lord's Prayer in unison in maternal tribute. Ohio florists generously donated carnations for each soldier in camp.[6]Following the centuries-old tradition of nations mobilizing for war, motherhood was drafted into service during World War I, but this time with the help of the new holiday.[7] The

MOTHER'S DAY 1918

Figure 4.1. Cartoonist Clifford Berryman illustrating the symbolic link between the celebration of Mother's Day and the support of the First World War. Courtesy of the U.S. National Archives and Records Administration, College Park, Maryland.

American celebration of Mother's Day, although relatively new as a nationally rec-ognized holiday, had tremendous sentimental appeal and was already a commercial success—a testimony to its easy marketability. The holiday offered an irresistible opportunity to serve civilian mobilization as the United States entered into World War I. It was an armed and ready weapon, if you will, in the government's war propaganda. Not only did the wartime celebration of Mother's Day encourage and valorize the sacrifice of American mothers, but it also helped recast the country's involvement in a foreign war as the ultimate defense of the home that American motherhood represented. The military's 1918 Mother's Day observance ingeniously channeled both the filial sentimentality of the day and the established practice of sending mothers letters and greeting cards toward a wartime goal.

Although operating on preexisting maternal imagery and traditions, the Mother's Day campaign still required weeks of planning by the AEF General Staff Headquarters and the collaboration of various U.S. welfare agencies operating throughout France. The *Stars and Stripes* ran successive articles covering the military's letter drive and shamelessly utilized the tried and true power of guilt to elicit the soldiers' cooperation:

> She knows—without your writing it or anybody else's writing it—that you are her son; and that, being her son, you cannot be anything but what is good and straight and clean and true and loyal. . . . But you will never forgive yourself if you begrudge the time to write to her—even if it's only to tell her you're well and to send her your love in just those brief words—on the day of all days in the year that is pre-eminently hers and hers alone—Mother's Day.[8]

If the literary image of a mother endlessly rereading her treasured letter was not convincing enough, an accompanying illustration portrayed a stereotypical apron-clad mother running breathlessly down the driveway, with a hand on her heart and the other outstretched to grab the letter from the postman. A Blue Star flag, identifying her sacrifice of a son to war, is proudly displayed below the American flag on the front porch behind her. From the open window, the soldier's little sister is peering out to share in the moment. A white picket fence and a small dog caught up in the excitement add the finishing touches.[9]

American relief organizations did their part to make the Mother's Day campaign a success by providing soldiers with the means and opportunity to write a letter home. Canteen workers assisted illiterate soldiers in composing their letters. Oth-ers encouraged men without a mother at home still to write to loved ones eager for any news from them. Women workers fervently distributed preprinted postcards to soldiers on leave in the French Riviera. The prepared prose compared the soldier's mother to the picturesque scenery of southern France, the ocean tides to her endur-ing love, the sunny skies to her continual good cheer, and the blooming flowers to her beautiful soul, one that inspired her son to revere womanhood and believe in God. Soldiers too distracted or apathetic to pen their own prose to their mothers had only to sign to their names to the postcard.[10]

Figure 4.2. Example of the floral industry capitalizing on the symbolic link between the celebration of Mother's Day and the support of the war. Florists' Review, 25 April 1918, 8.

The government-sponsored propaganda elevated the protection of motherhood to a palatable war objective. Top executives of the country's nascent film industry eager to ingratiate themselves with governmental agencies, as well as attract new audiences, volunteered their services in promoting mothers' patriotic sacrifices to war. On the big screen, mothers who nurtured a sense of duty and honor in their sons, thus inspiring them to fight for her and their home, were the heroines. In contrast, mothers who smothered their sons, raising a generation of cowards, symbolized the epitome of villainy. This battle to redefine the meaning of maternal patriotism in popular culture reduced mothers to passive objects of devotion as opposed to active political agents. The propaganda essentially portrayed the obedient mother and a patriotic son as the foundation of the American wartime family.[11]

The degree to which wartime propaganda affected or reflected American attitudes of motherhood and war varied. Many of the 1918 Mother's Day celebrations

Figure 4.3. Mother's Day Programs from 1918, 1919, and 1925, further illustrate the connection between motherhood and sacrifice during times of war. Courtesy of the International Mother's Day Shrine, Grafton, West Virginia.

showed a clear connection between maternal sacrifice and patriotism, the very message at the heart of the military's letter-writing campaign. As the result of the country's mobilizing efforts, millions of women rallied to support U.S. involvement in World War I, often based on their roles as mothers.[12] Twenty years later, a new generation of mothers rallied to support World War II under the country's massive mobilization efforts. It is unfair, however, to dismiss maternal wartime activism as the by-product of social coercion or governmental manipulation. Although war propaganda helped define and reinforce the link between motherhood, sacrifice, and patriotism during two world wars, it did not hold complete sway over American women. Its images and messages did not have the final say in how mothers expressed their relationship with war and its required sacrifices, regardless of the extent of their wartime activism. The American War Mothers (AWM) exemplified this complex relationship between motherhood and war in the early twentieth century. The early history of the AWM offers a glimpse into the intersection of motherhood, women's wartime activism, and the symbolic role of Mother's Day. What began with club women answering the state of Indiana's call for mothers to mobilize for World War I led to a national organization of women refusing to strictly emulate the passive object of devotion epitomized in wartime propaganda.

In 1925, President Calvin Coolidge signed the American War Mothers' Congressional charter, and in 1933, the organization moved its national headquarters to Washington, DC. True to its origins, the modern AWM designates itself as a perpetual patriotic organization, continuing to recognize and support the service of veterans and their families.[13] Although a mother's eligibility for membership during both world wars depended on her sacrifice of a child to war, that sacrifice did not mark the totality of the member's patriotic service. Theirs' were not unconditional sacrifices but ones deserving of reciprocity. The war mothers defined their unqualified obedience to the war effort strictly with the military obedience of their soldier sons and heroic daughters and not beyond.[14] In exchange for their children's service, its members expected a voice in government decisions and the absolute freedom to challenge the decisions that unduly risked their children's lives. That was an entitlement due them, they believed, one born of that initial sacrifice of sending a child off to war but certainly not restricted to it.

The AWM was not the only early-twentieth-century women's organization to justify patriotic activism during wartime or otherwise in the name of motherhood, but they were the only national women's organization to explicitly subsume the Mother's Day holiday and the related symbol of the carnation into their patriotic identity and service to American veterans. What organization was more fitting to celebrate a national holiday originating from a flag resolution, they believed, than an organization composed of the mothers who sent their sons to defend the very flag that hung on all governmental building and individual homes on the second Sunday in May?[15] With that assertion, they officially went to war with Anna Jarvis, albeit inadvertently at first. Yet just as they refused to limit their patriotism to the passive role of the maternal martyr, they too refused to surrender their celebration of Mother's Day due to the ravings of an irate Philadelphia woman. The AWM instead braced for battle over the physical and interpretative ownership of Mother's Day. Through the intertwining of patriotic and Mother's Day symbols, the strategic employment of the day's possessive plural spelling, and alliances with rival Mother's Day promoters, the war mothers attempted to erase Jarvis's claim to have founded the holiday.

The organization's history effectively reveals the failure of both Jarvis and the American government to protect the purity of their maternal message or predict the depth and consequences of its social resonance for women. While Jarvis anchored her Mother's Day celebration to women's domestic service and the propaganda campaigns of both world wars linked Mother's Day to women's willingness to serve a foreign war, neither could completely control how women chose to honor their maternal roles.

A MOTHER'S RELATIONSHIP TO WAR

The U.S. government seriously underestimated women's desire to have a voice in the country's foreign policies once war erupted in Europe. Whether they strove to keep the country out of war, worked to prepare it for war, or wholly supported entry into the war, American women constituted an independent force during World War I. Although persuaded by wartime propaganda, they challenged and shaped it to reflect their individualized models of patriotism. And motherhood offered an exclusive and fertile framework in which to define their relationship to war. During World War I, a woman did not need to experience motherhood personally to accept the premise that women's natural reproductive capacities or experience gained through rearing children instilled in them an intuitive drive to serve, sacrifice, nurture, and protect those in their care. Thus, both single and married women, mothers and potential mothers, pacifists and military advocates alike coexisted (albeit uneasily at times) under an "ideological umbrella of motherhood."[16] The history of the American War Mothers' model of maternal patriotism is clearly rooted within this era. Although hotly contested in regard to its appropriate expression, the popularly accepted link between motherhood and war cultivated during World War I made possible the AWM's national appeal.

During the inaugural meeting of the Woman's Peace Party (WPP) in 1915, suffrage leader Anna Howard Shaw vividly identified motherhood's mediating link between women and war when she equated the sacrifice and heroism demanded of childbirth to that required of soldiers on the battlefield. War, she warned, threatened to annul a mother's heroism, making futile the countless sacrifices made in the giving and rearing of a child. Shaw insisted,

Looking into the face of that one dead man we see two dead, the man and the life of the woman who gave him birth; the life she wrought into his life! And looking into his dead face someone asks a woman, what does a woman know about war? What, what, friends in the face of a crime like that, what does man know about war![17]

Members of the WPP, the first peace organization to be led exclusively by women in American history, rooted their calls for the abolishment of war in the sentiment eloquently stated by Shaw. As "the Mother Half of Humanity," they earned the right to be consulted in the settlement of foreign conflicts that potentially risked the lives of those they bore, fed, nursed, washed, dressed, and taught from infancy.[18] Pacifism, argued the WPP, was the logical and natural extension of a mother's dedication to the creation and preservation of life. How could the maternal role *not* induce in all American women a visceral response to the needless destruction of human life wrought by war? Thus the WPP advocated America's neutral mediation in the ceasing of European hostilities, warned of the escalating risks taken by the country's military preparedness campaigns, and protested school children's early socialization for war through mandatory military training.[19]

In August of 1914, 1,500 women dressed in symbols of mourning marched for peace in New York City. An immense crowd, estimated to be three people deep, lined both sides of Fifth Avenue to witness the event. The procession illustrated the women's determination to exert their influence "on a field of public action from which in the past they have been almost wholly withdrawn," reported the *New York Times*. "Those who did not look upon the prospect with much satisfaction must at least take cognizance of the fact, and prepare to reckon with it."[20] Such imagery portraying the condemnation of war as the maternal province of women resonated with Americans on the eve of World War I. In addition, popular antiwar songs artfully interlaced the tenets of pacifism and the unparalleled power of motherhood with their lyrics. Note the closing verse of the 1915 hit song, "I Didn't Raise My Boy to Be a Soldier": "Let nations arbitrate their future troubles, / It's time to lay the sword and gun away. / There'd be no war today, / If mothers all would say, / I didn't raise my boy to be a soldier."[21]

The ideology of motherhood may have legitimized women's public advocacy for peace, but motherhood's juxtaposition to pacifism on one side did not negate its juxtaposition to war on the other. Once entry into World War I appeared inevitable, maternal ideology infused women's wartime relief efforts with the same moral imperative it bestowed on the female-led peace movement. Consider here the activism of Anna Howard Shaw and Carrie Chapman Catt, national figures in the woman's suffrage movement. Although Shaw spoke at the 1915 peace conference and Catt personally presided over the gathering of three thousand representatives from an impressive array of women's organizations, neither of them officially joined the Women's Peace Party but rather joined the Women's Committee of the Council of National Defense (WCCND) when the United States formally entered the war. Instead of employing women's activism toward the peace movement, they encouraged and coordinated women's wartime relief efforts.[22]

Shaw's tenure as director of the committee, however, did not indicate her rejection of women's maternal relationship with war. The deployment of American men to the battlefields of France only raised the stakes of that relationship. When confronted with the inescapable realities of war, the preservation of life became contingent on a quick and decisive American victory, a victory reliant on both the heroism and sacrifice of mothers and sons on their respective fronts. Only a war fought in vain could render women's maternal commitment to the giving and preserving of life as meaningless. Subsequently, women's acceptance of their roles as "mother of heroes" and "mothers of martyrs" became one of the most compelling elements of World War I rhetoric.[23]

A mother's willingness to sacrifice her son was not the only measure of a mother's service to her family and country. For the Woman's Peace Party, the conservation of life and the protection of home necessitated the abolishment of all wars. These ideals were predicated on mothers' refusal to raise their sons to be soldiers. For those active in wartime mobilization, however, the conservation of life and the protection of home made war inevitable, even justified, and depended on the sacrifice of sons to war. Mothers may have never intended to raise their sons to be soldiers, and did not relish the thought of their death, but they certainly did not raise their sons to cower behind their skirts and leave defenseless the home built on a lifetime of their maternal devotion. In their view, a mother who claimed she never raised her son to be soldier had not earned the right to be defended by another mother's son.[24]

Most American women, of course, were not as sure of their convictions and struggled to define their relationship to war and reconcile their maternal identities to its demands. "I was told the other day that it was 'ignoble' for me to desire to save these boys, mine and others from the fighting and injury and death," confided one mother to another. "The habit of protecting them was formed too long ago to be dropped in a moment or to seem 'ignoble' so soon. I feel as if all my anchors were swept away and as if the charts were all topsy turvy."[25] The maternal boundary between peace and war remained a permeable one, facilitating a diverse range of women's emotional and physical investment in World War I. For some women, the unfixed boundary between the meaning of "noble" or "ignoble" motherhood made the recovery of their maternal bearings difficult.

World War II called American women to the service of their country once again. Within months after the attack at Pearl Harbor, the familiar rhetoric making the protection of motherhood a wartime goal returned in full force. On the floor of the U.S. House of Representatives, Congressman Charles Plumley of Vermont classified World War II as a mother's war:

> Other wars saw mothers fighting through their sons at the front. But in no other war in history were bombs as likely to burst beside a baby's bed as to shatter on a battlefield. In no other war were mothers on the battle line. Other times we were trying to win a war. Now we are fighting to win back a civilization. War has invaded the mother's kingdom—the home.[26]

An estimated eight million mothers saw their sons off to war with a heavy heart, knowing that they might never return home.[27] As during World War I, the country honored mothers who paid the ultimate sacrifice and their publicized grief fed the propaganda designed to personalize the war for all Americans. The tragic story of Mrs. Alleta Sullivan is an infamous example. The government exploited her grief over the loss of five sons at sea in November 1942. She toured the country speaking at war plants and shipyards, often accompanied by her husband and only surviving child, Genevieve, who later joined the U.S. Naval Women's Reserve, popularly known as WAVES (Women Accepted for Volunteer Emergency Services). Posters depicting the Sullivan brothers asked Americans if they have done their part for the war. A movie based on the men's stories promoted war bond drives. Meanwhile, Mrs. Sullivan implored war workers to speed up production: "I speak as a mother who lost five sons and they went down fighting. They were never afraid."[28] Her concerns were now with the other American sons in action: "We must give them everything they need."[29] Unlike during World War I, mothers like Mrs. Sullivan were not the target audience of the mobilization efforts. Their patriotism, and that of their soldier sons, was less of a concern this time around. The concern lay instead over a younger generation of women, including mothers of small children, who needed to answer Mrs. Sullivan's plea to speed up wartime production.[30]

The ideology of motherhood played a part in outlining women's relationship to the war as another generation of women redefined their roles as American mothers and patriots. Many younger mothers were torn between the pressure to seek employment, on the one side, and the glorification of their maternal duties as essential patriotic defense work of the American family, on the other. The War Manpower Commission had to balance the country's need for female labor against social concerns over the physical and psychological toll a mother's labor could bring on the family and, by extension, American society.[31] If women refused to enter the war industries, they risked crippling the war effort. Government campaigns sold war jobs to reluctant middleclass women by utilizing positive messages such as "The More Women at Work, the Sooner We'll Win," or more dire ones like "Every Idle Machine May Mean a Dead Soldier."[32]

Yet, if young mothers abandoned the home to answer the commission's patriotic call, they risked psychologically crippling their children and possibly the country's future. Psychological screening methods used for the first time by the drafts boards further increased the social anxieties over the precarious situation of American motherhood. Over two million men were deemed unfit for service during the war due to psychiatric reasons. They lacked, according to medical opinion, "the ability to face life, live with others, think for themselves and stand on their own two feet."[33] Experts were quick to blame mothers for the psychological weaknesses in their sons. Therefore, precautions had to be taken to ensure that the young mothers of today did not repeat the same mistakes in the rearing of the next generation. They had to resist the economic lure of wartime employment (and later, postwar employment) and fully embrace the values of family life.[34]

For mothers of grown children deemed psychologically healthy enough to serve in uniform, it was easier to reconcile their identities as patriotic Americans and good mothers. The devotion to one identity did not require the neglect of the other. Instead, the identities merged into one, just as they did for many mothers during World War I. By volunteering for relief efforts, filling defense jobs, or encouraging their sons and daughters to enlist in the military, they demonstrated their patriotism. By working to provide the military with all it needed to end the war and by insisting that War Department policies reflected the best interest of their soldier sons, they fulfilled their maternal obligation to guard the lives of their children. Moreover, on the second Sunday of May each year, it was their sacrifice and not the general wartime sacrifices experienced by all American mothers that earned the highest tribute. (Nazi Germany paid similar tributes to motherhood through elaborate Mother's Day celebrations.)[35] In his 1944 Mother's Day Proclamation, President Roosevelt called on the country to give public and private tribute to mothers by praying that "God will strengthen and protect all sons and daughters exposed to the dangers of war and that He will be near all mothers who need His comfort in the time of grief."[36]

The American War Mothers personified the maternal rhetoric of sacrifice through two world wars. As peace movements, patriotic organizations, and government war committees promoted the relationship between motherhood and war in abstraction, the AWM made it tangible. On one level, they perpetuated the traditional wartime roles of women as mothers entrusted to sacrifice their sons, mourn their deaths, and preserve their memories for future generations.[37] However, to be the mothers of heroes and martyrs held a deeper meaning for the women of the AWM, one beyond its traditionally passive representation. The war mothers found solace and an enduring identity within their model of patriotic motherhood. Above all, they possessed the power to delineate the obligations *owed to them* by a country that depended on their maternal work. Through the symbols they adopted to represent their goals, the war mothers endeavored to have their sacrifice recognized, rewarded, and remembered both independently and along with the sacrifices made by their military sons and daughters. The organization's celebration of Mother's Day epitomized their model of patriotic motherhood as it embraced so many of the holiday's sacrificial symbols. Throughout the early twentieth century, the AWM held steadfast to it fundamental claim to Mother's Day and the honor it bestowed on them above all others.

SACRIFICE, SERVICE, AND MOTHER'S DAY

Ironically, the American War Mothers owes its founding to an initial failure of the male war bureaucracy to draw on maternal ideology to mobilize women's support. The Wilson Administration often handicapped women's activism during World War I by requiring their oversight by male-dominated war committees or not providing their organizations with defined roles in the mobilization efforts. The difficulties with the U.S. Food Administration's first food drive serves as a prime example. In the summer of 1917, the head of the Food Administration, Herbert Hoover, announced a campaign centered on women signing pledge cards promising to follow the administration's food conservation objectives. He designed the campaign without consulting any of the women's groups he expected to serve as foot soldiers under the direction of state defense councils. Despite early warnings from the Women's Committee of the Council of National Defense that the plan lacked the social infrastructure required to be successful, Hoover blamed the faltering food drive on women's lack of patriotic zeal as opposed to his poorly designed and hastily discharged strategy. WCCND director Anna Howard Shaw laid the blame squarely on Hoover and the campaign's patronizing approach toward women: "They do not think of approaching them in an intelligent way, as they do men, but they use a sort of kindergarten method in which they tell them to do something without telling them any reason for it ... and think that women, like children, ought to obey without the whys or wherefores of anything."[38]

The AWM emerged out of the confusion over the implementation of the 1917 food drive. In Indiana, the frazzled and desperate food commissioner appealed to the Woman's Civic League of Indianapolis for help enlisting women in Hoover's food conservation program. League member Mrs. Alice M. French suggested appealing to women from a mother's point of view, especially a mother with a son in the service like herself. She quickly drafted a letter for the Food Commission, appealing to women's intelligence and selflessness by explaining the whys and wherefores of the food drive. She began the letter by first thanking the recipient for all the ways she, and women like her, had already responded nobly to the war effort: "We are sewing, knitting, making hospital supplies, and doing whatever we find to do to hasten the day of peace and the return of our soldier boys to our home." [39] French then linked the added duty of food conservation to a woman's patriotic maternal role: "It is a mother's privilege and pleasure to see the family well fed, and she will always have in mind the absent boy when she prepares a meal at home. Will *you* express your patriotism by helping the general plan for food conservation?"[40] Furthermore, she wished to make clear that the U.S. Food Administration's primary intention was only to provide women with educational literature. She assured them that signing the food-saving pledge cards was an expression of loyalty and nothing else, saying, "Women who signed the cards will be given many valuable, helpful suggestions—but not orders or commands."[41] The food commissioner allegedly saw the potential in the original idea of appealing to women as war mothers and sent a copy of the letter to Washington, DC. On September 29, 1917, French received a call at home from Don Herold, the publicity man for the Indiana Food Conservation Headquarters. A telegram from Herbert Hoover had instructed Herold to seek French's assistance in organizing all the war mothers throughout the state. She immediately agreed. Consequently, the AWM celebrates September 29, 1917, as Founder's Day. [42]

French recalled how mothers responded with enthusiasm over their enlistment in war activities, happy for an outlet for their pent-up sorrow and the opportunity to fight alongside their boys in the "most horrible war of the ages."[43] They were eager to expand their purview beyond the issue of food conservation from the very beginning, however. "This War cannot be carried on without the various touches of the woman's hand," wrote French in a letter promoting war mothers' participation in a War Council of all War Workers being sponsored by the state in Indianapolis.

There would be no army without our splendid boys, and we have every right to know what is being done for their success and welfare. We are giving our boys—our strength-our time—our money, and food. And we know in spite of these, there are many slackers who are giving most effective help to the enemy—by their indifference.[44]

In a meeting designed to specifically address the concerns of Indiana state workers, French never questioned the relevancy of war mothers' participation. Although the mothers did not represent the traditional paid war industry worker, they felt they had earned the right to oversee all war activities with the investment of their sons and daughters to war.

French's mobilizing of war mothers soon reached beyond the Indiana state line. Her personal appeals to various governors to enlist the service of the mothers in their states cumulated in the national incorporation of the AWM in 1918. Its national designation reflected the growing strength and stability of its members' maternal identities in relationship to the war. First of all, it officially ended the organization's affiliation with the Indiana State Food Administration, which had financially supported the early activities of the original Indiana War Mothers. As their interests grew beyond that of food conservation, the women quickly recognized the importance of sustaining the AWM's political and financial independence in order to pursue their own agenda.[45] Besides, the legitimacy of their wartime role was beholden only to the military service of their sons and daughters and not to the sponsorship of any male-dominated war commission or patriotic association.

Above all, the organization's national appeal symbolized its members' belief in the exceptionality of their maternal identities and the authority that commanded. To gain membership, women had to have a son or daughter who served in the U.S. military between the period of April 6, 1917, and November 11, 1918. This distinguished their experiences from previous generations of war mothers. By *war*, the AWM specifically meant the Great War. They were not the first American mothers to sacrifice their sons to war, of course, but they believed the far-reaching political and human costs of America's first world war significantly enlarged the scope of their involvement and influence. The most revealing evidence of the AWM's sense of exceptionally was their restricted concept of motherhood. *Mother* meant strictly a biological mother. Adoptive mothers and stepmothers did not become eligible for membership until 1974 and still under limited conditions.[46] French recalled the eligibility of stepmothers as the most controversial subject at the first national convention, provoking the longest discussion: "It was finally settled that since we were to become an honorary body of mothers after the War was over and that our perpetuation was to be by ties of blood—only blood mothers were eligible to membership."[47] They were, in other words, the honored mothers among all mothers, even other so-called "war mothers." The women were tied to the war and their soldier sons by more than the natural maternal love felt by every woman who rears a child. Theirs was a sacrifice nourished from within their womb and born of their body; when they surrendered their sons to the battlefields of France, they surrendered a piece of themselves. In the words of the AWM, "she bore children into whose minds and hearts she instilled a love of country that made of them noble patriots, and placed her upon a roll of honor unequalled in the ranks of American Motherhood."[48]

With their sister war mothers, AWM members found genuine solace in shared experiences. Their model of patriotic motherhood bound them to each other as much as it did to the war effort. This bond was clearly evident in all aspects of their service work, from the public display of patriotism to the most mundane chapter correspondence in which they stressed their sense of mutual obligation. "Make the welfare of our boys your business, talk about it, and make plans that will tend to hasten the end of this terrible war, and the speedy return of our boys to our home," French advised a fellow war mother. She continued:

I took the liberty to send a letter of sympathy from Indiana War Mothers to Mrs. Alice Dodd, the first of us to lose her son. We can help and sympathize with each other, and the government at Washington gives official recognition to our worth, and to our loyalty to our country. [49]

At the end of her letter detailing general chapter business, French mentioned her son, Donald R. French of the 334□8 Regiment, and then finished with this simple request: "I would like to know about your son."[50]

The American War Mothers had active chapters in over half of the states by the end the war. Despite the organization's original intention to evolve into an honorary society, many of those chapters were reluctant to suspend their patriotic work. They recognized the need for their continued service in the tormented souls of returning soldiers and the despairing hearts of grieving families: As expressed in the organization's 1928 ritual book, "many of our sons are suffering greatly from the effects of exposure and heavy burdens of war, and for years to come these results of the conflict will be before us; there are widows and orphans to be cared for, and Gold Star Mothers who may need our services. We caught the torch and it is our duty and pleasure to keep it burning."[51]In 1925, President Calvin Coolidge signed the congressional charter for the AWM, designating its central purpose as one of patriotic service to the country and its veterans. Each member pledged to be as loyal and steadfast in her dedication to her post-war mission as she was when she "smelled the smoke of battle."[52]

The organization's peacetime work sustained its members' wartime maternal identities with only minor adjustments. The mothers of heroes and martyrs had earned a permanent role in the country's military affairs, and through their construction of war memorials, social activism, and political agenda, they ensured that the American people never forgot it. War mothers, for example, testified in front of investigating committees over the horrible hygienic conditions they witnessed within veterans' hospitals and the mistreatment of soldiers by apathetic medical staff and Red Cross volunteers.[53] As founding partners of the Woman's Patriotic Conference of National Defense, they lobbied Congress on issues of military preparedness, believing it the best strategy to avoid future wars. As mothers, they were neither eager to send their sons or grandsons to fight in another world war nor willing to support "peace at any price."[54] Throughout the 1930s, the women even held the Roosevelt administration accountable for every offense they experienced. War mother Mrs. Charles Boll urged the president and first lady to formally apologize to the women after failing to speak at the group's 1936 national convention. The war mothers were apparently "indignant over the courtesy they received."[55] Mrs. Boll feared that the president's choice to take a vacation while the AWM delegates were in Washington may have cost him some votes.[56]

With the outbreak of World War II, the AWM effortlessly resumed its wartime partnership with the country's mobilization efforts. The women were more confident than ever, thanks to experience gained and lessons learned over twenty years of activism. They also welcomed a new generation of war mothers into their honored ranks. In 1942, President Roosevelt ratified the AWM charter to include mothers of son and daughters serving in World War II as eligible for membership—but still only those mothers "tied by blood."[57] The new members were just as dedicated as their older role models and expected to have a voice in the country's wartime policies and peace negotiations. In November of 1944, the war mothers requested a formal place at any or all conferences where the question of peace was to be discussed.[58]

The AWM's celebration of Mother's Day in the interwar years easily suited the model of patriotic motherhood that justified their continued social and political activism. On a symbolic level, the holiday reminded the public of its members' wartime sacrifices and reaffirmed their honored status among American mothers. On a practical level, the AWM's charitable work depended on the monies collected from the fundraising campaigns associated with the Mother's Day observance, beginning with its adaptation of the holiday's symbol of the white carnation. The floral emblem became the national flower of the organization in 1923 and worked on multiple levels for the women. In AWM rituals, the white carnation symbolized the war mother's unwavering faith and purity of life. In practice, the selling of carnations was a main fundraising source for the organization. Early AWM records reported individual chapters selling fifty to one hundred thousand carnations during a single campaign. After 1931, the national headquarters permitted individual chapters to keep all proceeds raised from annual carnation sales, provided that the money was reserved for service projects such as aid to veterans' hospitals, soldiers' loan funds, Americanization programs, and the erection of war monuments. The sums dedicated to the various service projects throughout the decade were impressive, thanks in part to the holiday fundraiser. With a national membership of seven thousand mothers in 1939, the AWM raised over $30,000 for hospitalization programs, over $64,000 for general relief projects, and over $6,000 to care for impoverished war mothers.[59]

General assistance to all war mothers, regardless of their direct membership in the AWM, remained a central service project for the organization, one also partially reliant on Mother's Day carnation sales. A 1925 fundraising promotion asked,

> The spirit that prompts the sale of these Carnations is full of sentiment and serves to keep fresh our appreciation of sacrifices and love so freely given by the Mothers in their services to our country.... Will *you* help make the public remember the American War Mother, who will ask the passerby to wear the Carnation offered by her, who gave her all in the World War, that they might live in happiness and plenty?[60]

A portion of the proceeds from the 1925 carnation sales went toward the construction of the American War Mother National Memorial Home in Aurora, Colorado, roughly sixteen miles outside of Denver. Dedicated in July 1926, the center provided lodging and assistance for mothers and wives of veterans recovering at the Fitzsimmons Army Hospital, housing over 150 mothers and wives during its first year of operation. Throughout the next thirty-five years, the AWM investing nearly $40,000 in physical renovations and additions to the home, yet another expense atop the organization's practice of forgiving the debts of those who were without the means to fund their stay.[61]

The American War Mothers originally dedicated the National Memorial Home in honor of its Gold Star mothers. The name derives partly from the wartime tradition of hanging a flag with a blue star on a home to indicate a son or daughter serving in the military. Upon a soldier's death, the blue star was sewn over with a gold one.[62] For a country that represents itself as a unity of stars, the flags were a powerful symbol of a mother and her soldier son's wartime sacrifice and service.[63] The Gold Star designation bestowed an additional tribute on mothers already deemed "unequalled in the ranks of American motherhood."[64] Even after the 1928 incorporation of an independent American Gold Star Mothers Association, the AWM maintained an official Gold Star department within its national organization. This included African American mothers who were denied membership into the whites-only American Gold Star Mothers Association.[65] In 1921, the *New York Times* chronicled the AWM's efforts to provide financial assistance to an African American Gold Star mother approaching her one-hundredth birthday. Her son had been her sole support before the war, but after his death in a frontline trench in France, her son's wife and young child received all his insurance benefits and then moved out of state, leaving the mother to fend for herself. The elderly woman was on the brink of starvation and about to lose her home to foreclosure when the war mothers heard of her plight and rallied to her side. "She is one of us," stated the AWM National President, "her son died for the same cause mine did."[66]

The adoption of the carnation symbol and the central role the flower played as a fundraiser was only the first step in the American War Mothers' assumption of Mother's Day. In 1925, Congress granted the organization official permission to hold its holiday observance at the Tomb of the Unknown Soldier in Washington, DC. A monument meant to venerate all the World War I soldiers who gave their lives in service to their country offered the ideal setting for the AWM to lay exclusive claim to a holiday meant to venerate all mothers. Against the backdrop of the tomb, the war mothers showcased their unequaled sacrifice, which set them apart from the average American mother and patriotic citizen. The combined imagery of solemn heroism and maternal grief reinforced the exceptionality of their relationship to war, reminiscent of Anna Howard Shaw's 1915 denunciation of men who dared question a woman's knowledge of war after looking into the face of her dead son: "What, what, friends in the face of a crime like that, what does man know about war!" [67]

Politicians, military leaders, and representatives of various patriotic organizations attended the AWM Mother's Day services every year, many of which were broadcast over the radio. Music, readings, and speeches espoused the dual themes of patriotism and motherhood. To honor the heroism of the unidentified soldier interred at "this shrine of patriotism" was to honor the heroism of the nameless mother who bore him and made possible his fight to preserve the American principles of democracy.[68] In essence, then, the American way of life truly rested on the model of patriotic motherhood in which the AWM embodied, at least according to the traditional rhetoric of the annual services. During their ceremonies, the war mothers cleverly symbolized that link between motherhood and the preservation of democracy with the traditional Gold Star mothers' "Aisle of Honor." Following the initial service held in the amphitheater at Arlington Cemetery, the observance moved to the Tomb of the Unknown Soldier, where the AWM president and representatives of other organizations traditionally placed a commemorative wreath. Those wishing to pay their respects to the Unknown Soldier walked through a gauntlet of Gold Star mothers holding garlands of laurel and carnations, the intertwined floral representations of military heroism and maternal commemoration. The Gold Star mothers lined the entire path from the amphitheater to the tomb. One could not honor the fallen soldier without first recognizing the mother who made his service possible, the mother who "bore children into whose minds and hearts she instilled a love of country that made of them noble patriots."[69]

The American War Mothers held its Mother's Day services at the Tomb of the Unknown Soldier until World War II restrictions on travel and other logistical problems required a change in venue. Yet the AWM never relinquished its right to hold Mother's Day services at the monument and continued to place wreaths on the tomb during the years of the war mothers' absence; after the war, they quickly reclaimed the site for their maternal tributes.[70] In the meantime, the AWM expected its annual observance to receive the same public attention and respect as it had when held in Washington, DC. Throughout the 1930s, for example, it was the war mothers' custom to personally invite the president and first lady to the service, although evidence suggests that the Roosevelts preferred to send messages in lieu of attendance.[71] Regardless, the AWM insisted on some degree of recognition from the White House even when its Mother's Day services were held in Indiana, far from the nation's capital. In April 1944, the national president, Mrs. Hahn, wrote of her disappointment over the president's failure to respond to her Mother's Day invitation from Indianapolis. One week had gone by without an official response from the White House:

It is rather disappointing not to have heard from you, we thought you would send us a message to be read at the service; after all, you know that it is the Mother's of this land that is furnishing this great army of yours to fight this war, we believe we have a right to ask you for a message at least to be read at this service. This is not a High School service, we have the army, the navy, the marines and air corps back of us here. Mr. President I have a fond hope in my heart that you will respond to this appeal.[72]

Although President Roosevelt decided to remain in Washington, DC, for the holiday, he did oblige the request for a personal message to be read at the AWM Mother's

Day service. In it, he thanked the war mothers for all their work and praised them as a true source of strength and inspiration for the country.[73] The gesture was no doubt meant to ease any hurt feelings and, more importantly, mitigate the potential political ramifications of the perceived slight. At the time, the AWM had a national membership of over twenty thousand, with over twenty-five organized state chapters and three hundred local chapters across the country.[74] Roosevelt's gesture apparently worked, and all was forgiven, at least for the moment anyway. "Mr. President this message will be kept in the archives of the American War Mothers, it will go down in history, we do not have any document in our files that will be valued as this one will be," affirmed Mrs. Hahn, "you have given us courage to carry on to do the work that lies ahead when our boys come home."[75]

ANNA JARVIS DECLARES WAR ON THE AMERICAN WAR MOTHERS

Jarvis's twenty-year Mother's Day standoff with the AWM was not over the latter's maternal claims of patriotism. In abstract, Jarvis admired the sacrifices of mothers during times of war, describing them once as the "heroes of heroes."[76] She frequently linked motherhood to wartime patriotism in her early attempts to gain political endorsements for her Mother's Day movement and genuinely believed that mothers provided a patriotic service to their country, one deserving of due consideration. She expressed that sentiment in a letter to President Wilson while he attended the 1919 Paris Peace Conference. As the leader of the "greatest international Mother Cause—the ALL Nation Mother's Day," Jarvis implored the president to remember the care and protection of the world's mothers in his negotiations:

> It seems as tho [sic] about everybody and everything are represented at the Peace Conference, excepting that most important person and economic factor of all, the fountainhead of the state—MOTHER. . . . There is no mawkish sentiment in asking that Mother be represented and considered at the Peace table.[77]

Thus, it was not the ideological link between motherhood and patriotism that instigated Jarvis's campaign against the AWM, but the patriotic parameters the war mothers drew around that relationship. What Jarvis challenged was the exclusivity of the organization's model of patriotic motherhood and its resulting sense of entitlement. Every mother, according to Jarvis, who dedicated herself to the preservation of the home, who quietly and unobtrusively attended the daily needs of her family, was a patriot in service to her country. Acts of patriotism were not limited to wartimes or defined by civic activism, nor were patriotic tributes reserved only for mothers of heroes and martyrs, regardless of how deserving their sacrifice. When the AWM's maternal entitlement included Mother's Day and its symbols, Jarvis immediately

Figure 4.4. The formation of the American War Mother's "Aisle of Honor" during
a Mother's Day service at the Tomb of the Unknown Soldier.
Library of Congress Prints and Photographs Division, Washington, DC.

interpreted the presumptuous behavior as a personal insult to her character and, ironically, an affront to holiday's intrinsically democratic observance. It was her patriotic duty, therefore, to expose the "vanity and hypocrisy" she saw in the organization's attempt to seize a memorial day meant to glorify all mothers equally. The war mothers' greed and incessant craving for political aggrandizement drove them to glorify their model of motherhood above all others, in Jarvis's opinion, and it was her responsibility to stop them.[78]

Initially, the AWM extended an olive branch of sorts to Jarvis, no doubt taken aback by the ferocity of her quick condemnation. During World War I, founder Alice French allegedly sent representatives from Indianapolis to Jarvis's Philadelphia home to offer her an honorary charter membership in the organization. She soundly refused. Jarvis's word is the only evidence that such a proposition ever existed, as AWM records do not back her claim.[79] Yet, Jarvis's story is a plausible one. For an organization wanting a legitimate claim to Mother's Day, offering an honorary membership to the day's popularly recognized founder was a sound strategy. Jarvis's acceptance could have granted the AWM unfettered use of the holiday's symbols and sentiments for their social and political goals. But the strategy failed and, without the hope of arriving at a mutual understanding, the battle over Mother's Day escalated exponentially in severity and scope. Jarvis's refusal to accept the war mothers' role in the celebration of Mother's Day led them to mount an aggressive campaign to erase her from the holiday's history.

The "war of words" officially began in May of 1924 with the inaugural AWM carnation drive. What the war mothers identified as a valuable fundraising campaign essential for sustaining their patriotic work, Jarvis classified as blatant profiteering. Through the Mother's Day International Association, she denounced the war mothers as infringers and unauthorized solicitors commercializing the sentiment of the Mother's Day and its symbol of the white carnation. But the war mothers held their ground, refusing to recoil from Jarvis's "malicious" and unfounded accusations. Their organization did not require Jarvis's permission to share in the public commemoration of motherhood, they retorted, since no organization can infringe on a day designated by a congressional joint resolution as a public holiday.[80] A higher power than Jarvis, therefore, had sanctioned their carnation sales.

Furthermore, the AWM's adoption of the carnation as an official emblem brought an air of authenticity to its carnation drives and reinforced the group's association with the holiday's maternal reverence. Yet Jarvis recognized the war mothers' appropriation of the white carnation symbol for exactly what it was, another tactic to lay siege to her copyright protections on Mother's Day. Why else would a group already represented by the insignias of different colored stars need to espouse another symbol? In 1925, Jarvis's indignation carried her assault against the AWM beyond its typical war of words into a direct confrontation when she crashed the organization's fifth national convention being held in Philadelphia in protest. The war mothers pressed for her arrest, but an enamored magistrate dismissed the charge of disorderly conduct. The *Philadelphia Record* reported the public compliment paid to Jarvis by the magistrate. "I understand that you made the white carnation the symbol of Mother's Day. I am glad you did this. Whenever I see a white carnation, I think of my own mother," he confessed. "You have done a very wonderful thing and all the glory belongs to you. You are discharged."[81]

Obviously, the annual service at the Tomb of the Unknown Soldier was another point of contention. Jarvis repeatedly appealed to the American people to protect the sacred meaning of both the tomb and Mother's Day from exploitation. "These women have the near-by Memorial Day of May 30th, why not use that sacred Memorial for their money-getting schemes?"[82] The women even ensnarled President Franklin Roosevelt in their Mother's Day disputes. Comically, a letter from Jarvis ardently protesting the AWM's Mother's Day observance often followed the war mothers' equally ardent request for the Roosevelts' attendance at the Arlington services. It became painfully clear to Jarvis, however, that the administration favored the interests of the AWM at the expense of her movement work. The president seemed to turn a deaf ear to her repeated pleas for assistance, despite her best efforts. Jarvis's mounting frustration was evident in her increasing demands for Roosevelt's recognition and her petty comments over the favoritism shown the AWM. She once sent a terse telegram to the president, consisting of only one question: "What recognition had President given to Mother's Day? Please Answer."[83]

In a letter to her cousin in 1933, she balked at the obscene sum of money the administration expended on the Gold Star mother pilgrimages. In the 1920s, the

AWM had joined the American Gold Star Mothers Association in lobbying Congress to fund the opportunity for mothers to travel overseas to view their sons' graves. The women described the hearts of Gold Star mothers' as "just breaking for the sight of the grave of their boy."[84] In 1929, Congress passed legislation enabling mothers and widows to travel to Europe courtesy of the American taxpayers. Between 1930 and 1933, over six thousand women of the estimated seventeen thousand deemed eligible made the subsidized pilgrimage to American cemeteries in Europe. The AWM estimated the total cost of the total 48 pilgrimages at over $5 million.[85]

Jarvis doubted the sincerity of the mothers who joined the pilgrimages. How quickly those same mothers who wanted to tear President Wilson apart for drafting their sons, and who presently neglected the graves of relatives in their hometowns, eagerly jumped at the offer of a free trip to Europe, she quipped.[86]

Jarvis's criticisms, however mean-spirited in nature, were not completely groundless. She believed the AWM to be a crass, political, money-getting group that exploited her work only to fund their exclusive organizational business and "good times."[87] To a certain degree, Jarvis was right. The AWM artfully assimilated the symbols and sentiment of Mother's Day into its model of patriotic motherhood, and in doing so, benefited both financially and politically. Before 1931, a significant portion of the carnation sale proceeds financed the national conventions and magazine publication instead of directly funding service projects, although one could argue that all the AWM projects directly benefited from the organization's general economic solvency. Nonetheless, Jarvis failed to appreciate the nuances of the AWM claim to Mother's Day. She regarded all unauthorized Mother's Day observances as tainted by commercialization, refusing to distinguish between the blatant profiteering of florists and the fundraising efforts of reputable philanthropic organizations like the AWM.

Despite her accusations, Mother's Day remained an intricate part of the war mothers' maternal identities. It enhanced their reputation, helped justify their political involvement, and financially sustained their social activism. The lengths to which the AWM went to defend its stake in Mother's Day from Jarvis, their biggest threat, revealed the value that the war mothers placed on the holiday. In 1925, under the leadership of national president Margaret McCluer, the AWM conducted an "objective" study of the history of Mother's Day. The main intent was to confirm, once and for all, the identity of observance's true founder. The AWM compiled the results of the extensive research in the booklet Memoirs of "Mothers' Day" by American War Mothers, published that same year. The publication was a mixture of poems and quotations paying tribute to motherhood and, above all, a commemoration of the American figures that the AWM credited for the nation's twentieth-century observance of Mother's Day. Those honored included Frank Hering of the Fraternal Order of Eagles as the holiday's first advocate, Senators E. J. Burkett and Thomas J. Helfin for leading the Congressional recognition of Mother's Day, and General Pershing for instigating the 1918 military observance of the day.[88] The AWM excluded Anna Jarvis from the historical account along with the other female figures often associated with the day's founding. Not even Julia Ward Howe, famed author of *The Battle Hymn of the Republic*, earned a passing nod of acknowledgment. The war mothers rationalized the absence of Jarvis's contributions to the Mother's Day story based on the lack of significant historical evidence. The results of the independent research determined that Jarvis played only a minor role in the day's creation. She was not the first to publicly call for a maternal memorial day, she was not directly responsible for the act of Congress legally establishing the holiday, and she failed to appreciate the model of patriotic motherhood responsible for popularizing the holiday during World War I.

The AWM's repudiation of Jarvis's proprietary hold on Mother's Day reflected their change of battle tactics, a basic reversal of the old adage, "if you can't beat them, join them." When Jarvis refused their initial offer of reconciliation, it left the war mothers with few options other than directly assaulting her creditability as official founder. The new strategy no doubt directed the organization's eager endorsement of Frank Hering as the holiday's legitimate founder in the 1920s. Hering, Jarvis's most hated Mother's Day rival, owed his continued association with the holiday in part to the work of the AWM. It was, after all, the organization's research that uncovered irrefutable proof that his promotion of a commemorative Mother's Day preceded Jarvis's movement by four years. In accordance, the war mothers officially crowned Hering the "Father of Mothers' Day" in 1925 and invited him to speak at the inaugural Mother's Day service at the Tomb of the Unknown Soldier.[89] Four years later, they publicly reaffirmed their commitment to Hering's founder status with the presentation of their highest honor, the AWM medal, symbolizing sacrifice, light, knowledge, strength, victory, and American patriotism.[90]

The relationship between Hering and the AWM was truly a symbiotic one. Each found in the other the means to silence their mutual antagonist and legitimize their entitlement to Mother's Day. For Hering, the steadfast alliance with the AWM helped redeem his tarnished reputation after his involvement in a charitable fundraising scandal resulted in a 1932 federal conviction. Through their connection with Hering, the war mothers cleverly canceled out Jarvis's charges of unauthorized solicitation of Mother's Day and its symbols. Moreover, the regular application of Hering's possessive plural spelling of the holiday neutralized Jarvis's threats of legal retaliation for the violation of her copyrighted possessive singular spelling.[91] Hering and the AWM, particularly under the leadership of Margaret McCluer, formed a formidable partnership that Jarvis desperately struggled to surmount. The pair, whom Jarvis referred to as the "red fish and the woman he works with" or more commonly as "Frank and his Maggie," comprised Jarvis's personal axis of evil set on making her a public imposter and a fraud.[92]

Nothing better exemplified the power of the American War Mothers to define the celebration of Mother's Day and its historical record than the sponsorship of a commemorative stamp in 1934. Its promotion of the holiday's twentieth anniversary brandished all the major components of the organization's appropriation of Mother's Day: the assertion of their unequaled maternal identity and patriotism, the validity of their social activism and fundraising goals, their allegiance with Hering and President Roosevelt, and their snubbing of Jarvis. Each played a role in the issuance of a three-cent postal stamp in honor of American motherhood. The war mothers' petitioning for a commemorative stamp began in earnest in January of 1934. Their first appeal to Franklin Roosevelt beautifully combined references to their esteemed wartime maternal sacrifices, current patriotic work, and the president's well-known interest in philately with the observance of Mother's Day:

> The aim of the American War Mothers this year is to create an endowment fund so we may care for the dependent and helpless Mothers of our organization, many of whom gave from one to nine sons to the service and many of whom wear one, two, three, and four Gold Stars. Five Mothers were taken from Alms Houses to make the Pilgrimage to the last resting place of their sons. The appeal to us for assistance is growing to such a great extent that we must have help.... Our appeal to you is to make [Mothers' Day] even greater this year by granting the issuance of a Commemorative Mothers' Day Stamp. Because of your great acquaintance in the Stamp World and with First Day Covers, and your knowledge of the results coming from them, we need not say more. When the War was raging and our boys facing death, they left this message over the battlefields, "No matter what happens to me, take care of Mother." Mr. President, we appeal to you to help us respond to that message.[93]

Surprisingly, both Roosevelt and Postmaster General James A. Farley resisted this poignant request and rejected the war mothers' proposal.[94]

The initial failure only hardened the women's resolve. In their next appeal, the language of clear indignation replaced the previous letter's sentimental prose. Less notable historic anniversaries have earned a commemorative stamp, they stressed, as well as events not designed to assist in the care of the country's needy: "Did Pocahontas do as much for the good of this nation as the millions of American mothers? . . . Is this not as worthy a project as a more commercial World's Fair, which was accorded an issue?"[95] If feelings of shame did not persuade Roosevelt and Farley, they hoped some practical political advice might change their minds. Glibly, the war mothers suggested that such a gesture as a commemorative stamp would be particularly popular in the current political climate: "It would, in effect, assuage in small part some of the rancor that resulted from the cuts in veterans' aid."[96]

Nine days after receiving the second request, the Post Office Department released its plans to commission a stamp officially honoring the twentieth anniversary of President Woodrow Wilson's 1914 Mother's Day proclamation.[97] President Roosevelt personally sketched the stamp's original design featuring the iconic image of Whistler's mother and the phrase, "In Memory and Honor of the Mothers of America." The Bureau of Engraving and Printing remained faithful to the President's rough sketch, with just the minor addition of the holiday's official floral emblem;

Figure 4.5. 1934 Commemorative Mother's Day Stamp. Author's Private Collection.

bureau designers placed a vase of white carnations at the feet of Whistler's mother after deciding against inserting a small bouquet into her clasped hands.[98] On May 2, 1934, the Post Office placed the first of the two hundred million printings of the Mother's Day stamp on sale in Washington. Postmaster General Farley predicted that the commemorative stamp, the first of its kind ever dedicated to motherhood, would become the most popular stamp ever issued.[99]

Both Hering and the war mothers profited politically and financially from their association the issuance of the commemorative stamp. The AWM spent months in preparation of that first-day sale. Under the guidance of two expert philatelists, the organization designed a special cachet (first-day issue envelope) to showcase the three-cent stamp and raise money to fund its endowments. Six stenographers labored for over two months addressing the specialty order cachets, ranging in price from fifteen to twenty-five cents, in order to guarantee their mailing on the first day of the stamp's sale.[100] Congress helped publicize the AWM's fundraising efforts by proclaiming the war mothers' official sponsorship of the stamp and by offering individual endorsements of the organization's patriotic work in the name of the nation's worthiest mothers. "Who in all the world has more claim on our hearts than a dependent mother, and especially the mother of a veteran who offered his life that civilization might not perish from the earth?" asked Indiana Congressman Leon Ludlow.[101]

For Hering, the stamp offered a chance to redeem a political reputation still tainted by scandal. Although the stamp officially commemorated the twentieth anniversary of President Wilson's proclamation, it also corresponded with the thirtieth anniversary of Hering's first Mother's Day plea in 1904. The signature covers accompanying the stamp's first-day sales included his honored role in the history of Mother's Day, courtesy of the AWM.[102] This national affirmation of his title as "Father of Mothers' Day" came at the most opportune time for Hering, just two years after his conviction for violating federal lottery laws and one year after President Roosevelt extended him executive clemency. [103]

According to historian Donald Reid, postal stamps are more than just the colorful curiosities of enthusiasts; they are a vital primary resource, as stamps often provide significant information for any historian in search of symbolic messages.[104] In the case of the commemorative holiday stamp, not everyone embraced its symbolic representation of Mother's Day or its tribute of American motherhood. Postmaster General Farley praised the stamp's central motif as inspired by one of the "most notable artistic achievements of all times," the portrait of James Whistler's mother. He found it a source of pride that the first postal service in the world to commemorate motherhood would showcase the work of an American-born painter and the likeness of his American mother. Many art critics, however, disagreed, denouncing the postal service for its drastic cropping of the famous maternal portrait. Others panned Farley's tactless promotion of the stamp as an ideal sentimental souvenir to affix to the traditional Mother's Day greetings. "Few Captains of Industry could have devised a better piece of promotion," noted *Time*.[105]

Jarvis, of course, eagerly joined the art critics, philatelic societies, and others with her own condemnation of the commemorative stamp. The day after the Post Office department announced its plans to commission a stamp, Jarvis sent a letter to presidential secretary Colonel Louis McHenry Howe requesting an immediate audience with Roosevelt. She asked that no further action be taken on the stamp matter until after her opportunity to warn the president of his role as an unwitting pawn in the AWM's charity racket:

This stamp is one of the cleverest tricks that any women surely ever put over on a President so gracious as to see them. . . . This misspelling of our name and [the changing of the] Founder of Mother's Day to a fellow of their own partnership in money getting schemes, are surely things that Our President did not recognize.[106]

Jarvis intricately dismantled the symbolic message of the stamp to expose it as a vehicle for profiteering. First of all, she felt its central motif was as a ridiculous representation of Mother's Day since Mrs. Anna McNeill Whistler bore absolutely no connections with the holiday's history, unlike her own mother, Ann Reeves Jarvis. Moreover, she understood better than anyone else the reasons behind the distorted image of Whistler's mother that angered art critics. Simply put, Whistler's body interfered with the stamp's primary design as an advertisement for carnation sales. Poor Mrs. Whistler needed her feet amputated in order to provide space for the vase of carnations. Jarvis naturally accused the peddling women of the AWM and the imposter Hering for forcing the mutilation of Whistler's mother. It was no

Figure 4.5. First Day Cachet designed by the American War Mothers.
Author's Private Collection.

doubt designed to enhance their annual carnation sales along with the promotion of their latest cachet money scheme. And if amputating Mrs. Whistler's feet was not enough, mocked Jarvis, the stamp swindlers stole her wedding ring as well.[107]

Her pleas and protests to Roosevelt and Farley met with limited success. She did successfully prevent the words "Mother's Day" from appearing on the stamp, requiring its listed title to be changed to "Commemorative Stamp." But in the end, that was a hollow victory. The Postal Service and AWM still informally promoted the stamp as commemorating Mother's Day, instead of the general commemoration of American mothers. That did not surprise Jarvis. She knew that her rivals required the name to market the stamp. "The Postmaster General says, 'people like the stamp.' It is not the stamp they like but Mother's Day, as it is supreme to any mere postal stamp," she stated.[108] Although the war mothers' assault against her reputation and Mother's Day work did not surprise Jarvis, its speed certainly scared and frustrated her. Within a single decade, the AWM went from the assumption of the white carnation emblem to the expulsion of Jarvis's name from the holiday's history as commemorated by the 1934 Mother's Day stamp.

AN UNEASY TRUCE

The maternal rhetoric of the two world wars influenced the American War Mothers' founding and shaped its members' understanding of their relationship to war. They believed that their sons were fighting abroad to protect democracy at home, the very home built on a mother's love, labor, and sacrifices. But their image of

Who ran to help me when I fell,
And would some pretty story tell,
Or kiss the place to make it well?
My mother.

Figure 4.7. Mother's Day card designed by the American War Mothers as part of the organization's 1934 fundraiser. Author's Private Collection.

motherhood was not the simple product of wartime sentiment and mobilization efforts. The devotion of the women who joined the AWM had a depth of meaning not captured through the one-dimensional maternal figures typically portrayed in propaganda. They expected more than platitudes for their sacrifices. The dedication they gave to the wars warranted a country's devotion in return, and the organization's symbols were designed to remind the country of the service paid and the service owed to them as a special category of American mothers. The experiences they shared as mothers of heroes and martyrs elevated their maternal status above those who thrived under the democracy their sons and daughters fought and died to protect. They not only earned but also deserved specific entitlements as patriots and as mothers. "We were much consulted and LISTENED to," recorded AWM historian Marguerite White. "We were THE American War Mothers who had provided the boys and girls who had fought in the Great War . . . Mothers, this is our heritage."[109]

Their maternal entitlement included Mother's Day and all it enabled them to accomplish. For over twenty years, Jarvis challenged the AWM's custodial claim on the celebration of Mother's Day. She never understood why the war mothers required her day when they had so many others patriotic celebrations from which to choose.[110] They had Navy Day in October, Armistice Day in November, Army Day in April, Peace and Memorial Days in May, Independence Day in July, and after 1936, a Gold Star Mother's Day on the last Sunday in September. All were worthy holidays, of course, but they did not fully express the war mothers' dual identities. As an organization of "war veterans," the AWM rightfully shared in the patriotic holidays meant to honor those men and women who served their country in war. But as an organization of mothers, they wished always to put the interest of their children before their own, including their patriotic tributes. They did not want the celebration of their patriotism to overshadow that of their soldier sons and daughters. As for Gold Star Mother's Day, that remained an exclusive observance reserved for only a select portion of war mothers. Yet, Mother's Day perfectly suited the war mothers' broader model of patriotic motherhood, and they seized on the opportunity to sustain their ideals of exceptionalism through its celebration. Essentially, the holiday conferred a symbolic affirmation of their patriotic and maternal identities while it concretely provided the means to express that dual identity through service work for veterans and their families. As mothers, the holiday elevated them above all other women. But as patriotic mothers, their sacrifices elevated them above all other mothers—at least on the second Sunday of May.

In the end, the war mothers' need to use Mother's Day as an expressive outlet for their patriotic and maternal identities failed to change Jarvis's opinion of them. However, despite the animosity that Jarvis harbored over the AWM's annual Arlington observances and its endorsement of Frank Hering, she did eventually reconcile with the organization's original founder, Alice M. French. Jarvis did not hold "my dear Mrs. French" accountable for the "persons of dishonorable methods and greed" that led the AWM throughout the 1920s and 1930s.[111] And, unlike many of her fellow war mothers, French graciously acknowledged Jarvis's role in the holiday's creation. Norman Kendall included Mrs. French's touching words of gratitude in his 1937 Mother's Day history: "Miss Anna Jarvis is the founder of Mother's Day and [the holiday] will remain as long as [a] mother's love shall live."[112]

CHAPTER FIVE

A NEW MOTHER'S DAY FOR MODERN MOTHERS

I n the midst of the Great Depression, the celebration of Mother's Day grew to meet the social costs of the economic crisis. Maternal sentimentality, with all its quaint imagery of home and unconditional love, failed to fully mask the reality of families struggling for survival: families living far from the idealized domesticity portrayed in greeting cards and on department store placards. "Many on Mother's Day will be wearing carnations and sending flowers to Mother—a beautiful custom," agreed the Golden Rule Foundation, a philanthropic organization based in New York City. Yet at the same time, it warned, "Mothers—millions of them throughout the land—in homes of the unemployed are praying, not for flowers but for flour; not for confections but for bread; not for greeting cards and telegrams but for food, clothes, medicine and the simple necessities of life."[1]

In 1933, Congress cemented the relationship between the holiday and the support of charitable organizations by amending the original 1914 Mother's Day Resolution. In addition to the customary display of the American flag and the traditional tokens of affection to mothers, Senate Resolution 16 called on Americans to celebrate Mother's Day through contributions to churches, fraternal organizations, and welfare agencies providing relief for families victimized by the economic recession, especially the country's "unprecedented large numbers" of mothers and children lacking life necessities due to the unemployment or the death of the male wage earner.[2] The amended resolution immediately bolstered the work of benevolent organizations hoping to extend the holiday celebration into month-long campaigns for individual causes. They lobbied eagerly for the resolution's early passage so as to make the most effective use of the opportunity.[3]

As philanthropic groups constructed promotional and fund-raising campaigns around Mother's Day, they consciously altered the design and meaning of its celebration. They added more to the postsentimental critique of Mother's Day than just the admonishment of its commercialization. They offered legitimate alternatives for the commemoration of motherhood through the endorsement of progressive reform in honor of mothers. Throughout the 1930s, the American Mothers Committee of the Golden Rule Foundation (AMC; GRF)[4] and the Maternity Center Association (MCA) promoted a new Mother's Day that they believed better represented the expectations of motherhood, the needs of mothers and children, and the role of women in the modern era. When the AMC and MCA made Mother's Day central to their campaigns for welfare relief and better health care for American mothers, they inexorably adapted the original intent of a Mothers' Day founded on a model of social motherhood to their modern social agendas. They determined it was finally time, after two decades of empty sentimentality, to make mothers a serious concern of Mother's Day.[5]

Not surprisingly, Jarvis did not view the new Mother's Day campaigns as a modern homage to her mother's legacy. When she successfully rewrote Ann Reeves Jarvis's Mothers' Day story to fit her own holiday model, she deliberately excluded a civic dimension to the maternal role. At its heart, Mother's Day remained a home day for Jarvis, a day reserved as a "thank-offering" from sons and daughters to the mother who lovingly dedicated her life to their well-being.[6] She therefore perceived the charitable appropriation of Mother's Day as a direct threat to the sanctity of the home and the celebration of motherhood. During her final years, Jarvis once more served as the sentimental foil to organizations attempting to reinvent the meaning of Mother's Day to fit their modern maternal model. She included the American Mothers Committee, the Golden Rule Foundation, and the Maternity Center Association alongside the commercial industries on her list of identifiable anti-mother propagandists. Under the new guise of philanthropy, the groups used the same manipulative tactics as other rivals: financial gain, unauthorized celebrations, occasional adoption of the day's plural spelling, and federal sanction and protection for their work.

Although already accustomed to the commercial exploitation of Mother's Day by the 1930s, the intensity of the charitable intrusion on the holiday admittedly surprised Jarvis at first.

She was both "amazed" and "dismayed" at how the public allowed professional welfare workers to exploit the day's sentiment; she especially deplored the "committees of prominent men and women" who had commercialized the day in the name of "needy mothers."[7] She was an immediate and vocal critic of the congressional additions to the traditional Mother's Day resolution. She tirelessly tried to halt the annual passage of the "vicious legislation" throughout the 1930s, mainly through a voluminous letter-writing campaign that included regular appeals to President Roosevelt to help stop the "rabid greed of welfare agencies."[8]

Even though Jarvis's contemporary critics dismissed her suspicion of professional charity promoters, her demands for transparency in the political affiliations, financial records, and social policies of these organizations provide revealing commentary on the transitioning perspectives of motherhood and the celebration of Mother's Day. The American Mothers Committee and the Maternity Center

Association's views of modern motherhood allotted a level of intrusion into the home by the benevolent, medical, or civic authorities with which they allied themselves. In contrast, the sentiment behind Jarvis's Mother's Day observance bestowed unconditional praise on a mother's familial influence, effectively preserving her autonomy. Thus, when the GRF and MCA attempted to reduce Mother's Day to a "beggars' day," according to Jarvis, they demeaned all American mothers; the sting of charity had no place on a day meant for "gratitude to the living, and reverent memories for the deceased."[9]

OBSERVING MOTHER'S DAY THE GOLDEN RULE WAY

"Philanthropy still looms as a Major Big Business," declared Lyman L. Pierce in 1938. "This phenomenon does not just happen. It is not an effortless process. Institutions and organizations which make no effort to stimulate this process are onlookers rather than participants."[10] As the president of a fund-raising firm and one of the crowned inventors of the modern charitable drive, Pierce offered hope to philanthropic organizations struggling to find donors during the economic crisis. He confidently predicted that the amount of charitable gifts and bequeaths could soon reach pre-Depression level, as the American people's overall incomes had increased 61 percent since 1932. In order to tap into the new monetary growth, however, benevolent societies needed to centralize their methods to better approach potential donors. Without a well-organized campaign, Americans would continue to spend their discretionary income on luxury items instead of altruistic causes. Expenditures for theater tickets and cigarettes had increased by over 40 percent since 1932, for example, while expenditures for automobiles, whiskey, and beer had increased between 200 percent and 300 percent.[11]

The Golden Rule Foundation, incorporated in 1929, was one of the first philanthropic associations to publicize the growing discrepancy between the level of family expenditures on charities and the number of impoverished families throughout the country. As of 1933, an estimated fifteen million people depended on public relief, six million of whom were children under the age of sixteen. Yet, in the face of such obvious need, Americans spent twice as much on alcohol, tobacco, and narcotics each year as they gave to churches and private philanthropies. Federal appropriations for emergency relief were not enough to meet the social crisis, warned the foundation; moreover, such government appropriations did not "absolve private citizens from contributing for the support of the sick, the orphaned, the aged, and others in permanent need."[12] Since its inception, the GRF understood the power of a well-crafted charity drive that Lyman Pierce described. Every December, the foundation sponsored a Golden Rule Week designed to raise social awareness and charitable funds. Families were asked to prepare fugal meals for one week to "release for constructive philanthropy" the money typically spent on "wasteful if not injurious luxuries."[13] The foundation offered complete menus for three different levels of frugality, as well as suggested dinnertime conversations about the rewards of charitable giving.[14]

The primary focus of the December Golden Rule Week had remained the nation's undernourished children. But thanks to Mother's Day's growing popularity, the second Sunday in May offered another opportunity to specifically address the desperate plight of American mothers and raise funds for both women and their children. The same year that Congress amended the Mother's Day resolution, the GRF reported that twenty thousand mothers died annually due to complications in childbirth. The appalling statistic ranked the country's maternal death rate the highest among the industrialized countries of the world. Foundation President Charles Vickrey stressed in his published overview of the nation's dire situation, *The Golden Rule Book*, how each death at childbirth was a serious loss to the country: "The women who die from this cause are lost at the time of their greatest usefulness to the state and to their families; and they give their lives in carrying out a function which must be regarded as the most important in the world."[15] As a professional philanthropist, Vickrey effectively led the foundation's charitable postsentimental co-option of Mother's Day in the 1930s. The day's emotional praise of motherhood afforded a perfect opportunity for the GRF to tug at the hearts of Americans and hopefully turn holiday celebrants into charitable donors instead of simple consumers of flowers, confections, and greeting cards. Once the foundation captured the country's attention, it could fundamentally alter the meaning of maternal tribute and its celebratory expression by teaching Americans how to observe Mother's Day "the Golden Rule Way."[16]

Essentially, the Golden Rule Foundation operated as an administrative clearinghouse in support of a network of philanthropic organizations. Those interested in making charitable gifts or bequests could contact the foundation for advice on where the greatest need existed, as well as a list of reputable benevolent institutions and an overview of their work; donors could either designate specific charities as beneficiaries of their gifts or allow the foundation to disperse undesignated funds to where its studies revealed "acute unmet human needs." [17] Beginning in 1931, the GRF requested that donors make monetary gifts in honor of Mother's Day to its new Golden Rule Mothers Fund for the direct relief and welfare of the "Forgotten Mothers" and children of the unemployed. Of special concern for the foundation were mothers and children living beyond the reach of most community chests, such as those struggling to survive in the isolated mountain cabins of Appalachia and the camps of the southern coalfields.[18] As the honorary chairwoman of the foundation's National Mother's Day Committee, Eleanor Roosevelt reinforced the GRF's call for action in her speaking engagements as the First Lady of New York. In March of 1931, she encouraged an audience of collegiate women to do more for mothers this Mother's Day than the customary purchasing of flowers and other commercial tokens. "Whether your mother is living or dead, we are asking you to do just a little something for the suffering mothers of the United States," she urged.[19]

The GRF expanded its Mother's Day fundraising campaign with the creation of the American Mothers Committee in 1933. The committee's original purpose was "to bring to the attention of the general public, particularly young people, the rewards of the career of Motherhood," and it accomplished that task primarily through the annual designation of an American Mother of the Year. The AMC's national search provided weeks of additional publicity for the Golden Rule Mothers Fund each year. By 1943, the committee had organized subcommittees in every state, the District of Columbia, and the territories of Alaska, Hawaii, and Puerto Rico. Each subcommittee led individual searches for potential award recipients by distributing nomination forms through local networks of community and religious organizations and the regional media. The committee then chose its national winner from the subcommittees' narrowed pool of nominees; those not selected as the American Mother of Year were still honored as a mother of the year in their individual state or territory.[20]

While Vickery valued the American Mother of the Year award primarily for the publicity it generated for the foundation, the annual campaign held a deeper significance for the women of the AMC. Throughout the early twentieth century, committee members defined a career in motherhood as broadly as they envisioned the holiday's purpose and their role within its celebration. It was their intention to give the Mother's Day observance a "spiritual quality which highlights the standards of ideal motherhood and recognizes the important role of the mother in the home, the community, the nation and the world."[21] Subsequently, the AMC designed its American Mother of the Year award to formally recognize both the private and public dynamics of women's maternal identities. Every recipient had to illustrate a balanced maternal identity by excelling in the six essential qualifications:

First, that she be a successful mother, as evidenced by the character and achievements of her individual children; Second, that she be an active member of a religious body; Third, that she embody those traits highly regarded in mothers: courage, cheerfulness, patience, affection, kindness, understanding and a homemaking ability; Fourth, that she exemplify in her life and conduct the precepts of the Golden Rule; Fifth, that she have a sense of responsibility in the civic affairs and that she be active in service for public benefit; Sixth, that she be qualified to represent the Mothers of America in all responsibilities attached to her role as the National Mother.[22]

For the AMC, the annual award was more than a publicity gimmick for the GRF Mothers Fund. With every American Mother of the Year campaign, the committee reinforced a model of motherhood that escaped the boundary of the home and thus the sentimental specifications of Jarvis's Mother's Day.

An award reception held on Mother's Day marked the climax of the entire holiday campaign, drawing even more national attention. The American Mothers Committee described the 1935 reception for Lucy Keen Johnson, its first American Mother of the Year recipient, as "simple but celebrity-studded."[23] The day of tribute for Mrs. Johnson began at ten in the morning with a Girl Scout troop escort from her suite at the Waldorf-Astoria to a Mother's Day service at a local church and ended with an award reception featured on NBC's nightly radio broadcast. During the ceremony, GRF President Vickrey praised Mrs. Johnson's maternal qualifications as American Mother of the Year, and AMC Honorary Chairwoman Sara Delano Roosevelt presented her with the committee's official "Motherhood Medal." Lucy Johnson graciously accepted her award in front of a nationwide audience in honor of all mothers: "I take this medal not for myself alone but for the millions of American mothers today who are making a great nation of this fair land of ours." The NBC broadcast also featured holiday greetings from Sara Roosevelt and her son.[24]

Mrs. Johnson's life spoke directly to the maternal model promoted by the AMC. She was the wife of a prominent lawyer until the age of thirty-eight, when she was left a widow with six children (five of them stepchildren). To support her family, she took a position as dean of women at her alma mater, Wesleyan College in Macon, Georgia, which meant moving all seven of them into one of the women's dorms. She served as a "foster mother" to Wesleyan co-eds for fifteen years, retiring only after the last of her four sons and two daughters graduated from college. Mrs. Johnson met the AMC's final three qualifications by successfully balancing her family and career with a dedication to the Methodist Church and her leadership of various community service projects. When viewing the totality of her accomplishments, Mrs. Johnson's maternal peers overwhelmingly agreed that her career as a mother fully embodied the holiday's true spirit. She had shown through her children, career, faith, and civic commitment the impressive reach of a woman's maternal influence. In a tragic twist to the story, Mrs. Johnson became a "mother" again when a daughter died in childbirth, leaving the newborn in Mrs. Johnson's care just three months before she received her award.[25] All of Mrs. Johnson's successors illustrated the same integration of their private and public maternal roles throughout the early twentieth century. Regardless of the variations in their educational levels, religious faiths, economic class, and race, every award recipient rejected the arbitrary isolation of her maternal role and identity in a single sphere of influence.[26]

JARVIS VERSUS THE "CHARITY CHARLATANS"

In May 1933, Jarvis detailed the latest threat to her Mother's Day movement in a lengthy letter to her cousin. "In New York City there is a clique of charity profiteers that some day will be revealed as operators rivaling Wall Street," she wrote. "These men and women that you might think would stand for truth and right are as hard boiled and indifferent to justice as any to be found."[27] It became difficult for Jarvis to battle Charles Vickrey's Mother's Day "gold hunting" drives when he gained the assistance of such influential figures as Sara and Eleanor Roosevelt. She asked her cousin to request literature from the Golden Rule Foundation and forward it to her so she could follow Vickrey's Mother's Day campaign: "His plans for getting funds are daring and far-reaching, as you may see when you receive his printed matter. I have told him I think he is one of the biggest rascals out of Sing Sing."[28] To Jarvis,

Vickrey was simply another holiday profiteer hiding behind a Christian cause. She awaited the day when his greed would expose him as a fraud and infringer, just as it did for Frank Hering in the 1932 Fraternal Order of the Eagles lottery scandal. In the meantime, she needed to keep close account of "Golden Rule Charlie's" many golden schemes that began in earnest after the congressional endorsement of charitable giving on Mother's Day.[29]

Jarvis insisted that Vickrey was the mastermind behind the congressional amendment to the Mother's Day resolution, having been the one who pushed Senator Royal Copeland of New York to introduce it. Copeland, in her opinion, was merely a puppet of the GRF and other charities seeking to avoid prosecution for infringement; she marveled at how easy it was for people to fall for the projects of "designing persons" and their "craftiness."[30] Jarvis wrote over fifty personal letters and telegrams in an attempt to stall the legislation in 1933, including at least three direct appeals for President Roosevelt to stave off the "hordes of hungry, scheming charity promoters."[31] She pleaded with the president to remember that Mother's Day was her "movement and life" and deserved his protection.[32]

Jarvis's constant petitioning failed to prevent the repeated passage of the amended holiday resolution throughout the 1930s. Only once did she presumably succeed in pressuring the president to remain at least publicly neutral on the topic when he chose not to issue a special Mother's Day proclamation in 1935. In typical political style, President Roosevelt trusted any tribute that the American people paid to mothers would come spontaneously from their hearts, making any formal direction from a presidential proclamation unnecessary.[33] Nonetheless, with the both Sara and Eleanor Roosevelt's involvement with the GRF and other benevolent organizations, requests for the president's annual support of the new Mother's Day resolution found greater executive favor than Jarvis's repeated protests.[34]

Jarvis's criticism of the Golden Rule Foundation was just as multifaceted as her condemnation of other antimother propagandists. On a personal level, she deemed Vickrey and Senator Copeland's sponsorship of the senate resolution as a blatant end run around her copyrights, which was the same stunt attempted by Robert Spero and Senator Julius Berg's bill to officially replace Mother's Day with Parents' Day in the state of New York. She denounced the foundation's American Mother of the Year contest and its American Mothers Committee as publicity ploys meant to camouflage the holiday's economic exploitation. She accused Vickrey of misappropriating donations to pay the salaries of the hired promoters (namely himself) and to finance the lavish luncheons thrown for New York socialites. Vickrey's shady actions were well hidden behind the list of prominent names serving on the foundation's various committees, she believed. "It is amazing how men of repute will permit their women homefolk to be identified with professional promoters, and be the latter's tools, peddlers and street barkers," she quipped.[35] Jarvis doubted any of the money went to assist the women and children for which Vickrey expressed such heartfelt concern. In 1938, she demanded an account of all receipts and disbursements of the $10,000 the foundation reportedly earned through its award campaign that spring; she hoped that the public exposure would finally make "Golden Rule Charlie" accountable for his numerous deceptions on the American people.[36]

Regardless of her opposition to the congressional corruption of the original Mother's Day resolution, Jarvis was not categorically opposed to charitable causes directly associated with Mother's Day. She included benevolent work with prisoners within her Mother's Day movement by encouraging prisoners to seek the mutual emotional uplift found with sending a personal Mother's Day message home. She personally requested holiday paroles for repentant sons and daughters to visit their mothers. Reuniting a mother with her child, whether through a letter or in person, was a gift in accord with the day's maternal reverence, as it was motivated by gratitude and love. According to Jarvis, no one could "challenge the sincerity of the love for mother of the prisoner, the 'down and out,' or others to whom the world seems a bitter game."[37]

Since she designed the Mother's Day observance to applaud mothers' influence within the home, a gift made out of pity had no place in the observance of Mother's Day. "Let us have one day of the year when even the 'poor mother' may feel exalted and not have the word 'poor' rubbed in to her thru the brutal word 'charity.' Mother's Day remembrances are as awards for benefactions received," implored Jarvis.[38] Mothers deserved messages and acts of appreciation and affection "given from hand to hand, and not thru the thrifty, salaried charity schemer."[39] Ultimately, then, her resentment of the GRF's Mother's Day campaigns also included the distorted holiday sentiment that accompanied its obvious grafting in the name of the "Forgotten Mothers."

Vickrey naturally dismissed Jarvis's accusations. In a letter to President Roosevelt's private secretary in 1933, Vickrey appeared more amused than overtly threatened by her efforts to stop the foundation's holiday drive:

I understand that our friend of many years, Miss Jarvis of Philadelphia . . . has been adding considerable variety if not excitement to your day's work. I am indeed sorry if I have been the occasion of throwing upon you or the President any unpleasant correspondence. . . . I can assure you however that the nation as a whole deeply appreciated the service rendered by the President in placing Mother's Day, by his Proclamation, this year and in the future on a little higher plane than in the past.[40]

He apparently viewed the foundation's successful incorporation of charitable giving into the observance as a noticeable improvement over Jarvis's sentimental design. Yet, the GRF's celebration of Mother's Day did not exist on the same "higher plane" as the American Mothers Committee's observance. It was difficult for the foundation's larger fundraising drive to avoid the national depiction of mothers as victims of an economic situation beyond their control. As with the welfare work of Frank Hering and the Eagles, the promotional rhetoric typically portrayed mothers as passive beneficiaries rather than active agents of change.

The AMC, in comparison, attempted to ameliorate the foundation's message of maternal vulnerability and passivity with the American Mother of the Year celebration of maternal strength and activism. When the GRF chose to restrict the scope of the committee's involvement to the selection of the American Mother of the Year, however, it effectively overshadowed the women's distinctive tribute to American motherhood. This eventually led to a relational breakdown between the AMC and its parent organization. By 1950, the committee had grown tired of its auxiliary role and sought independent incorporation, first within New York and then nationally in 1954. "With independence came the realization of a longtime dream . . . to utilize, in a year round and much needed program, the wonderful capabilities of the remarkable women chosen as State Mothers [and National Mothers] each year," explained its national president.[41] The American Mothers were now ready, she boasted, to face the "future with courage and determination."[42]

"LET'S MAKE MOTHER'S DAY MEAN A BETTER CHANCE FOR MOTHERS EVERYWHERE": THE MATERNITY CENTER ASSOCIATION

In 1915, doctors and health commissioners convened a committee to investigate the disturbingly high infant mortality rate in New York City. Three decades of public health efforts, such as purified milk stations and infant welfare clinics, had improved the survival rates of babies between one and twelve months of age, but they did not halt the steady climb of death rates for babies in the first month of life or the maternal death rate. The committee concluded that the lack of prenatal care and complications during childbirth explained the disparate survival rates for mothers, newborns, and older infants and toddlers. Older children died mainly from gastrointestinal illnesses resulting from contaminated milk and substandard hygiene conditions, while newborns died within hours or days due to premature births, congenital disorders, and accidents during delivery. Although a midwife, general practitioner, or an obstetrician attended most women during childbirth, mothers rarely received prenatal care before their third trimester unless obvious complications occurred. Moreover, maternal deaths associated with puerperal septicemia (childbed fever) revealed the necessity of postpartum care in saving the lives of new mothers. The committee, therefore, recommended an extensive coordination of the city's then-chaotic maternity programs to provide prenatal care as early as possible and medical monitoring for both mother and baby in the weeks following the delivery. With its new focus on mothers, New York City health reformers led the way in associating maternal health with infant health in the public consciousness.[43]

Nationally, complications resulting from childbirth were a leading cause of death for women between the ages of fifteen and forty-four in the early twentieth century, second only to tuberculosis. The U.S. maternal mortality rate of sixty-two per ten thousand live births in 1916 ranked the country fourteenth among sixteen industrial nations in its ability to provide safe maternity care.[44] In New York City, overcrowding, poor sanitation, and poverty exacerbated the risks for mothers. As a result, the city's network of female public health professionals, settlement house workers, and women's clubs responded first to the health crisis.

The Maternity Center Association, in particular, owed its founding to the initial work of Frances Perkins. In 1917, two New York obstetricians approached Perkins seeking her assistance in establishing a network of maternity centers throughout the city to provide prenatal care and education programs for mothers. Perkins knew firsthand the potential risks all women faced during pregnancy. Two years earlier, she had prepared herself to die in childbirth when she was forced to undergo an emergency caesarian; she survived the ordeal, but sadly her son did not. Perkins's experience naturally encouraged her activism on behalf of maternal health, and she eagerly threw herself into the proposed idea of developing a Maternity Center Association. In 1918, Perkins recruited some of the city's wealthiest patrons, many of them young mothers themselves, to officially sponsor the MCA's creation and fund its starting operation. By the end of Perkins's one-year tenure as executive secretary, the association employed twenty-six public health nurses operating out of sixteen clinics.[45] Two years later, its administrative board coordinated thirty maternity centers and over thirty employed public health nurses throughout Manhattan. Of the 8,742 pregnant women and infants cared for at the centers in 1921, there was a 29.2 percent reduction in the deaths of newborns and a 21.5 percent reduction in maternal deaths when compared to New York City's overall mortality rates.[46]

Thanks to the increased awareness of the city's maternity crisis, the majority of hospitals and health organizations, like Lillian Wald's Henry Street Visiting Nurse Service, began assuming more responsibility for prenatal and postnatal care of patients by the early 1920s.[47] The overlapping of services encouraged the MCA to change its original mission and function primarily as an educational and experimental agency.[48] In accordance, the association centralized its work in 1921 to a single center on the city's East Side where four thousand babies on average were born each year. This enabled the MCA to concentrate on the development of prenatal and postnatal screening techniques, serve as a national teaching center for public health nurses, and above all offer educational programs for women on the importance of prepartum and postpartum medical care.[49]

The Maternity Center Association's focus on maternal education and medical intervention mirrored the larger changes in the public health movement's perspective on maternal behavior and its relationship to infant mortality. Since the late nineteenth century, discussions of infant mortality had focused primarily on the urban poor and working-class populations who experienced some of the country's highest rates. Reformers debated the causal link between infant death, conditions of poverty, and ethnic traditions (or "dysfunctional" immigrant behavior) in hopes of eradicating the principal culprit of the health crisis. In reality, of course, there remains no single solution to such a complex social problem; nonetheless, the broader discourse on "the problem of infant health" narrowed in scope to become "the problem of motherhood" by the 1920s. As mentioned previously, public health reformers and doctors specializing in the new fields of obstetrics and pediatrics increasingly agreed that mothers were unable to successfully rear children without the proper education and guidance of experts, and the failure of 730,000 men to physically qualify for service in World War I helped hasten that consensus. A woman's natural instincts and capacity for unconditional love failed to sufficiently prepare her for modern motherhood. According to the new model, she now required adequate training in the latest scientific principles of motherhood and childcare, as well as steadfast medical supervision. Once mothers applied the new tenets of scientific motherhood, experts predicted that the nation's children would not only survive infancy but also continue to thrive, regardless of the mitigating factors of poverty and ethnic diversity.[50]

The funds made available under the 1921 Sheppard-Towner Act (also known as the Maternity and Infancy Act) enabled the MCA to improve its clinical and educational services and expand its national reputation. The Sheppard-Towner Act marked the first federal welfare program in the United States. It funneled matching federal funds to states willing to subsidize prenatal screening clinics and "well-baby" programs. The act also stressed the necessity of maternal education and underwrote the cost of distributing educational literature and employing nurses to provide group and individual instructions on all aspects of maternal and infant health.[51] Public health nurses, like those the MCA trained and employed, were the heart of the maternal and infant health initiatives that the Sheppard-Towner Act funded. Throughout the country, they served as emissaries of the new scientific knowledge to mothers. The U.S. Children's Bureau extolled the public health nurse as the first line of defense against the mothers and grandmothers who loved their babies very much but whose ignorance nonetheless killed an estimated one hundred thousand babies each year:

It is the public health nurse who follows the case into the home and there on the spot, with the utensils and the conditions which the mother has at her disposal, she teaches the principles of the care of the baby in the most effective way. She is the final link in the chain that connects the scientific investigator in his laboratory with the children he is working to save. She is the messenger who brings the last word of science to the place where it must be applied if our knowledge is to be effective.[52]

The MCA served the expectant mothers of New York in the same way. Its staff of administrators, volunteers, and public health nurses understood the value of being the "final link in the chain" between medical knowledge and its practical application to the daily lives of women and children, and together they strove to save the lives of mothers and babies that would have otherwise died due to inadequate care.

Community unavoidably shaped the MCA's perspective on maternity care. The association trained its nurses to never view the maternity patient as an isolated individual:

She is a part of a family that lives in a community with other families. Whatever effects the whole health situation in that community influences the lives and health of the mothers and babies. To give good maternity care the nurse must know these influences.[53]

In contrast to obstetricians who tended to view maternity care within a narrow clinical framework, the MCA offered a holistic perspective, one born of its intimate relationship with the community it served. The nurses who visited the tenement homes of their clients could not ignore the mitigating social and economic factors affecting an expectant mother's health. The association reminded the nurse of her responsibility to ensure both a mother's emotional and physical health during pregnancy: "Her problems should therefore be your problems until you have helped her solve or adjust to them."[54]

The nurses were also conscious of their instruction's relevancy to the women they visited at home or met in their group classes. As health professionals, they believed the adherence to medical advice would save the lives of women and children they served, but personal experiences forced them to acknowledge the limitations that poverty and familial obligations placed on the clients' ability to follow that life-saving advice. Consequently, no patient was dismissed because she failed to follow all of the nurse's directions. The nurse simply recommended "the next best thing" until she found the one thing that a reluctant mother was disposed to do in order to improve her health and that of the baby.[55] Nurses were prepared to adjust their recommendations to fit the immediate needs of their patients, even if they contradicted the standing instructions of advising physicians. As a general rule, for example, the MCA counseled hospital deliveries over home births. Its nurses, nonetheless, carefully weighed the benefits of a hospital birth against the obvious disruption that a mother's extended absence from her family would cause and, when deemed warranted, made arrangements for a home delivery and the necessary postpartum care.[56]

Although the association's nurses experienced a larger degree of autonomy than their counterparts working in hospitals or private offices, they were still limited within the purview of preventative health care and under the supervision of the association's obstetricians. Nurses were trained to screen for potential complications in their prenatal visits to clients, in other words, but were not permitted to formally diagnose or administer treatment independent of the obstetrician's instructions. Consequently, the nurses placed a significant importance on their duties as educators. The MCA designed Mothers' Club Talks for expectant mothers on every aspect of maternity health and infant care. The classes covered technical information about how a fetus develops, what to expect during a prenatal examination, how to prepare for delivery, and instructions on breastfeeding. Topics also included general information on a woman's diet and exercise during pregnancy, what to buy in preparation for the baby's arrival, and how to change a newborn's diaper or give him or her a bath. As a further enticement for mothers, the association offered refreshments, games, and most importantly, childcare during the Mothers' Club Talks. When necessary, the nurses conveyed the same information through home visits for the mothers still unable or reluctant to attend the scheduled classes.[57]

The MCA wished to ultimately empower women through its educational programs. By encouraging mothers to not only adhere to the medical advice but also to understand the basic scientific principles behind the advice, it hoped to inspire women to take an active interest in their own health, as well as the health of their families and communities.[58] "In giving these talks," the association instructed its nurses,

> make them simple and direct—using technical terms but explaining them. Make sure that your mothers know the reason for every procedure advised. Encourage them to ask questions. Remember that every pregnant mother is a potential "neighbor-nurse" in the months to come.[59]

In addition to its work within New York City, the MCA gained a national reputation as a training center for public health nurses. Nurses from all over the country came for instruction and field experience in maternity care; a total of 2,500 public health nurses trained with the MCA between 1921 and 1928, some staying as long as six months. By 1929, requests to study at its field clinic outgrew the physical capacity of the center, prompting the association to arm its nurses with teaching literature and exhibits and send them throughout the country to lead training seminars. The association also continued to revise its handbook for public health nurses, *Routines for Maternity Nursing and Briefs for Mothers' Club Talks*, first published in 1920. It distributed over fourteen thousand copies within the first five years of its publication, along with five hundred thousand copies of its pamphlet series, *Twelve Helpful Talks*, designed specifically for expectant mothers.[60]

A study conducted in 1929 showcased the success of the association's educational programs and training techniques, revealing how its patients were three times less likely to suffer fatal complications in childbirth than area women not under its care. The MCA credited the success to its educational instruction to mothers and its ability to coordinate medical care with local physicians and hospitals to ensure that each patient received the medical care best suited for her individual needs. The association's notable achievements encouraged its medical staff to promote the idea of a scientifically trained nurse-midwife to the city's larger medical community. They argued that professional nurse-midwives could expand the city's maternity care by performing normal deliveries instead of serving merely as attendants, thereby providing a service to both mothers and obstetricians.[61]

THE AMERICAN MEDICAL ASSOCIATION VERSUS THE
MATERNITY CENTER ASSOCIATION

The repeal of the Sheppard-Towner Act in 1929 and the professional jealousies of the American Medical Association (AMA) forced the Maternity Center Association to reevaluate its local and national role as champions of maternal and infant health care in the 1930s. The Sheppard-Towner Act had exclusively designated funds for preventive health services so as not to interfere with the private practices of doctors. Up to that period, general physicians had not offered such preventive care measures, instead focusing their efforts on curing those already sick. When the U.S. Children's Bureau first sponsored the act, it promoted the legislation as a necessary measure to fill gaps in health services that private doctors were unwilling to provide and therefore was not a direct threat to their professional livelihood. After the act's passage, however, the AMA encouraged private physicians to incorporate preventive health services into their practice and become the "family health advisor as well as the family physician."[62] Not only would the new measures facilitate a lucrative expansion for a physician's practice, but it would also effectively end the government's unwelcomed foray into the business of health care. As predicted, the growing number of obstetricians, pediatricians, and general family doctors who offered prenatal and postnatal care to patients in the 1920s enabled the AMA to successfully argue that the Sheppard-Towner Act was no longer necessary and directly threatened the livelihood of private doctors.

In 1927, Congress voted not to renew the health legislation, and by 1929, all federal funds for the public clinics and educational programs created under the Sheppard-Towner Act officially stopped. Unfortunately, the AMA's victory did more than remove the government's involvement in maternal and infant health care. It invariably undermined the medical authority of public health organizations like the association and its staff of public health nurses. As the AMA declared prenatal and postnatal care to be its exclusive domain, the public health nurse lost her valued position as the first line of defense against high infant and maternal mortality rates. According to the AMA, only a doctor was qualified to evaluate an expectant mother's health and determine the course of her treatment.[63]

The American Medical Association's drive to protect its political influence and the livelihood of its members placed the Maternity Center Association on the defensive. The association's cooperative relationship with private physicians and public hospitals had been a key to its success throughout the 1920s. The AMA's new assertion of dominance, however, threatened that relationship.[64]

With the repeal of the Sheppard-Towner Act, then, the New York medical community had less incentive to support the MCA's maternity work, particularly the advocating of professional nurse-midwives. The association quickly recognized the tenuous balance between its own aspirations and the requisite deference to the powerful medical fraternity.[65] On the one hand, the MCA was not willing to completely surrender its local and national leadership in the arena of maternal and infant health. On the other hand, it could not risk alienating private physicians by appearing to trespass too far into their territory. It was in this context that the popular Mother's Day observance offered the MCA a solution to its pressing dilemma. By appropriating the holiday in the 1930s, the association found a way to nurture a new professional relationship with private physicians, secure its continued influence within the national campaign to provide quality maternity health care, and shield its controversial nurse-midwifery program.

Initially, the MCA used Mother's Day to reemphasize its role as the messenger of scientific knowledge to expectant mothers. It had already recognized the holiday's usefulness for raising awareness and support of its maternity work in the 1920s. In 1929, for example, the association placed a Mother's Day ad in the fashion section of the *New York Times*, asking readers to contribute to its efforts to save the lives of mothers instead of the floral industry's profit margins:

Help the Maternity Center Association teach the value of maternity care to the public and to the mothers so that they will demand it for themselves. Help the Maternity Center Association teach public health nurses so that they may be able to give this maternity care. Won't you send a contribution—whatever you can?[66]

Two years later, the association was ready to expand its Mother's Day promotion into a nationwide educational campaign on behalf of the estimated sixteen thousand mothers who lost their lives each year to inadequate maternity care. Of that tragic total, insisted the MCA, ten thousand had died from preventable complications. Had the mothers known the value of prenatal care and sought the services of skilled medical professionals, they would have survived to celebrate Mother's Day another year.[67] The association, therefore, set out to re-channel the sentimentality of the observance into a practical service to mothers. Advocates of its national plans denounced the traditional observance of Mother's Day as "almost sacrilegious" or an "emotional jag"—a day for people to simply "go to church, shed a tear, eat a big dinner and forget about it."[68] When faced with such a health crisis, the MCA and its supporters concluded that the sentimental celebration offered no tangible value to the real lives of mothers.

In 1931, the association launched the first of six national Mother's Day campaigns designed to accomplish three main goals: raise awareness of the country's high maternal death rates, educate women on the importance of maternity care, and help communities develop the necessary strategies to provide mothers (particularly poor mothers) access to such care.[69] The association's aim to create a New Mother's Day observance, one more "productive of results in terms of human lives saved," recaptured the original Mothers' Day legacy of Ann Reeves Jarvis, Julia Ward Howe, and Juliet Calhoun Blakeley.[70] As an organization that sought medical and community solutions to high maternal and infant mortality rates, the MCA's campaigns were reminiscent of Ann Reeves Jarvis's Mothers' Day Work Clubs in the 1850s. Both trusted the guidance of medical authorities and touted education as the best tool in empowering mothers to guard their own health and ensure the survival of their children. The association's national slogan "Let's Make Mother's Day Mean a Better Chance for Mothers Everywhere," faintly echoed the "Better Mothers, Better Homes, Better Children, Better Men and Women" motto of the nineteenth-century clubs.[71]

As an organization predominantly represented by women, the MCA also exemplified the collective power of women and mothers outside the private sphere once envisioned by Howe and Blakeley. Although the nursing staff consisted of single women, married women (and presumably mothers) served in the majority of administrative offices and dominated the membership of every governing board, with the exception of the medical board and finance committee.[72] Frances Perkins poignantly described the women she worked with during the MCA's first years as "caught up in the operation of the basic emotion known as maternal feeling . . . They felt, therefore, warm, sympathetic and tender toward every other child in the world."[73] They embraced, in short, the public dynamic of their maternal roles.

The association's Mother's Day campaigns reached a national audience under its effective female leadership. Campaign publicity included advertisements, cartoons, and articles in thousands of national periodicals and a series of special radio talks. Speeches presented at its first annual Mother's Day luncheon in New York City were nationally broadcast over forty-five CBS radio stations. Between 1931 and 1933, the campaign's publicity efforts centered on the appalling maternal mortality rates. Typical stories published in magazines and newspapers stressed the country's failure to save the mothers who died needlessly in childbirth every year.[74] A promotional cartoon featuring Uncle Sam rocking a recently orphaned baby illustrated the association's early attempts to rally (or at least shame) the nation into addressing the serious health problem. With both hands on a cradle, Uncle Sam looks solemnly at a sign exposing the United States' disgraceful maternal death rate. "Uncle Sam is troubled—16,000 mothers every year fail to answer roll call on Mother's Day," grimly notes the caption.[75]

During a time when many newspapers customarily refused to print the word *pregnancy*, the holiday campaigns succeeded in exposing a national audience to the dangers of inadequate maternity care, often providing facts and information that had never before appeared in public print. The immediate response was overwhelming. In the wake of the first campaign, over three thousand expectant mothers wrote the MCA to request its educational literature, and civic organizations around the country promised to incorporate the issue of maternal and infant health into their community service. The popularity of the 1931 holiday thoroughly convinced the association of the nation's eagerness for "something more substantial than vacuous sentimentality" on Mother's Day.[76]

The core of the educational campaigns remained the message for all expectant mothers to seek the medical services of a doctor as soon as they were aware of the pregnancy. In this way, the association remained an ally of private physicians. It

Uncle Sam is troubled—16,000 mothers every year fail to answer roll-call on Mother's Day. They die having babies. Of these 10,000 could be saved, if people knew the importance of adequate maternity care. Among 22 nations the maternity death rate in the United States is highest.

Figure 5.1. Maternity Center Association, New Mother's Day Campaign Publicity Kit 1931. ©Childbirth Connections. Used With Permission.

was assumed that women who could afford the expense of a private obstetrician or pediatrician would choose to do so, thus allowing public health organizations and community welfare programs to continue aiding poor mothers who would otherwise have gone without proper prenatal and postnatal care.[77] Despite its public deference to the members of the AMA, however, the MCA was willing to hold private physicians and hospitals accountable for the quality of maternity care they provided patients. In 1934, the New York Academy of Medicine released a report admitting the medical fraternity's culpability in the city's maternal death rate between 1930 and 1932.

According to the academy's own exhaustive investigation, chronicled in a *Good Housekeeping* article, New York City still experienced the highest maternal mortality rate of the world's largest cities. Of the 2,341 maternal deaths that occurred over the three-year period, the report concluded that 1,343 were preventable. The academy blamed the brunt of the unnecessary deaths on doctors, an estimated 61 percent culpability (the study attributed 36 percent of the deaths to the ignorance or incompetence of mothers). The reasons for the startling lapse in quality of medical care included the lack of obstetric training for general practitioners in medical schools, the overeagerness of doctors to use drugs to induce labor or anesthetics to ease the pain of labor, and exorbitant doctors' fees that kept prenatal care out of the reach of many middleclass families. The curtailing of public health programs, of course, further exasperated the critical situation.[78]

In the same year as the New York Academy of Medicine's study, the association's Mother's Day campaign exhibited a stronger emphasis on the importance of community activism in ensuring all mothers access to quality maternity care. It had included the role of community organizations in its Mother's Day campaigns from the start. Groups wishing to lead their own holiday campaigns could request a free publicity kit from the association to aid in their efforts. The kit provided complete outlines for town meetings, church sermons, radio talks, political proclamations, newspaper articles, and advertisements, all designed to empower a group's effort to secure better maternity care in their individual communities. Every Mother's Day campaign drew hundreds of requests for the promotional kit.[79]

In 1934, the MCA consciously narrowed its focus on community activism and initiated a contest to encourage organizations across the country to appraise the quality of maternity care in their local communities:

Merely deploring this condition will not change it. Wishing will not change it. An effort everywhere is needed by parents, physicians and nurses; first, to know precisely the facilities of their own communities, and, second, to make these facilities measure up to the standards of adequate care. Clubs and civic organizations can provide the machinery for coordinating such an effort.[80]

Prizes were awarded to individual groups who presented the most thorough account of its community's maternal services, as well as plans for further improvement. Yet the contest was not as successful as originally hoped. While many communities requested the survey material, few were able to complete the process sufficiently. Most cited a problem with local doctors either too busy or apathetic to assist in the complicated appraisal of maternity services.[81]

Nonetheless, the focus on community action and civic responsibility remained a central theme of the Maternity Center Association's holiday campaigns between 1934 and 1937. Influential state and national figures, such as former New York governor Al Smith, First Lady Eleanor Roosevelt, and Secretary of Labor Frances Perkins added their support to the association's efforts by serving as dedicated spokespersons for the campaigns. "The thing is not a question of whether you are going to support and be interested in the work of the Maternity Center Association," attested Eleanor Roosevelt, "because I don't see how any sane human being could help but be interested in the care of mothers and the real knowledge that must be taught them and taught the people who are going to take care of them."[82]

Although Perkins had only served as the MCA's executive secretary for one year, she remained informally connected to its work throughout the rest of her career. She later referred to the association as her single "most successful piece of social work."[83] While serving as secretary of labor, Perkins also represented the association as an honorary vice president and joined the first lady as a vocal advocate for government intervention in the cause of maternal health. When asked in 1935 to defend the U.S. Children's Bureau's involvement with the MCA's Mother's Day campaigns, Perkins frankly answered: "Because children need a mother's care."[84] Studies had proven that the death of the mother decreased the odds of survival for the infant during its first year of life, she asserted, "so it is a matter of life and death to children that maternal mortality should be reduced. For this reason the Children's Bureau has from the very beginning been interested in the care of mothers."[85]

If unable to inspire communities to hold city governments and local medical professionals accountable for inadequate standards of maternity services, the MCA offered detailed advice to empower expectant mothers to demand quality pre- and postnatal care for themselves. The educational literature for the 1935 Mother's Day campaign included instructions on how to distinguish a skilled physician from a quack, how to select an adequate hospital maternity ward, and what qualified as complete maternity care—defined as the medical supervision and care of a mother from the beginning of pregnancy until her full postpartum recovery. This policing of maternity care did not directly threaten the American Medical Association, as illustrated by the association's authorship of "Choosing Your Doctor" in the Mother's Day campaign literature. In the long run, of course, the AMA had a professional and economic incentive to support the MCA's efforts to weed out poorly trained physicians from the ranks of the medical community.[86]

The association's training of professional nurse-midwives throughout the 1930s elicited a different response from the New York medical fraternity. In 1931 and 1932, the MCA opened the Lobenstine Midwifery Clinic and the Lobenstine Midwifery School after its failed attempt to coordinate a nurse-midwifery program with city hospitals. The fully licensed clinic and school provided nurses with instruction and field experience in prenatal, labor and delivery, and postpartum care. Advocates saw the professionally trained nurse-midwife as the perfect solution for communities lacking in maternity services. Allowing nurse-midwives to care for women expecting normal pregnancies would better meet the medical needs of poor and rural women, as well as reserve the obstetrician's expertise for the complicated cases requiring intensive medical intervention. Doctors on the association's medical board reassured their colleagues that a nurse-midwife would improve their practice, not compete against it. "If nurse-midwives performed normal deliveries," they argued, then "obstetricians would deal with fewer complications during and after childbirth, perform fewer Caesarian sections, have more time to read medical journals and attend medical meetings, and become richer."[87]

Yet the argument failed to convince many obstetricians that nurse-midwives did not pose a direct threat to their private practices. In response, the Lobenstine clinic agreed to only treat patients who could not afford private care, mainly women from the district's African American and Puerto Rican populations. Furthermore, the MCA promised that its graduates would not stay to practice in the city but would be sent to rural communities or overseas where qualified doctors did not exist.[88]

In another measure to protect the fledging nurse-midwifery program, the MCA did not aggressively publicize it. Thus, the association's holiday promotions of quality maternal care did not include the benefits that trained nurse-midwives offered over the services of private physicians. The Lobenstine school and clinic trained their nurse-midwives in the same holistic approach to maternity care that they trained the traditional public health nurses. They too recognized that pregnant women did not exist in isolation and that economic, emotional, and environmental factors affected the health of the mother and unborn child. Moreover, its graduates had more firsthand experience delivering babies than most of the country's doctors. Where the average medical student was lucky to observe six deliveries before graduation, the Lobenstine nurse-midwives attended twenty. Women attended by nurse-midwives subsequently experienced shorter labors and less medical intervention, such as the drugs and forceps that obstetricians routinely used, and were more likely to deliver safely at home than women solely under the care of a private physician.[89] But out of a sense of professional self-preservation, the MCA's Mother's Day campaigns excluded nurse-midwifery as a viable option for women seeking quality maternity care.

JARVIS VERSUS THE "EXPECTANT MOTHER RACKET"

As with the Golden Rule Foundation, Jarvis doubted the legitimacy of the Maternity Center Association's Mother's Day campaigns. She considered it another camouflaged attempt to divert public and private subsidies into the pockets of unscrupulous figures, all in the name of needy mothers, and she demanded a public accounting of the association's Mother's Day solicitations. Her efforts to halt the MCA's holiday campaigns pitted her against a virtual who's who of New York politicians, health reformers, and socialites who dominated the association's various committees and boards. This included Eleanor Roosevelt and Frances Perkins, of course. Jarvis nevertheless remained fearless in her assault against the association's exploitation and ideological corruption of her sentimental Mother's Day observance, despite the obvious political power and social influence of its supporters. In her opinion, "the committee of prominent ladies" that supported the MCA used the cause of expectant motherhood as bait to lure in salaries and luxuries for its professional charity promoters and not for the direct benefit of needy mothers.[90] "Somebody should page

Dillinger and tell him what a 'piker' he was to bother with the little stuff in banks. Had he allied himself with Mother's Day committees of prominent ladies," she quipped, "he might be high and mighty as they on earth instead of where he is."[91]

She estimated the association's total assets between $250,000 and $600,000, a portion of which was obtained through its annual Mother's Day carnation peddling and other unethical holiday solicitations. She included in the tally the association's potential access to the $8 million allocated to public health services under the 1935 Social Security Act, courtesy of Secretary Perkins.[92]

The increasing ranks of prominent ladies that promoted the association's Mother's Day campaigns each spring further added to Jarvis's frustration. She insisted that these wives of renowned politicians, businessmen, financers, news-paper/magazine owners, doctors, lawyers, and even a New York Giants baseball player, had enough personal wealth to save all the victims of poor maternity care themselves. Thus, they did not need her day. Instead they used her Mother's Day for their begging and then publicly chastised her for protesting year after year. In response, Jarvis enjoyed agitating the committee women (who began dodging her phone calls) by sending registered evening telegrams to their husbands, informing them of their wives' dubious behavior.[93] "Men do not like their wives oftentimes giving their time to these clubs, and are glad of an excuse to stop them," she explained.[94] Even President Roosevelt received telegrams addressing his wife's sordid charity work.

Whereas Jarvis slightly tempered her criticism in correspondence to President Roosevelt, the letters addressed directly to the first lady and Secretary Perkins patently accused the women of illegally usurping Mother's Day. In 1935, Jarvis charged Eleanor Roosevelt with "grand larceny of human reputation and achievement" for misrepresenting and encroaching on her movement work: "My indignation is supreme in this hour of my full knowledge of your crafty plotting to seize property and work in no way having the favor or a penny of yours or any of your Outfit."[95]

Later that same year, she compared Perkins's sanctioning of the association's Mother's Day operations to Mussolini's seizing of property in Africa, as both acts were motivated purely by greed. "The association and prominent dames and yourself would not permit your names and work to be defiantly used by unfriendly strangers as you have used names and work and celebrations of Mother's Day," wrote Jarvis. "Try the game on the American Red Cross, Daughters of the American Revolution, Grand Army of the Republic, American Legion and see where you women come off."[96] Furthermore, she advised Perkins to resign before she became tempted to divert federal funds through Social Security or the U.S. Children's Bureau to aid her private maternity concerns: "It is too bad for our government you have not risen above the commonplace charity racket of [the] Maternity Center Association."[97] She cordially ended her letters to both women with, "Very Truly, Anna Jarvis, Founder, Mother's Day."

CRITIQUE OF SCIENTIFIC MOTHERHOOD

Ultimately, it was more than just the flagrant disregard of Jarvis's legal copyright that fueled her crusade against the maternal organization. Jarvis's celebration of motherhood, however limited in scope, exalted the natural abilities of mothers to rear their children and reign supreme over the domestic sphere. Thus she reserved the second Sunday in May for the expression of unabashed gratitude; the day was never meant to elicit pity for poor mothers or promote programs to combat women's maternal incompetence. Subsequently, Jarvis's criticism of the Maternity Center Association exposed the potential danger that advocates of scientific motherhood posed to the sanctity of the home and a woman's maternal autonomy. Moreover, it revealed the fine line that the MCA traversed between empowering expectant mothers to be proactive in their prenatal and postnatal health care and wanting to legitimize its own professional authority over that care.

The association built its holiday campaigns on the belief that women educated on the importance of maternity care would demand a better standard of treatment for all the mothers in their communities. Once they gained access to that health care, however, the MCA expected women to fully surrender to the medical professionals providing it. The association's promotion of scientific motherhood drew criticism from contemporaries besides Jarvis and, most recently, from modern historians. Contemporary critics feared the damage brought by the involvement of medical experts and government programs in the lives of mothers and their children. In his early criticism of the Sheppard-Towner Act, Senator James A. Reed of Missouri denounced the public intrusion into the private matter of child rearing, insisting that government meddling could not replace "mother love" or the wisdom gained from maternal experience. He subsequently proposed renaming the welfare legislation "A Bill to Organize a Board of Spinsters to Teach Mothers How to Raise Babies."[98]

Recent historians have voiced similar criticisms, documenting the hidden costs of women's adherence to the tenets of scientific motherhood in the early twentieth century. Such costs included the undermining of mothers' confidence and autonomy, as well as the erosion of women's trust in traditional female support networks.[99] Yet, despite all that the scientific model promised, women did not welcome the requisite medical supervision with equal enthusiasm. Letters to the U.S. Children's Bureau illustrated mothers' frustration with conflicting medical advice or the incompetence of specific physicians. A few even questioned the assumption that scientific medical care was synonymous with progress, asking why the young mothers of today experienced difficult pregnancies and deliveries despite the advantage of the best doctors and access to the latest literature. "Our mothers and grandmothers who had from seven to ten children apparently did not have this trouble," insisted one woman.[100] Regardless of the negative experiences described in women's letters, the bureau upheld the importance of women's reliance on doctors. The recommendation to "consult a physician" remained its primary response to the mothers writing for help or advice.[101]

As advocates of medical prenatal care, the MCA also weakened women's traditional view of pregnancy and childbirth as purely natural events and thus an experience shared by generations of women: "Many expectant mothers will be told that their mothers and grandmothers 'let nature take care of itself.' But in this modern day we know that when 'left to nature' there is much waste and many losses of both mothers and babies."[102] In other words, a modern mother could no longer confidently turn to female neighbors and relatives for advice on matters of maternity and childcare, as the MCA deemed such lay assistance as dangerous.

Indicative of this modern view was the one significant difference between the members of Ann Reeves Jarvis's Mothers' Day Work Clubs in the nineteenth century and the modern public health nurses of the MCA. Although both carried a similar message about the importance of education and hygiene in improving maternal and infant health, Reeves Jarvis's club members spoke as mothers, thereby tempering their advice with their own maternal experiences. Public health nurses, in comparison, were generally single women. Their authority to dispense childcare advice to mothers rested on their professional training, not maternal experiences; therefore, the medical reframing of maternity to emphasize science over experience promoted the nurses' professional status. Yet many mothers, particularly working-class and poor mothers, valued maternal experience over "book learning" and often questioned or completely rejected the unsolicited advice of public health nurses. The mothers' rejection of the new maternal standard only strengthened many health professionals' view of them as ill-equipped to properly raise their children, viewing the women's lack of interest in scientific childcare methods as a sign of their ignorance, not as evidence of their maternal confidence or honest consideration of the advice's practical application to their lives.[103]

The medical chauvinism of the scientific model of motherhood also played a role in the era's movement to "Americanize" the immigrant population crowding the country's urban centers. Most public health professionals and child welfare reformers agreed on the importance of maternal education, some going as far as to describe it as a positive eugenics measure in the larger campaign of "race betterment."[104] Indeed, immigrants composed a significant portion of the association's clientele, and its nurses often discussed the particular difficulty in earning the immigrant women's trust. Once the nurses gained the women's confidence, the MCA believed immigrant mothers would "correct all sorts of superstitions and habits" and accept modern standards of hygiene and childcare.[105] This is not to suggest that the MCA viewed its work as a form of social control. Many immigrant mothers welcomed the advice; they were eager to become a "modern mother" and thankful for any assistance that enabled their children to thrive in American society. But for every immigrant mother who joined a Mothers' Club or willingly entertained a visiting health nurse in her home, there was a mother who cringed at the nurse's superior tone and resented the restrictions placed on her ability to follow the traditional childcare practices by which she was reared.

Proponents of scientific motherhood based their model on the assumption that all mothers and children had either an adequate standard of living or that an educated mother could neutralize the harmful ramifications of poverty on a child's development. In reality, poor and working-class mothers, immigrant and native-born alike, often did not possess middle-class standards of hygiene and childcare, despite the best available instruction and personal aspirations. The focus on maternal education as the salvation of the modern child essentially helped absolve civil institutions of any culpability in the health of all American children. It was far easier to blame the nation's high infant mortality rates, or generations of defective youths, on impoverished mothers instead of the mitigating economic, physical, and social environments in which those mothers reared their children.[106]

The Mother's Day observances that relied on the sentimental and postsentimental models naturally displayed these different perspectives. The sentimental model glorified women as natural caretakers of the home and praised the power of mother love. Instead of using Mother's Day to admonish mothers who did not know enough to seek pre- and postnatal care, especially working-class mothers and those of racial or ethnic minorities, Jarvis's Mother's Day offered unconditional, and thereby equal, praise for all mothers. "A day that has shown it has a 'heart' and 'living' interest for all classes, races, creeds, native and foreign-born, high and low, rich and poor, scoffer and churchman, man, woman and child, is Mother's Day," described Jarvis.[107] In contrast, the scientific model demanded deference to medical experts and the intrusion of public agencies to protect children from the rampant maternal ignorance, carelessness, and incompetence. The MCA's Mother's Day campaigns may have honored motherhood through rallying community activism in its name, but in the end it also risked the collective confidence of mothers by encouraging their dependency on (typically) male medical authorities.

In order to increase enrollment in its educational and prenatal programs, for example, the MCA relied initially on scare tactics in its holiday publicity. Promotional ads described the "pathetic life" of thousands of babies left motherless each year, forced to rely on foster-mothers, orphanages, and relatives as poor substitutes: "The tragedy, the waste, the heartbreak is immeasurable."[108] Campaign literature frequently altered the holiday's white carnation emblem from its intended symbol of a mother's love to a graphic symbol of death, with sixteen thousand white carnations representing the sixteen thousand mothers who annually perished due to complications in childbirth.[109] In an era where the majority of mothers delivered without serious complications, despite the high maternal death rates, such sensational headlines were meant to shake a mother's faith in pregnancy and childbirth as a natural process. The association's Mother's Day educational literature, fortunately, instructed mothers how to banish all their worries. "Pregnancy is natural and should be normal," it assured. "The birth of a baby should not impair the health of any woman who has had good care from the beginning.

The important thing is to engage a good doctor early and to follow his advice in every detail, every day."[110]

As noted, Jarvis was not alone in her criticism of the MCA's holiday campaigns, especially in its first three years. *Good Housekeeping* editor William Frederick Bigelow admitted the magazine's reluctance to assist charitable organizations in their efforts to turn a day of love and homage for one's mother into another day of almsgiving:

> We admitted that the whole thing was founded on sentiment, and that the day was being commercialized, but just the same we wanted Mothers' Day let alone. A lot of big, grown men—and women, too, though they seem a bit nearer to the mother heart—would feel a bit sheepish at ordinary times to say, even with a flower, "Mother, I love you," but not on this day. It is easy then— and those words need so much to be said that their saying should be easy.[111]

Thus the MCA's early campaigns designed to mainly raise public awareness of the critical state of maternity care did not attract the magazine's endorsement. The sensational and headline-catching stories about dying mothers and orphaned children did not suit *Good Housekeeping's* sentimental portrayal of Mother's Day.

Although shocking imagery of mothers perishing in childbirth never completely left the MCA's promotional repertoire, the association ultimately recognized that such descriptions created needless dread about maternity and chose to soften its rhetoric in 1934. "Merely deploring this condition will not change it," the associated admitted.[112] Once the MCA changed its strategy and offered a more positive or constructive educational campaign, *Good Housekeeping* finally agreed to publicize the association's Mother's Day observance. "WE YIELD—or does one say bow?—to the inevitable," proclaimed Bigelow. "Mother's Day is going off the sentimental standard." [113] He readily approved of the MCA's plea for community service in the name of motherhood; more importantly, he recognized the appeal of the campaign's proactive holiday message for the magazine's middleclass female readership, especially the readers who already trusted its resident medical experts' monthly advice columns on health and childcare: "We see in this movement, which we heartily endorse, nothing that can do harm to the original purpose of Mothers' Day. Just the opposite. If it succeeds, there will be more mothers for sons and daughters to love and honor as the years go by."114

Ironically, the MCA's deference to obstetricians and family practitioners gradually weakened its nurses' authority over their clients. By the 1930s, the association's medical board had severely restricted a nurse's ability to make independent medical assessments or administer any treatment beyond the basis hygienic intervention, such as performing enemas or distributing sodium bicarbonate for heartburn. Medical board members agreed that a nurse's visit was only of value if her detailed reports were verified by a hospital or doctor caring for that patient.[115] In a relatively short period of time, doctors successfully moved the pre- and postnatal medical

Figure 5.2. Maternity Center Association, New Mother's Day Campaign Publicity Kit 1931.
©Childbirth Connections. Used With Permission.

supervision pioneered by the MCA into their private practices, making the role of the public health nurse functionally insignificant in maternity cases.[116]

The association's holiday campaigns fostered this fateful transfer of power. Consider, for example, who was showcased in the following excerpt from *The Story of the New Mother's Day*, titled "Message to Expectant Mothers and Fathers":

Every pregnant mother needs a doctor—the best one available—to care for her from the time she believes she is pregnant until he says she is able to resume her regular activities and responsibilities and to care for her baby. Her doctor will make a complete examination. He will take her blood pressure and examine her urine, measure her in order to determine whether the passages are large enough for the baby to be born without difficulty. He will make an internal examination, too. He will want to see her every three or four weeks or oftener throughout pregnancy to examine her urine and take her blood pressure, so he may know all about her condition as the baby is developing and be able to give her the best of care when the baby is born. He will help her decide whether to go to a hospital or to stay at home for the baby's birth. He will want to see her and the baby several times after the labor. He will examine her two and three months later to make sure everything is all right before she undertakes the full care of her home and baby.[117]

The public health nurse that the U.S. Children's Bureau once heralded as the essential link between medical principles and the practical care of women and children had thus lost her place twenty years later.

However many advantages that medical science has provided mothers and their children since the early twentieth century or however dedicated the MCA was in providing the best care possible for its clients, the association's goal of empowering women as active participants in their health care and the care of their children faced its own limitations. Just as the sentimental model of motherhood restricted maternal power to the domestic sphere, the scientific model of motherhood offered a degree of maternal power that seemingly stopped once an expectant mother entered the doctor's office. And despite the MCA's training of professional nurse-midwives in a holistic approach to maternity care, the association's Mother's Day campaigns pushed expectant mothers toward the care of obstetricians and hospital births, rather than empower them to evaluate alternative approaches.[118] Consequently, Jarvis's scathing criticisms of the MCA deserve a closer appreciation as she hinted at the troubling contradictions of the association's Mother's Day message. Hidden beneath her inane rants over the "committee of prominent ladies" and the "expectant mother racket" was a sincere disdain for a model of motherhood that belittled a mother's autonomy and weighed her worth solely against a cold clinical standard.

"MAKE MOTHER'S DAY SAFE FOR MOTHER": JARVIS'S ATTEMPT TO RECLAIM MOTHER'S DAY

In 1931, a *New York Times* reporter asked Eleanor Roosevelt and fellow Golden Rule Foundation chairwoman Mrs. John Finley to comment on Jarvis's accusations and threats of legal action against their Mother's Day campaign. Jarvis's reaction to their organization's charitable efforts appeared to sincerely puzzle Mrs. Roosevelt. "I think she misunderstands us," she explained. "She wanted Mother's Day observed. We want it observed, are working for its observation, and are really aiding her."[119]

To which Mrs. Finley added, "We are helping her to a better observance of the thing she loves. In so far as she is working for a better observance of the day we are working with her."[120]

Obviously, it was more than just a simple misunderstanding to Jarvis. And in all fairness, her fervent defense of her Mother's Day observance was not wholly unjustified—despite the frequent ridicule her eccentric behavior elicited from her contemporaries. Jarvis understood the Golden Rule Foundation's and Maternity Center Association's postsentimental critique of her day on multiple levels. When the foundation called for a "better observance" of Mother's Day and the association created a new Mother's Day story, each insinuated that her sentimental model, and especially her national leadership as official founder, was obsolete and meaningless in the modern era. When public accusations, verbal confrontations, and threats of legal action failed to stop, or even slow, the momentum of the organizations' charitable drives, Jarvis sought alternative strategies to gain an advantage against her critics. This included using the GRF's and MCA's own tactics against them.

As a challenge to the GRF, Jarvis considered naming her movement's own "American Mother" and ventured at least three separate times to bestow the honorary title on Sara Delano Roosevelt. Through Mrs. Roosevelt, the country could truly focus its minds on a "special personality of an outstanding mother," she wrote the president in 1933. "Your Excellency's mother has given to our country the gift of a son that should make her honor now before it is too late for her life."[121] Jarvis's reasons for targeting Sara Roosevelt were obvious. Not only was Mrs. Roosevelt the honorary chairwoman of the American Mothers Committee, she was known to offer assistance to the MCA in gaining her son's unofficial endorsement of its Mother's Day campaign, as well.[122] The wooing of Sara Roosevelt into her Mother's Day movement offered Jarvis a chance to gain favor with the president and hopefully distract from the competing Mother's Day events that Sara Roosevelt sponsored. Her various attempts to formally honor Mrs. Roosevelt in 1933, 1934, and again in 1937 failed to secure her the coveted relationship with the president and his mother, however.[123] The setback encouraged her to rethink her strategy in combating her charitable rivals.

In 1938, Jarvis addressed the MCA's criticism of her Mother's Day as an "emotional jag" and "vacuous sentimentality" by promoting her holiday observance as a genuine example of sentiment in action.[124] She was never against protecting the health of mothers and the home under their care. She once bragged that her uncle, Dr. James Reeves of "international repute," had battled maternal mortality long before the MCA began its crusade to save the country's poor dying mothers. (She never included the role her mother played in her uncle's efforts, of course).[125] What Jarvis denounced was the way in which the MCA exploited Mother's Day for the aggrandizement of its wealthy supporters and the professional ambitions of its medical advocates. "It is too bad 14,000 mothers continue to die yearly for 10 years, when so much of Mother's Day money and Federal funds, public contributions, and wealthy socialites on committees for Maternity Relief should bring different results," she retorted.[126] It was obvious to Jarvis that the "expectant mother racketeers" failed to sincerely honor American mothers on Mother's Day and instead chose to honor themselves.

In response, Jarvis launched her own public service campaign to honor and promote the welfare of mothers in an attempt to reclaim the holiday from the charitable organizations. She acknowledged that there was no greater appeal than "to do something for Mothers," thus she asked the country to make the second Sunday in May safe for mothers: "Through your Clubs, through your churches, through your papers, through your many contacts, preach the gospel of 'Live and Let Live,' and make *Mother's Day Safe for Mother* and succeeding days safer for all of us."[127] Jarvis did not mean making mothers safe from the ravishment of poverty or inadequate health care, however. Her warning concerned the 140,000 killed or permanently injured in traffic accidents and the 36,000 home accidents that occurred each year. "Practically all of these accidents either involved a mother herself, or someone dear to her, and brought her heartache and sorrow," stressed Jarvis.[128] Like her philanthropic rivals, she appealed to President Roosevelt for his formal endorsement of her safety drive, explaining how the authenticity of her holiday campaign rose above all the others, as she did not seek funds in order to benefit salaried charity promoters or fund elaborate social events. In contrast, she solicited the people's due diligence, not funds or pity, in protecting their mothers from harm on the city streets and within private homes. She asked the country's sons and daughters to express their appreciation for their mothers with the gift of safety. "We do not talk 'charity,' but 'gratitude' and 'goodwill' as the finer words for Mother's Day," she wrote President Roosevelt.[129]

The success of Jarvis's 1938 safety campaign remains unknown, but evidence suggests she attempted the same campaign the following year, at least within the state of Pennsylvania. In a letter to the Pennsylvania Association of County Fairs, she asked its president to join her efforts to wipe out the national crime of highway and home accidents. She believed that their combined resources and influence could make a national difference. "Let us be a U.S. Leader thru Mother's Day," she implored.[130] The phrasing of her request was very telling. After dedicating three decades of her life to her movement, she was not willing to allow her Mother's Day observance, or her national leadership, to become irrelevant within a growing modern society. Sadly, her failing health and declining assets made it difficult to continue her movement work throughout the last decade of her life.

ANNA JARVIS'S FINAL YEARS AND THE BURDEN OF THE MOTHER'S DAY MOVEMENT

O n the eve of Mother's Day in 1944, Mrs. Charlotte Douglas Suru-Mago of Denver, Colorado, wrote a letter to President Roosevelt on behalf of her mother.
Mrs. Suru-Mago's mother had previously written the mayor of Philadelphia
for verifications of rumors she heard concerning Anna Jarvis's economic
and physical decline. The mayor's office confirmed the facts of Jarvis's failing health. Although they did not believe she was destitute, they knew she
currently resided at the Marshall Square Sanitarium in West Chester, Pennsylvania.
The woman's mother remained concerned about Jarvis and her quality of life. Having once been a student of Jarvis's when she first taught school in Grafton, West
Virginia, the woman carried a deep affection for her former teacher and beloved
Mother's Day founder. To help ease her mother's worry, Mrs. Suru-Mago agreed
to write the president: "I wonder if you know that Miss Anna Jarvis, the one who
gave to America and the whole world the beautiful thought of a day for Mothers,
has not long to live? And I wonder if you would like to know where she is, (though
doubtless you do) and would not be willing to thank her this Mother's Day for all
of us in America?"[1] It is unknown what response, if any, Mrs. Suru-Mago and her
mother received from the president or if Jarvis ever learned of the women's efforts
on her account. Moreover, it is unclear if the Roosevelt administration knew of
Jarvis's ultimate fate since, after a decade of correspondence between Jarvis and
the White House, the letters had stopped by 1944.[2]

Jarvis's diligent guardianship of Mother's Day eventually consumed her financially, physically, and emotionally. Beginning in the late 1930s, stories of her faltering
health and finances became fixtures of the annual Mother's Day press coverage. In
1938, *Time* reported her increasingly erratic public behavior and bizarre private
habits at the age of seventy-four. The article referenced her "violent telegrams" to
President Roosevelt and her practice of walking the streets with a black satchel

Figure E.1. Time *magazine included this picture of Jarvis in its May 1938 article featuring the accounts of her alleged erratic public behavior and increasingly reclusive lifestyle. Courtesy of the West Virginia and Regional History Collection, West Virginia University.*

full of press releases and publicity photos of herself as a young woman.[3] Over the years, the magazine contended, Jarvis had grown more reclusive, preferring to spend much of her time secluded in her home behind heavy curtains, listening to the radio in the hopes of one day hearing her dead mother's voice speak to her. One needed to know the secret number of bell rings that alerted the maid to answer the door in order to visit the "old Philadelphia busybody."[4] And for added exclusivity, she allegedly installed a mirror on the third floor that allowed her to see who was at the front door without having to peer out the window.[5]

In rebuttal, Jarvis issued a four-page press release through the Mother's Day International Association condemning the *Time* article as libelous and challenging the multiple allegations it made against her efforts to defend her life's work and its exaggerated depiction of her personal conduct. She denied ever intentionally sending President Roosevelt violent telegrams and reminded her critics that she had been a visitor to the White House since President William McKinley's administration. Her business affairs required her to carry a satchel full of important documents, none of which included pictures of herself, however, as she purposely avoided having her likeness taken. As for her seclusion behind heavy curtains, Jarvis insisted she made no attempts to hide from anyone. Her telephone number and mailing address were clearly listed on her association's letterhead.[6]

Figure E. 2. Memorial services held in West Laurel Hill Cemetery Philadelphia, Pa., May 8, 1949, for Jarvis. The floral design displayed on top of monument was a contribution from Andrews Methodist Episcopal Church, Grafton, W.Va. The memorial marked the first celebration of Mother's Day since her death in November 1948. Courtesy of the West Virginia and Regional History Collection, West Virginia University.

Her documented public antics and verbal assaults throughout the years, nonetheless, have left the issue of her mental stability open for interpretation. In Jarvis's defense, surviving family papers offer insight on the private responsibilities she carried in addition to her movement work that likely influenced her emotional health over the years. After the death of her father in 1902 and her brother Claude in 1926, Jarvis served as executrix of both estates. It was a position she took seriously, not just for her own livelihood but that of her visually handicapped sister Lillian, who reluctantly remained under her elder sister's care. As Jarvis battled those who threatened her Mother's Day movement, she simultaneously fought to ensure the solvency of the family fortune, often choosing to legally represent herself during property disputes in Grafton and Philadelphia.[7]

At times, the financial responsibility weighed heavily on her peace of mind, especially after the death of her brother of heart disease at sixty-eight years of age. "My brother's affairs are simply overwhelming, with a new burden every day," she confided to a friend. "I thought I had worked hard in the past for other things, but nothing ever equaled the work and burdens of the present. I trust we may have something before we both expire (my sister and self)."[8] Records estimate the value of Claude Jarvis's estate as high as $700,000 at the time of his death; this included

Figure E.3. Memorial Plot. Courtesy of the West Virginia and Regional History Collection, West Virginia University, Morgantown, West Virginia.

the three-story brick home the siblings shared, his taxi business, and a trust fund. Jarvis spent several years defending the estate from creditors, as well as claims that her brother had a common-law wife who was entitled to a share. Capricious Lillian then added to her sister's stress by accusing her of mishandling the estate and purposely withholding the fortune that Claude had allocated for his baby sister. Lillian had always resented the family portrayal of her as an invalid dependent on family charity. During the years that Jarvis traveled promoting her movement, Lillian had managed the affairs of her brother's home in her sister's absence; thus she felt justified in demanding her share of Claude's estate.[9] By the 1930s, however, the probate proceedings had consumed the bulk of the sisters' inheritance and Jarvis admitted to the difficultly she had in funding her movement work.[10]

Nevertheless, Jarvis refused to economically exploit the Mother's Day observance despite her evaporating fortune. Understandably, then, it was difficult for her to watch commercial industries and rival organizations generate huge profits while her Mother's Day International Association struggled to afford basic office supplies. It violated her sense of justice and fair play, fanning her indignation. "Grafters have gotten the funds we should have had for our work," she railed. "Every cent of their profit first trickled out of the pocket of the founder of Mother's Day, but not one cent ever came back."[11] In spite of the bitterness that persistently plagued her, Jarvis remarkably sustained her holiday movement until physically unable to continue. She had invested too much of her identity into the day's observance to willingly relinquish her relationship with it without a fight. In frustration, she wondered why the devastating consequences of the unauthorized uses of Mother's Day fell on her and "not to them that deserve it?"[12]

Jarvis became the truly tragic figure in the Mother's Day story, a casualty of the postsentimental assault on the holiday's maternal sentimentality. In November of 1943, Jarvis wandered into a Philadelphia hospital seeking assistance. A *Newsweek* article described her as weak, nearly blind, and impoverished. It was obvious to the magazine how the years of bitter fighting against the forces of commercialization had "crushed her in body and soul."[13] A group of twelve supporters quickly formed the Anna M. Jarvis Committee (AMJC) to oversee Jarvis's business affairs and fund her residence at the Marshall Square Sanitarium. Tragically, the committee failed to convince Lillian to leave the dilapidated family home and join her sister. A police officer discovered her dead two months later during a routine check. The seventy-six-year-old woman was lying on the kitchen floor next to a lighted gas stove, icicles reportedly hanging from the ceiling. The Philadelphia coroner listed the cause of death as carbon monoxide poisoning.[14] Meanwhile, Jarvis's mental and physical health slowly deteriorated over the next four years. The AMJC chairman described her condition in the months leading to her death as pitiful, as she had become completely blind, almost deaf, and bedridden. Media accounts described her growing senility as well, evidenced by her refusal to accept Lillian's death and the denial of her own blindness. She allegedly accused sanitarium workers of purposely keeping her in a dark room.[15]

But Jarvis was not utterly alone in the final years of her life, regardless of her personality flaws that Lillian once defined as her "continual quarrelling, her abnormal conceit, and a tendency to be disrespectful to her superiors."[16] She had many national and international admirers throughout her career. During the peak of her holiday movement in the 1920s, she purchased the house next door to the home the siblings shared for the additional storage required to keep up with the volume of literature and correspondence she both wrote and received. Workman reportedly removed five tons of paper from the home twenty-five years later.[17] Moreover, her general popularity never completely faded throughout her lifetime. Even after she entered the sanitarium, she continued to receive Mother's Day greetings from around the world. In 1947, the AMJC handled over 1,200 pieces of mail addressed to Jarvis from government officials including President Truman, leaders of religious and social organizations, and letters from individual well-wishers. She enjoyed displaying her favorite letters in her room and showing them off to visitors and sanitarium workers. Her most prized greeting came from a small boy who heard of her situation and sent her a one-dollar bill he had been saving. "I am six years old and I love my mother very much. I am sending you this because you started Mother's Day," he wrote.[18]

While Jarvis lived, the AMJC sustained her Mother's Day work, which included the annual letter-writing campaign to the president of the United States and every state governor. It also solicited the necessary funds to pay her medical expenses,

Figure E. 4. A close up of the commemorative bronze plaque on Anna Jarvis's headstone as it looks today. Author's Private Collection.

with the possible assistance of the floral industry. *Newsweek* reported a $1,580 contribution from a national florist organization as a belated act of gratitude for the woman who had given them so much.[19] When Jarvis died on November 24, 1948, it was again the official committee who made all the final arrangements. The members buried her in an orchid dress with a string of pearls around her neck and a spray of carnations adorning the casket. Following a private funeral, she was buried next to her mother, sister, and brother in the West Laurel Hill Cemetery outside of Philadelphia. The committee disbanded two years later after securing the perpetual care of the Jarvis family gravesite and dispensing the remains of the estate to Jarvis's sole heir, the granddaughter of her oldest brother, Josiah.[20]

Ultimately, Anna Jarvis's greatest success became the source of her greatest heartache. On the one hand, she triumphantly led a national and international movement to establish a maternal memorial day as forty-three foreign countries celebrated Mother's Day at the time of her death. She also secured a place in history as the holiday's founder. On the other hand, her battle to restrict the holiday's observance to its sentimental specifications came at a substantial cost, and she eventually grew to regret her role in the day's creation.[21] Yet Jarvis's failure to suppress multiple interpretations and expressions of the Mother's Day observance, despite her best efforts, serves to highlight further the intrinsic source of the day's cultural longevity. The holiday's symbolic celebration of the maternal role provides all of us who observe it the power to ponder the true meaning of motherhood in modern society and construct for ourselves a maternal ideal worth memorializing.

APPENDIX

P opular histories of Mother's Day and the Jarvis family disagree on the number and names of children born to Granville Jarvis and Ann Reeves Jarvis. Below are the records of the Jarvis children as documented by other scholars and within the personal recollections of Anna Jarvis.

Historian Howard Wolfe identifies twelve Jarvis children in his book, *Behold Thy Mother: Mother's Day and the Mother's Day Church:*

1. Josiah W. P. Jarvis (February 28, 1853–unknown, 1919)
2. Anna A. Jarvis (February ?, 1854–December ?, 1856)
3. Clara Jarvis (August 22, 1855–December 12, 1862)
4. Columbia Jarvis (December 6, 1856–unknown)
5. Claude S. Jarvis (August 27, 1858–December 23, 1926)
6. Ralph Jarvis (March 4, 1860–March 10, 1862)
7. Maria A. Jarvis (unknown, 1861–October 12, 1862)
8. Wesley Jarvis (unknown 1863–unknown)
9. Anna Jarvis (May 1, 1864–November 24, 1948)
10. Thomas R. Jarvis (May 11, 1866–August 17, 1873)
11. Elsinore Lillian Jarvis (October 14, 1867–January 28, 1944)
12. Ellen Jarvis (died at birth, date unknown)

Olive Dadisman, the curator of the Anna Jarvis Birthplace in Grafton, West Virginia, has identified thirteen Jarvis children through census reports and county records:

1. Alonzo Eskridge Jarvis (September 28, 1851–April 14, 1853)
2. Josiah William Jarvis (February 28, 1853–unknown 1919)
3. Annie Elizabeth Jarvis (September 24, 1854–December 6, 1856)
4. Clara Jarvis (August 22, 1855–February 12, 1862) *
5. Columbia Margaret Jarvis (December 6, 1856–February 14, 1862)
6. Claude Solomon Jarvis (August 22, 1858–December 23, 1926)
7. Ralph Stewart Jarvis (March 1, 1860–March 10, 1862)

8. Marry A. Jarvis (March 28, 1862–November 18, 1862)
9. Margaret Jarvis (April 20, 1863–July ?, 1863)
10. Anna Jarvis (May 1, 1864–November 24, 1948)
11. Thomas Reeves Jarvis (May 12, 1866–August 17, 1873)
12. Elsinore Lillian Jarvis (October 14, 1867–January 28, 1944)
13. Ellen Jarvis (stillborn 1868)

*Although county birth records identify Clara Jarvis as the child of Granville and Ann Jarvis, she is not listed in the 1860 federal census with her siblings.

Anna Jarvis identified eleven Jarvis children in her unfinished biography of her mother's life located in the Anna Jarvis Papers, West Virginia and Regional History Collection, West Virginia University, Morgantown, West Virginia. She did not record the exact birth or death dates for any of the children:

1. Alonzo Jarvis
2. Josiah Jarvis
3. Ralph Jarvis
4. Annie Jarvis
5. Claude Jarvis
6. Marry Jarvis
7. Columbia Jarvis
8. Margaret Jarvis
9. Anna Jarvis
10. Thomas Jarvis
11. (Elsinore) Lillian Jarvis

SELECTED BIBLIOGRAPHY

ARCHIVAL MATERIALS

American War Mothers. Digital Collection. Kentucky Historical Society. Accessed on November 12, 2013 at www.history.ky.gov.

French, Alice Moore. Collection. Indiana Historical Society, Indianapolis.

Jarvis, Anna. Papers. West Virginia and Regional History Collection. West Virginia University Libraries, Morgantown, West Virginia.

Jarvis Family Documents. Jarvis Birthplace Museum, Webster, West Virginia.

Maternity Center Association. Papers. Archives and Special Collections. A. C. Long Health Sciences Library. Columbia University Medical Center.

Miller, Clay V. Papers. West Virginia and Regional History Collection. West Virginia University.

Mother's Day Collection. International Mother's Day Shrine, Grafton, West Virginia.

Mother's Day File. Henderson County Public Library, Henderson, Kentucky.

Pamphlet Collection. University of Notre Dame Archives. University of Notre Dame.

Roosevelt, Franklin D. Papers. Franklin D. Roosevelt Library, Hyde Park, New York.

Wannamaker, John. Papers. Gibbons Card File. Pennsylvania Historical Society, Philadelphia.

Wolfe, Howard. Collection. International Mother's Day Shrine, Grafton, West Virginia.

PAMPHLETS AND FORMAL PUBLICATIONS BY PRIVATE ORGANIZATIONS

Greenhoe, Theodore Marvin. *In Memory, Frank E. Hering, 1874–1943*. South Bend, IN, [1943?].

Golden Rule Foundation. *Observing Mothers Day the Golden Rule Way*. New York City: Goldren Rule Foundation,1933.

Hansen, Bob. *The Eagles*. Milwaukee: Faternal Order of Eagles, 1960.

Hering, Frank E. *The Facts in the Case: A Message from Frank E. Hering.* South Bend, IN, 1932.

Maternity Center Association. *Campaign Suggestions for Mother's Day, May 12, 1935.* New York City: Maternity Center Association, 1935.

———. *Maternity Center Association 1918–1943.* 1943.

———. *Maternity Center Association Log 1915–1975.* 1975.

———. *Routines for Maternity Nursing and Briefs for Mothers' Club Talks.* 1935.

———. *The Story of the New Mother's Day.* 1935.

McCann, Charles P. *Mother's Day Began with the Eagles.* [1940?].

McCluer, Margaret N., and Adelaide Riffle. *Memoirs of "Mothers' Day" Its Origins and Ways of Observing.* [Washington, DC]: American War Mothers, 1925.

Mother's Day International Association. "Mother's Day Community Program." 1924.

———. "The All Nation Mother's Day." 1924.

———. "The Mother's Day Movement." [1912?].

Parents Magazine. *George Joseph Hecht: A Lifelong Commitment to Children* [S.I.]: Parents Magazine Press, 1975.

Poling, Lillian D. *Mothers of Men: A Twenty-Five Year History of the American Mothers of the Year 1935–1959.* Bridgeport, Connecticut: Kurt H.Volk, 1959.

Sasseen, Mary Towles. *Mother's Day Celebrations.* Henderson, Kentucky, 1893.

Walz, Audrey Boyers. *The Story of Mothers' Day.* Mount Morris, New York: Allied Printing, [1943?].

White, Marguerite H. *American War Mothers: Fifty Year History 1917–1967.* Washington, DC: American War Mothers, 1981.

Vickrey, Charles V. *The Golden Rule Book.* New York: The Golden Rule Foundation, 1933.

UNPUBLISHED MANUSCRIPTS

Doherty, Robert Wesley. "Alfred H. Love and the Universal Peace Party." PhD diss., University of Pennsylvania, 1962.

Howard, Esme J. "Navigating the Stormy Sea: The Maternity Center Association and the Development of Prenatal Care 1900–1903." Master's thesis, Yale University School of Nursing, 1994.

Snider, Joseph Franklin. "The Early History of Grafton." Master's thesis, West Virginia University, 1945.

Twerdon, Sarah. "The Maternity Center Association as a Vehicle for the Education of Motherhood." Master's thesis, Columbia University, 1947.

Wolfe, Howard. "The Second Sunday." Howard Wolfe Collection, International Mother's Day Shrine, Grafton, West Virginia, 1983.

———. "The White Carnation." Howard Wolfe Collection, International Mother's Day Shrine, Grafton, West Virginia, 1984.

BOOKS AND JOURNAL ARTICLES

Apple, Rima D. "Constructing Mothers: Scientific Motherhood in the Nineteenth and Twentieth Centuries." In *Mothers and Motherhood: Readings in American History*, edited by Rima D. Apple and Janet Golden, 90–110. Columbus: The Ohio State University Press, 1997.

———. *Mothers and Medicine: A Social History of Infant Feeding 1890–1950*. Madison: The University of Wisconsin Press, 1987.

———. *Perfect Motherhood: Science and Childrearing in America*. Brunswick: Rutgers University Press, 2006.

———. "'Trai—,ning' the Baby: Mothers' Responses to Advice Literature in the First Half of the Twentieth Century." In *When Science Encounters the Child: Education, Parenting and Child Welfare in 20th Century America*, edited by Barbara Beatty, Emily Cahan, and Julia Grant, 195–214. New York: Teachers College Press, 2006.

———, and Janet Golden, eds. *Mothers and Motherhood: Readings in American History*. Columbus: The Ohio State University Press, 1997.

Barker, Kristen. "Birthing and Bureaucratic Women: Needs Talk and the Definitional Legacy of the Sheppard-Towner Act." *Feminist Studies* 29, no. 2 (Summer 2003): 333–355.

Barney, Sandra Lee. *Authorized to Heal: Gender, Class, and the Transformation of Medicine in Appalachia, 1880–1930*. Chapel Hill: The University of North Carolina Press, 2000.

Beatty, Barbara, Emily D. Cahan, and Julia Grant. *When Science Encounters the Child: Education, Parenting, and Child Welfare in 20th-Century America*. New York: Teachers College Press, 2006.

Beekman, Daniel. *The Mechanical Baby: A Popular History of the Theory and Practice of Child Raising*. Westport: Lawrence Hill and Company, 1977.

Bonifer, Michael, and L. G. Weaver. *Out of Bounds*. New York: Piper, 1978.

Campbell, D'Ann. *Women at War with America: Private Lives in a Patriotic Era*. Cambridge: Harvard University Press, 1984.

Clifford, Deborah Pickman. *Mine Eyes Have Seen the Glory: A Biography of Julia Ward Howe*. Boston: Little, Brown and Company, 1978.

Conwell, Russell. *The Romantic Rise of a Great American*. New York: Harper and Brothers Publishing, 1924.

Coontz, Stephanie. *The Way We Never Were: American Families and the Nostalgia Trap*. New York: Basic Books, 1992.

Cross, Gary. "Just For Kids: How Holidays Became Child Centered." In *We Are What We Celebrate: Understanding Holidays and Rituals*, edited by Amitai Etzioni and Jared Bloom, 61–73. New York: New York University Press, 2002.

Curti, Merle. *Peace or War: The American Struggle 1636–1936*. New York: W. W. Norton and Company, 1936.

Dally, Ann. *Inventing Motherhood: The Consequence of an Ideal*. New York: Shocken Books, 1982.

Dennis, Matthew. *Red, White and Blue Letter Days: An American Calender*. Ithaca: Cornell University Press, 2002.

Douglas, Ann. *The Feminization of American Culture*. New York: Doubleday, 1977.

Douglas, Susan, and Meredith Michaels. *The Mommy Myth: The Idealization of Motherhood and How It Has Undermined All Women*. New York: Free Press, 2004.

Downey, Kristen. *The Woman Behind the New Deal: The Life of Frances Perkins, FDR's Secretary of Labor and His Moral Conscience*. New York: Doubleday, 2009.

Duffy, John. *The Sanitarians: A History of American Public Health*. Urbana: University of Illinois Press, 1990.

Dye, Nancy Schrom, and Daniel Blake Smith. "Mother Love and Infant Death, 1750–1920." *The Journal of American History* 73, no. 2 (September 1986): 329–353.

Ehrenreich, Barbara, and Deirdre English. *For Her Own Good: Two Centuries of the Experts' Advice to Women*. New York: Anchor Books, 2005.

Elshtain, Jean Bethke. *Women and War*. New York: Basic Books, 1987.

Ettinger, Laura E. *Nurse-Midwifery: The Birth of a New American Profession*. Columbus: The Ohio State University Press, 2006.

Etzioni, Amitai. "Holidays and Rituals: Neglected Seedbeds of Virtue." In *We Are What We Celebrate: Understanding Holidays and Rituals*, edited by Amitai Etzioni and Jared Bloom, 1–42. Cambridge: Harvard University Press, 2000.

——, and Jared Bloom, eds. *We Are What We Celebrate: Understanding Holidays and Rituals*. New York: New York University Press, 2004.

Evans, Sara M. *Born for Liberty: A History of Women in America*. New York: Free Press Paperbacks, 1997.

Evans, Suzanne. *Mothers of Heroes, Mothers of Martyrs: World War I and the Politics of Grief*. Montreal: McGill-Queen's University Press, 2007.

Faust, Drew Gilpin. *This Republic of Suffering: Death and the American Civil War*. New York: Vintage Books, 2008.

Filene, Peter G. *Him/Her/Self: Gender Identities in Modern America*. Baltimore: The John Hopkins University Press, 1998.

Frank, Stephen M. *Life with Father: Parenthood and Masculinity in the Nineteenth-Century American North*. Baltimore: The Johns Hopkins University Press, 1998.

Gillis, John R. *A World of Their Own Making: Myth, Ritual and the Quest for Family Values*. Cambridge: Harvard University Press, 1996.

Graham, John. *The Gold Star Mother Pilgrimages of the 1930s: Overseas Grave Visitations by Mothers and Widows of Fallen U.S. World War I Soldiers*. Jefferson, North Carolina: McFarland and Company, 2004.

Grant, Julia. "Bringing Up Boys: Science, Popular Culture and Gender." In *When Science Encounters the Child: Education, Parenting, and Child Welfare in 20th Century America*, edited by Barbara Beatty, Emily Cahan, and Julia Grant, 215–234. New York: Teachers College Press, 2006.

———. *Raising Baby by the Book: Education of American Mothers*. New Haven: Yale University Press, 1998.

Greenberg, David. *Presidential Doodles: Two Centuries of Scribbles, Squiqqles and Scrawls from the Oval Office*. New York: Basic Books, 2006.

Griswold, Robert, J. *Fatherhood in America: A History*. New York: Basic Books, 1993.

Hall, Florence Howe. *Julia Ward Howe and the Woman Suffrage Movement*. Boston: Dana Estes and Company, 1913.

Hardyment, Christina. *Dream Babies*. Oxford: Oxford University Press, 1984.

Hatch, Jane M. *The American Books of Days*. New York: H. W. Wilson, 1978.

Hays, Sharon. *The Cultural Contradictions of Motherhood*. New Haven: Yale University Press, 1996.

Hazeltine, Mary Emogene. *Anniversaries and Holidays: A Calender of Days and How to Observe Them*. Chicago: American Library Association, 1944.

Hillard, G. S. *Life and Campaigns of George B. McClellan Major-General U.S. Army*. Philadelphia: J. B. Lippincott and Company, 1864.

Howe, Henry. "The Times, The Rebellion, West Virginia." In *War Stories: Civil War in West Virginia*, edited by David L. Philips and Rebecca L. Hill, 1-26. Leesburg, Virginia: Gauley Mount Press, 1991.

Howe, Julia Ward Howe. *Reminiscences 1819–1899*. Boston: Houghton Mifflin Company, 1899.

———. "Appeal to Womanhood Throughout the World." *The Voice of Peace*, September 1874, 92–93

———. "Mother's Day." The Voice of Peace, April 1873, 7.

———. "Letter from Julia Ward Howe." *The Voice of Peace*, April 1874, 13.

———. "Pamphlet of the Woman's Peace Festival, Held June 2." *The Voice of Peace*, May 1874, 29.

———. "Reply of Julia Ward Howe." *The Voice of Peace*, September 1875, 89–90.

———. "To the Friends of Peace." The Voice of Peace, July 1876,49–50.

Hulbert, Ann. *Raising America: Experts, Parents, and a Century of Advice About Children*. New York: Alfred A. Knopf, 2003.

Johansen, Shawn. *Family Men: Middle-Class Fatherhood in Early Industrializing America*. New York: Routledge, 2001.

Johnson, James P. "Death, Grief and Motherhood: The Woman Who Inspired Mother's Day." *West Virginia History* 39 (1978): 187–194.

———. "How Mother Got Her Day." *American Heritage* 30 (April/May 1979): 15–21.

Jones, Kathleen W. "Mother Made Me Do It: Mother-Blaming and the Women of Child Guidance." In *"Bad" Mothers: The Politics of Blame in Twentieth Century America*, edited by Molly Ladd Taylor and Lauri Umansky, 99–124. New York: New York University Press, 1998.

———. "Mother's Day: The Creation, Promotion and Meaning of a New Holiday in the Progressive Era." *Texas Studies in Literature and Language* 22, no. 2 (Summer 1980): 175–198.

Keeling, Arlene W. *Nursing and the Privilege of Prescription 1893–2000.* Columbus: The Ohio State University Press, 2007.

Kendall, Norman. *Mothers Day: A History of Its Founding and Its Founder.* Grafton, West Virginia: D. Grant Smith, 1937.

Klaus, Alisa. *Every Child a Lion: The Origins of Maternal and Infant Health in the United States and France 1890–1920.* Ithaca: Cornell University Press, 1993.

Kobler, John. *Ardent Spirits: The Rise and Fall of Prohibition.* New York: G. P. Putnam's Sons, 1973.

Krythe, Maymie R. *All About American Holidays.* New York: Harper and Brothers, 1962.

Ladd-Taylor, Molly. *Mother-Work: Women, Child Welfare, and the State 1890–1930.* Urbana: University of Illinois Press, 1995.

LaCerda, John, "Mother of Mother's Day." Coronet Magazine, May 1945, 10–13.

LaRossa, Ralph. *The Modernization of Fatherhood: A Social and Political History.* Chicago: University of Chicago Press, 1997.

———, Charles Jaret, Malati Gadgil, and G. Robert Wynn. "The Changing Culture of Fatherhood in Comic-Strip Families: A Six-Decade Analysis." *Journal of Marriage and Family* 62, no. 2 (May 2000): 375–387.

———, and Donald C. Reitzes. "Continuity and Change in Middle Class Fatherhood, 1925–1939: The Culture-Conduct Connection." *Journal of Marriage and Family* 55, no. 2 (May 1993): 455–468.

———, and Jaimie Ann Carboy. "A Kiss for Mother, a Hug for Dad." *Fathering* 6, no. 3 (Fall 2008): 249–265.

Lesser, W. Hunter. *Rebels at the Gate: Lee and McClellan on the Front Line of a Nation Divided.* Naperville, Illinois: Sourcebooks, 2004.

Lewis, Jan. "Mother's Love: The Construction of An Emotion in Nineteenth-Century America." In *Mothers and Motherhood: Readings in American History,* edited by Janet Golden, 52–71. Columbus: The Ohio State University Press, 1997.

Lindenmeyer, Kriste. *"A Right to Childhood": The U.S. Children's Bureau and Child Welfare 1912–1946.* Urbana: University of Illinois Press, 1997.

Lubove, Roy. *The Struggle for Social Security 1900–1935.* Cambridge: Harvard University Press, 1968.

Margolis, Maxine. *Mothers and Such: Views of American Women and Why They Changed.* Berkeley: University of California Press, 1985.

Martin, George. *Madam Secretary Frances Perkins.* Boston: Houghton Mifflin Company, 1976.

Mason, Mary Ann. *From Father's Property to Children's Rights: The History of Child Custody in the United States.* New York: Columbia University Press, 1994.

May, Elaine Tyler. *Homeward Bound: American Families in the Cold War Era*. New York: Basic Books, 1988.

McClellan, George B. *McClellan's Own Story*. New York: Charles Webster and Company, 1887.

———. *Report on the Organization and Campaigns of the Army of the Potomac: To Which Is Added an Account of the Campaign in Western Virginia with Plans of Battlefields*. New York: Sheldon and Company Publishers, 1864.

McNulty, Eleanor. "Miss Anna Jarvis Recounts the Founding of Mother's Day," *Children: The Magazine for Parents*, May 1927, 30.

Mechling, Jay. "Advice to Historians on Advice to Mothers." *Journal of Social History* 9 (Fall 1975): 44–63.

Meckel, Richard A. *Save the Babies: American Public Health Reform and the Prevention of Infant Mortality 1850–1929*. Ann Arbor: University of Michigan Press, 1990.

Michel, Sonya. "American Women and the Discourse of the Democratic Family in World War II." In *Behind the Lines: Gender and the Two World Wars*, edited by Margaret Randolph Higonnet, Jane Jenson, Sonya Michel, and Collins Weitz, 154–167. New Haven: Yale University Press, 1987.

Muir, Diana. "Proclaiming Thanksgiving throughout the Land." In *We Are What We Celebrate: Understanding Holidays and Rituals*, edited by Amitai Etzioni and Jared Bloom, 194-212. New York: New York University Press, 2004.

Muncy, Robyn. *Creating a Female Dominion in American Reform 1890–1930*. Urbana: University of Illinois Press, 1991.

Myers, Robert J. *Celebrations: The Complete Book of American Holidays*. New York: Doubleday and Company, 1972.

Nathanson, Jessica, and Laura Camille Tuley. *Mother Knows Best: Talking Back to the "Experts."* Toronto: Demeter Press, 2008.

Piehler, G. Kurt. "The War Dead and the Gold Star: American Commemoriation of the First World War." In *Commemorations: The Politics of National Identity*, by John R. Gillis, 168–185. Princeton: Princeton University Press, 1994.

Pierce, Lyman L. "Philanthropy—A Major Big Business." *Public Opinion Quarterly Journal*, January 1938, 140–145.

Pleck, Elizabeth H. *Celebrating the Family: Ethnicity, Consumer Culture, and Family Rituals*. Cambridge: Harvard University Press, 2000.

———. "Who Are We and Where Do We Come From: Rituals, Families and Identities." In *We Are What We Celebrate: Understanding Holidays and Rituals*, edited by Amitai Etzioni and Jared Bloom, 43–60. New York: New York University Press, 2002.

Reid, Donald M. "The Symbolism of Postage Stamps: A Source for the Historian." *Journal of Contemporary History* 19, no. 2 (April 1984): 233–249.

Reinfeld, Fred. *Commemorative Stamps of the U.S.A.* New York: Thomas Y. Crowell Company, 1954.

Rice, Susan Tracy, and Robert Haven Schauffer. *Mothers' Day: Its History, Origin, Celebration, Spirit, and Significance as Related in Prose and Verse*. New York: Dodd, Mead and Company, 1929.

Robinson, Barbara. "Mother's Day: What a Good Woman (or Two) Can Do," *Mature Years*, Spring 1993, 12–18.

Roosevelt, Franklin D. *The Public Papers and Addresses of Franklin D. Roosevelt*. Vol. 3 of *The Advance of Recovery and Reform*. New York: Russell and Russell, 1934.

———. *The Public Papers and Addresses of Franklin D. Roosevelt*. Vol. 4 of *The Court Disapproves*. New York: Russell and Russell, 1935.

Rosenzweig, Linda W. *The Anchor of My Life: Middle-Class American Mothers and Daughters 1880–1920*. New York: New York University Press, 1993.

Rothman, Sheila. *Woman's Proper Place: A History of Changing Ideals and Practices 1870 to the Present*. New York: Basic Books, 1978.

———. "Women's Clinics or Doctors' Offices: The Sheppard-Towner Act and the Promotion of Preventative Health Care." In *Social History and Social Policy*, edited by David J. Rothman and Stanton Wheeler, 175–201. New York: Academic Press, 1981.

Rupp, Leila. *Mobilizing Women for War: German and American Propaganda 1939–1945*. Princeton: Princeton University Press, 1978.

Ryan, Mary P. *The Empire of the Mother: American Writing About Domesticity 1839–1860*. New York: Harrington Park Press, 1985.

———. *Womanhood in America: Colonial Times to the Present*. New York: Franklin Watts, 1983.

Scanlon, Jennifer. *Inarticulate Longings: The Ladies' Home Journal, Gender and the Promise of Consumer Culture*. New York: Routledge, 1995.

Schlossman, Steven. "Perils of Popularization: The Founding of Parents' Day Magazine." In *History and Research in Child Development*, edited by A. Boardman Smuts and J. W. Hagen, 65–77. Chicago: University of Chicago Press, 1986.

Schmidt, Leigh Eric. *Consumer Rites: The Buying and Selling of American Holidays*. Princeton: Princeton University Press, 1995.

Schott, Linda. "The Woman's Peace Party and the Moral Basis for Women's Pacifism." *Frontiers: A Journal of Women Studies* 8, no. 2 (1985): 18–24.

Shaffer, John W. *Clash of Loyalties: A Border County in the Civil War*. Morgantown, West Virginia: West Virginia University Press, 2003.

Skocpol, Theda. *Protecting Soldiers and Mothers: The Political Origins of Social Policy in the United States*. Cambridge: The Belknap Press of Harvard University Press, 1992.

Smith-Rosenberg, Carroll. *Disorderly Conduct: Visions of Gender in Victorian America*. Oxford: Oxford University Press, 1985.

Smith-Rosenberg, Carroll, and Charles Rosenberg. "The Female Animal: Medical and Biological Views of Woman and Her Role in Nineteenth-Century America." *The Journal of American History* 6, no. 2 (September 1973): 332–356.

Stearns, Peter N. *Anxious Parents: A History of Modern Childrearing in America*. New York: New York University Press, 2003.

Steinson, Barbara J. *American Women's Activism in World War I*. New York: Garland Publishing, 1982.

———. "'The Mother Half of Humanity': American Women in the Peace and Preparedness Movements in World War I." In *Women, War, and Revolution*, edited by Carol R. Berkin and Clara M. Lovett, 259–284. New York: Holmes and Meier Publishers, 1980.

Stephens, Loren. "The Ties That Bind." In *The Business of Holidays*, edited by Maud Lavin, 139–145. New York: Monacelli Press, 2004.

Storms, Robert C. *Partisan Prophets: A History of Prohibition Party*. Denver: National Prohibition Foundation, 1972.

Tenney, Stanley A. "Taylor County in the Civil War." In *A History of Taylor County West Virginia*, edited by Taylor County Historical and Genealogical Society, 60–63. 1982.

Terry, Jennifer. "'Momism' and the Making of Treasonous Homosexuals." In *"Bad" Mothers: The Politics of Blame in Twentieth Century America*, edited by Molly Ladd-Taylor and Lauri Umansky, 169–190. New York: New York University Press, 1998.

Tharp, Louise Hall. *Three Saints and a Sinner: Julia Ward Howe, Louisa, Annie and Sam Ward*. Boston: Little, Brown and Company, 1956.

Tice, Karen. "School-Work and Mother-Care: The Interplay of Maternalism and Cultural Politics in the Educational Narratives of Kentucky Settlement Workers, 1910–1930." *Journal of Appalachia Studies* 4, no. 2 (Fall 1988): 191–224.

Ulrich, Laurel Thatcher. *Good Wives: Images and Reality in the Lives of Women in Northern New England 1650–1750*. New York: Vintage Books, 1991.

Wallechinsky, David, and Irving Wallace. *The People's Almanac*. New York: Doubleday and Company, 1975.

Williams, Edgar, J. *The White Carnation and Mother's Day*. Detroit, Michigan: Northwestern Printing Co., 1950.

Wills, Anne Blue. "Pilgrims and Progress: How Magazines Made Thanksgiving." *Church History* 72, no. 1 (March 2003): 138–158.

Wilson, L. D. "James Edmund Reeves, M.D." *Transactions of the Medical Society of West Virginia*, 1896, 1–9.

Wolfe, Howard. *Behold Thy Mother: Mother's Day and the Mother's Day Church*. Kingsport, Tennessee: Kingsport Press, 1962.

Zeiger, Susan. "She Didn't Raise Her Boy to Be a Slacker: Motherhood, Conscription, and the Culture of The First World War." *Feminist Studies* 22 (Spring 1996): 7–39.

Zelizer, Viviana A. *Pricing the Priceless Child: The Changing Social Value of Children*. Princeton: Princeton University Press, 1994.

NOTES

INTRODUCTION

1   Mother's Day International Association, "The Mother's Day Movement," [1912?], 6, Mother's Day Collection, International Mother's Day Shrine, Grafton, West Virginia.

2   Mother's Day International Association, "The Mother's Day Movement," 2–3; Howard Wolfe, *Behold Thy Mother: Mother's Day and the Mother's Day Church* (Kingsport, Tennessee: Kingsport Press, 1962), 233; and Howard Wolfe, "The White Carnation," (1984) 1, 8, 10, Howard Wolfe Collection, International Mother's Day Shrine, Grafton, West Virginia. "The White Carnation" is an unpublished collection of documents and correspondences of Anna Jarvis's and her Mother's Day International Association transcribed by Howard Wolfe. "Women Who Count," *Washington Post*, July 23, 1911.

3   The National Retail Federation estimated that consumers spent just over 15 billion dollars on Mother's Day gifts in 2008. Flowers, greeting cards, and special dinners ranked as the top three gift categories. The National Retail Federation, "Consumers Will Still Spend For Mother's Day, Just Not As Much, According to NRF Survey," accessed October 28, 2013, accessed on November 14, 2013 at www.nrf.com/modules. php?name=News&op=viewlive&sp_id=505.

4   For further discussion on the social meaning of holidays see: Amitai Etzioni and Jared Bloom, eds., *We Are What We Celebrate: Understanding Holidays and Rituals* (New York: New York Press, 2004); Matthew Dennis, *Red, White and Blue Letter Days: An American Calendar* (Ithaca: Cornell University Press, 2002); and Elizabeth H. Pleck, *Celebrating the Family: Ethnicity, Consumer Culture, and Family Rituals* (Cambridge: Harvard University Press, 2000). For an overview of the history of motherhood see: Sharon Hays, *The Cultural Contradictions of Motherhood* (New Haven: Yale University Press, 1996); and Rima D. Apple and Janet Golden, eds., *Mothers and Motherhood: Readings in American History* (Columbus: Ohio State University Press, 1997).

5   Amitai Etzioni, "Holidays and Rituals: Neglected Seedbeds of Virtue," in *We Are What We Celebrate: Understanding Holidays and Rituals*, 6.

6   Ann Dally, *Inventing Motherhood: The Consequence of an Ideal* (New York: Shocken Books, 1982), 17.

7   Dally, *Inventing Motherhood*, 21; and Etzioni, "Holidays and Rituals," 9–10.

8   Gary Cross, "Just for Kids: How Holidays Became Child Centered," in *We Are What We Celebrate: Understanding Holidays and Rituals*, ed. Amitai Etzioni and Jared Bloom (New York: New York Press, 2004), 63; Etzioni, "Holidays and Rituals," 15; and Pleck, *Celebrating the Family*, 2–9.

9   Elizabeth H. Pleck, "Who Are We and Where Do We Come From: Rituals, Families, and Identities," in *We Are What We Celebrate: Understanding Holidays and Rituals*, 45.

10 Cross, "Just for Kids," 61–73; and Pleck, *Celebrating the Family*, 45.

11 Pleck, *Celebrating the Family*, 6.

12 Stephanie Coontz, *The Way We Never Were: American Families and the Nostalgia Trap* (New York: Basicbooks, 1992), 151–155; Peter G. Filene, *Him/Her/Self: Gender Identities in Modern America* (Baltimore: The Johns Hopkins University Press, 1998), 43; and Kathleen Jones, "Mother's Day: The Creation, Promotion and Meaning of a New Holiday in the Progressive Era," *Texas Studies in Literature and Language*, 22, no. 2 (Summer 1980): 175–195.

13 Etzioni, "Holidays and Rituals," 11.

14 Mother's Day International Association, *The Mother's Day Movement*, 3; and Wolfe, "The White Carnation," 89.

15 Pleck, *Celebrating the Family*, 242–243, 245.

16 "What Mothers Think of Mother's Day," *Children: The Magazine for Parents* (May 1927): 29. Title changed to *Parents Magazine* in the 1930s.

17 "What Mothers Think of Mother's Day," *Children: The Magazine for Parents*, 30.

18 "What Mothers Think of Mother's Day," *Children: The Magazine for Parents*, 29.

19 "What Mothers Think of Mother's Day," *Children: The Magazine for Parents*, 30.

20 Jane M. Hatch, *The American Book of Days* (New York: H. W. Wilson, 1978), 439; Mary Emogene Hazeltine, *Anniversaries and Holidays: A Calendar Day and How to Observe Them* (Chicago: American Library Association, 1944), 50; Maymie R. Krythe, *All About American Holidays* (New York: Harper and Brothers, 1962), 123–124; and Robert J. Myers, *Celebrations: The Complete Book of American Holidays* (New York: Doubleday and Company, 1972), 143–145.

21 Coontz, *The Way We Never Were*, 152.

22 Wolfe, *Behold Thy Mother*, 196, 208.

23 "Mother's Day," *New York Times*, May 7, 1922; "Hits Mother's Day Prices; Miss Jarvis, Founder of the Observance, Reproves Confectioners," *New York Times*, May 18, 1923; "Mother's Day Organizer in Police Court," *The Decatur [IL]Sunday Review*, September 13, 1925; "Woman's Leader Freed of Charge," *The Hamilton [OH] Daily News*, September 15, 1925; "Second Sunday in May: Mother's Day Finds Promoter of Idea Poor, Hospitalized, and Still Bitter," *Newsweek*, May 8, 1944; Oscar Schisgall, "The Bitter Author of Mother's Day," *Reader's Digest*, May 1960; John Horton, "Mother's Day Founder Might Be Appalled Today," *Cleveland Plain Dealer*, May 11, 2008; Cristina Rouvalis, "For the Mother of Mother's Day, It's Just Never Been Right," *Pittsburgh Post-Gazette*, May 11, 2008; and Katherine Jamieson, "Oh, Mother!" *Bust*, April/May 2009. This is just a tiny selection of Mother's Day news coverage over the years where her fight against the holiday's commercialization is the main theme.

24 Wolfe, "The White Carnation," 62.

25 "The Mother's Day Campaign: An Account of the Publicity Used by the Maternity Center Association," *American Journal of Nursing*, 31, no. 7 (July 1931): 839.

26 Ralph LaRossa, *The Modernization of Fatherhood: A Social and Political History* (Chicago: University of Chicago Press, 1997), 200; and Pleck, *Celebrating the Family*, 15–17, 41, 49–51.

27   George J. Hecht, "Why Not Parents' Day?" *Children: The Magazine for Parents*, May 1929, 16.

28   "Tampering with Mother's Day," n.d., Anna Jarvis Papers, West Virginia and Regional History Collection, West Virginia University, Morgantown, West Virginia.

29   "Tampering with Mother's Day," Anna Jarvis Papers.

30   Anna Jarvis to President Franklin Roosevelt, April 27, 1934, Franklin D. Roosevelt Library, Hyde Park, New York.

31   Wolfe, "The White Carnation," 180.

CHAPTER ONE: THE FOREMOTHERS AND FOREFATHER OF MOTHER'S DAY

1   *56 Cong. Rec.* 8276 (1914).

2   Presidential proclamation, May 9, 1914, Mother's Day Collection, International Mother's Day Shrine, Grafton, West Virginia.

3   Mother's Day International Association, *The Mother's Day Movement*, [1912?], 3, Mother's Day Collection, International Mother's Day Shrine, Grafton, West Virginia; "History: The American Flag, Mother's Day Flag Resolution, Etc.," [1934?], Mother's Day Collection, International Mother's Day Shrine, Grafton, West Virginia; and Howard Wolfe, "The White Carnation" (1984), 1, Howard Wolfe Collection, International Mother's Day Shrine, Grafton, West Virginia.

4   David Wallechinsky and Irving Wallace include Robert K. Cummins of Baltimore, Maryland, among the founders of a Mother's Day observance. In 1892, he proposed an annual memorial service at the Universalist Church of Our Father in honor of Mrs. Emily Pullman, the mother of the Pullman sleeping car inventor, George Pullman. The service, held annually on May 22 to commemorate the date of Mrs. Pullman's death, eventually expanded to memorialize all mothers. Because so little is currently known about the services proposed by Cummins, I do not include him as one of the founders. Anna Jarvis, however, was aware of the claim that a man in Baltimore (she did not directly give his name) proposed a Mother's Day in the late nineteenth century. Although she never publicly denounced the claim, she did dismiss it as irrelevant in a personal correspondence to a family friend in 1938. Wolfe, "The White Carnation," 173–174; and David Wallechinsky and Irving Wallace, *The People's Almanac* (New York: Doubleday and Company, 1975), 939.

5   Molly Ladd-Taylor, *Mother-Work: Women, Child-Welfare, and the State, 1890–1930* (Urbana: University of Illinois Press, 1995), 1.

6   Ladd-Taylor, *Mother-Work*, 1.

7   Stephanie Coontz, *The Way We Never Were: American Families and the Nostalgia Trap* (New York: Basic Books, 1992),152.

8   Carroll Smith-Rosenberg, *Disorderly Conduct: Visions of Gender in Victorian America* (New York: Oxford University Press, 1985), 13.

9   Julia Grant, *Raising Baby by the Book: The Education of American Mothers* (New Haven: Yale University Press, 1998), 15–24; Christina Hardyment, *Dream Babies* (Oxford: Oxford University Press, 1984), 33–86; Sharon Hays, *The Cultural Contradictions of Motherhood*

(New Haven: Yale University Press, 1996), 29–35; and Jan Lewis, "Mother's Love: The Construction of an Emotion in Nineteenth Century America," in *Mothers and Motherhood: Readings in American History*, ed. Rima D. Apple and Janet Golden (Columbus: Ohio State University Press, 1997), 52–71.

10 Lewis, "Mother's Love," 58.

11 Hays, *The Cultural Contradictions of Motherhood*, 30. The following sources provide further discussion of nineteenth century maternal ideals: Mary P. Ryan, *The Empire of the Mother: American Writing about Domesticity, 1839–1860* (New York: Harrington Park Press, 1985), 45–70; and Maxine L. Margolis, *Mothers and Such: Views of American Women and Why They Changed* (Berkeley: University of California Press, 1985), 11–61.

12 Lewis, "Mother's Love," 59–60.

13 Ann Douglas, *The Feminization of American Culture* (New York: Doubleday, 1977), 75.

14 Sara M. Evans, *Born for Liberty: A History of Women in America* (New York: Free Press Paperbacks, 1997), 119–143; and Mary P. Ryan, *Womanhood in America: Colonial Times to the Present* (New York: Franklin Watts, 1983), 133–134.

15 Barbara Robinson, "Mother's Day: What a Good Woman (or Two) Can Do," *Mature Years*, Spring 1993, 15; and Howard Wolfe, *Behold Thy Mother: Mother's Day and the Mother's Day Church* (Kingsport, Tennessee: Kingsport Press, 1962), 190–191, 267.

16 Robinson, 15; and Wolfe, *Behold Thy Mother*, 190–191, 267.

17 Richard A. Meckel, *Save the Babies: American Public Health Reform and the Prevention of Infant Mortality, 1850–1929* (Ann Arbor: The University of Michigan Press, 1990), 1; and Nancy Schrom Dye and Daniel Blake Smith, "Mother Love and Infant Death, 1750–1920," *Journal of American History* 73, no. 2 (September 1986): 353.

18 Anna Jarvis, "Recollections of Ann M. Jarvis" [1905?], Draft A and Draft B, Anna Jarvis Papers, West Virginia and Regional History Collection, West Virginia University, Morgantown, West Virginia. The unpublished, unpaged, manuscript consists of two rough drafts of an account of Ann Reeves Jarvis's life and death. I identify the drafts as Draft A and Draft B throughout. James P. Johnson, "Death, Grief, and Motherhood. The Woman Who Inspired Mother's Day," *West Virginia History* 39 (1978): 187–194.

Popular histories of Mother's Day and the current written accounts of the Jarvis family identify only eleven or twelve Jarvis children. However, the various sources disagree on the identity of the children and names that appear on some lists do not appear on others—including the personal account of Anna Jarvis. Howard Wolfe's genealogical account of the Jarvis family is the main source cited by most histories. He identifies twelve Jarvis children; see *Behold Thy Mother*, 261. I base my history on the work of Olive Dadisman, the Curator of the Anna Jarvis Birthplace Museum. She has uncovered, to date, the records for thirteen children born to Granville and Ann Reeves Jarvis. See appendix.

19 Jarvis, "Recollections of Ann M. Jarvis," Draft A.

20 Anna Jarvis identified measles as the cause of Columbia Jarvis's death but did not specify the exact cause of death for Clara, Ralph, and Marry Jarvis. It is assumed that they too died of measles. Jarvis, "Recollections of Ann M. Jarvis," Draft A; and Johnson, "Death, Grief, and Motherhood," 189.

21 Jarvis, "Recollections of Ann M Jarvis," Draft B.

22 Jarvis, "Recollections of Ann M Jarvis," Draft B.

23 The western counties of Virginia seceding from the Confederate state during the Civil War. West Virginia became a state on June 20, 1863

24 Sandra Lee Barney, *Authorized to Heal: Gender, Class, and the Transformation of Medicine in Appalachia, 1880-1930* (Chapel Hill: The University of North Carolina Press, 2000), 41–70, 100–104.

25 Ladd-Taylor, *Mother-Work*, 19; Dye and Smith, "Mother Love and Infant Death," 337–346; and Karen Tice, "School-Work and Mother-Care: The Interplay of Maternalism and Cultural Politics in the Educational Narratives of Kentucky Settlement Workers, 1910–1930," *Journal of Appalachian Studies* 4, no. 2 (Fall 1998): 191–224.

26 The original spelling of Mothers' Day Work Club is unclear. *Mothers* appears in its plural form, possessive plural, and possessive singular forms throughout various publications. I use the possessive plural form, as I believe it best reflects the intention for collective action.

27 Meckel, *Save the Babies*, 11–39.

28 Norman Kendall, *Mothers Day: A History of Its Founding and Its Founder* (Grafton, WV: D. Grant Smith, 1937), 11, 3.

29 According to Sandra Lee Barney, nearly half of physicians practicing in West Virginia by the late nineteenth century held no medical degrees. In contrast, Dr. James Reeves began his medical training under two different preceptors and attended medical lectures at Hampden Sydney College in Richmond, Virginia. He eventually graduated from the University of Pennsylvania in 1860. He went on to have a successful career in the field of public health eventually establishing the American Public Health Association and both the West Virginian State Medical Society and the State Board of Health. Barney, *Authorized to Heal*, 22; L. D. Wilson, "James Edmund Reeves, M.D.," *Transactions of the Medical Society of West Virginia*, 1896, 1–9; and Wolfe, *Behold Thy Mother*, 250–251.

30 Robinson, "Mother's Day," 13–14; and Howard Wolfe, "The Second Sunday" (1983), 21–22, Howard Wolfe Collection, International Mother's Day Shrine, Grafton, West Virginia; and Wolfe, *Behold Thy Mother*, 182–183.

31 Barney, *Authorized to Heal*, 41–70, 122–151.

32 Kendall, *Mothers Day*, 8.

33 Kendall, *Mothers Day*, 9.

34 Kendall, *Mothers Day*, 10; and Wolfe, "The Second Sunday," 24–25. The following sources detail the death of Thornsbury Bailey Brown but do not include the story of Jarvis's prayer: Joseph Franklin Snider, "The Early History of Grafton" (master's thesis, West Virginia University, 1945), 9–10; Stanley A. Tenney, "Taylor County in the Civil War," in *A History of Taylor County West Virginia*, ed. Taylor County Historical and Genealogical Society (Grafton: Taylor County Historical and Genealogical Society, 1986), 62; W. Hunter Lesser, *Rebels at the Gate: Lee and McClellan on the Front Line of a Nation Divided* (Naperville, Illinois: Sourcebooks, 2004), 53–54; and John W. Shaffer, *Clash of Loyalties: A Border County in the Civil War* (Morgantown: West Virginia University Press, 2003), 70–71.

35 Robinson, "Mother's Day," 13–14; Wolfe, *Behold Thy Mother*, 182–183; and Wolfe, "The Second Sunday," 21–22.

36 The exact cause of death for all the Jarvis children is currently unknown. Because of the war and the children's ages (seven years, six years, two years, eight months and three months), it is likely that they succumbed to disease.

37 Robinson, "Mother's Day," 14; and Wolfe, *Behold Thy Mother*, 185–186.

38 Wolfe, *Behold Thy Mother*, 185–186; Wolfe, "The Second Sunday," 22–26.

39 Kendall, *Mothers Day*, 4; and J. Edgar Williams, *The White Carnation and Mother's Day* (Detroit: Northwestern Printing Company, 1950), 44.

40 Wolfe, *Behold Thy Mother*, 186.

41 Kendall, *Mothers Day*, 4.

42 Kendall, 4.

43 Howard Wolfe's entire study of the Jarvis family and Mother's Day is not without merit. Wolfe dedicated over twenty years to his research, and his history is the most detailed of the Jarvis family and Anna Jarvis's Mother's Day movement to date. He preserved a significant portion of Anna Jarvis's personal papers and the Mother's Day International Association documents that exist in both the West Virginia and Regional History Collection at West Virginia University and in the archives at the International Mother's Day Shrine. Whenever possible, I cite additional sources that support Wolfe's accounts; many are likely the same sources used by Wolfe.

44 Wolfe, "The Second Sunday," 20.

45 Shaffer, *Clash of Loyalties*, 3.

46 Lesser, *Rebels at the Gate*, 61–73; Shaffer, *Clash of Loyalties*, 64–68; and Tenney, "Taylor County in the Civil War," 62–63.

47 John Duffy, *The Sanitarians: A History of American Public Health* (Urbana: University of Illinois Press, 1990), 110; and Drew Gilpin Faust, *This Republic of Suffering: Death and the American Civil War* (New York: Vintage Books, 2008), 137–170.

48 Shaffer, *Clash of Loyalties*, 4, 84–128.

49 Henry Howe, "The Times, The Rebellion, West Virginia," in *War Stories: Civil War in West Virginia*, ed. David L. Phillips and Rebecca L. Hill (Leesburg, Virginia: Gauley Mount Press, 1991), 2–26; and Shaffer, *Clash of Loyalties*, 93.

50 Kendall, *Mothers Day*, 9; "Certificate of Exemption on Account of Having Furnished a Substitute," issued by the Board of Enrollment of the 2nd District of the State of West Virginia to Granville E. Jarvis of Taylor County, August 29, 1864, Mother's Day Collection, International Mother's Day Shrine, Grafton, West Virginia. Howard Wolfe's local history of the Civil War places Union General George B. McClellan's headquarters in the Jarvis home in late June of 1861. See *Behold Thy Mother*, 179. That information has not been formally corroborated. Contemporary accounts, including McClellan's published histories, verify the general's presence in Grafton between June 25 and June 29, 1861, but there are no direct references to the specific town of Webster (four miles south of Grafton) or the Jarvis family. G. S. Hillard, *Life and Campaigns of George B. McClellan Major-General U.S.*

Army (Philadelphia: J. B. Lippincott and Company, 1864), 92–98; George B. McClellan, *Report on the Organization and Campaigns of the Army of the Potomac: To Which is Added an Account of the Campaign in Western Virginia with Plans of Battlefields* (New York: Sheldon and Company Publishers, 1864), 19–26; and George B. McClellan, *McClellan's Own Story* (New York: Charles Webster and Company, 1887), 58.

51   Shaffer, *Clash of Loyalties*, 129, 154, 163.

52   Jarvis, "Recollections of Ann M. Jarvis," Draft B. The following sources provide more background on Granville Jarvis's business success and failures: Wolfe, *Behold Thy Mother*, 176; Wolfe, "The Second Sunday," 29–30; and Johnson, "Death, Grief, and Motherhood," 192.

53   Jarvis, "Recollections of Ann M. Jarvis," Draft A; and Johnson, "Death, Grief and Motherhood," 192.

54   Johnson, "Death, Grief, and Motherhood," 192.

55   Snider, "The Early History of Grafton," 76.

56   Kendall, *Mothers Day*, 9; Snider, "The Early History of Grafton," 76; and Wolfe, "The Second Sunday," 30.

57   Jarvis, "Recollections of Ann M. Jarvis," Draft A and Draft B; and Snider, "The Early History of Grafton," 59.

58   Wolfe, "The Second Sunday," 30, 32.

59   Kendall, *Mothers Day*, 11–12; and Wolfe, "The Second Sunday," 33.

60   Theda Skocpol, *Protecting Soldiers and Mothers: The Political Origins of Social Policy in the United States* (Cambridge: The Belknap Press of Harvard University Press, 1992), 328.

61   Kendall, *Mothers Day*, 32.

62   "The First Anniversary of Mother's Day," *New York Times*, June 3, 1874; and Deborah Pickman Clifford, *Mine Eyes Have Seen the Glory: A Biography of Julia Ward Howe* (Boston: Little, Brown and Company, 1978), 187.

63   They did not include the story of Ann Reeves Jarvis either, but by the 1920s, Anna Jarvis had already publicized her mother as the true source of the day's inspiration, citing the Sunday school prayer she overheard as a child. Mary Emogene Hazeltine, *Anniversaries and Holidays: A Calendar of Days and How to Observe Them* (Chicago: American Library Association, 1994), 78; Susan Tracy Rice and Robert Haven Schauffer, eds., *Mothers' Day: Its History, Origin, Celebration, Spirit, and Significance as related in Prose and Verse* (New York: Dodd, Mead and Company, 1927),vii–x, 3–7; and Robert J. Myers, *Celebrations: The Complete Book of American Holidays* (New York: Doubleday and Company, 1972), 143–150. All three sources include the history of "Mothering Sunday."

64   Jane Hatch, *The American Book of Days* (New York: H. W. Wilson, 1978), 439; and Maymie R. Krythe, *All About American Holidays* (New York: Harper and Brothers, 1962), 127.

65   Julia Ward Howe, *Reminiscences 1819–1899* (Boston: Houghton Mifflin Company, 1899), 336; "Official Report of the third Annual Meeting of the Woman's Peace Festival," *The Voice of Peace*, July 1875, 49–50; Robert Wesley Doherty, "Alfred H. Love and the Universal Peace Party" (PhD diss., University of Pennsylvania, 1962), 90; Merle Curti, *Peace or War: The American Struggle 1636–1936* (New York: W. W. Norton and Company, 1936), 116; and Coontz, *The Way We Never Were*, 152.

66 "Mothers' Peace Day Celebration, Swarthmore, Pa. May 29, 1909," *The Peacemaker and Court of Arbitration*, June 1909, 139.

67 Because of Howe's notoriety, I feel it is out of the chapter's scope to provide a detailed biography. Unlike the relatively unknown Ann Reeves Jarvis, Howe wrote an autobiography, and she has been the subject of several books and articles. The following sources provide an overview of Howe's life: Howe, *Reminiscences*; Florence Howe Hall, *Julia Ward Howe and the Woman Suffrage Movement* (Boston: Dana Estes and Company, 1913); Louise Hall Tharp, *Three Saints and a Sinner: Julia Ward Howe, Louisa, Annie and Sam Ward* (Boston: Little, Brown and Company, 1956); and Clifford, *Mine Eyes Have Seen the Glory*.

68 Tharp, *Three Saints and a Sinner*, 252; and Jarvis, "The Recollections of Ann M. Jarvis," Draft A and Draft B.

69 Taken from a speech titled "How to Extend the Sympathies of Women," in Hall, *Julia Ward Howe*, 238–239. The Association for the Advancement of Women was an organization designed to facilitate women's collective discussion of a variety of subjects and issues of mutual concern through annual congresses across the country. Howe served as president of the organization for nineteen years. Clifford, *Mine Eyes Have Seen the Glory*, 200–201.

70 Howe, *Reminiscences*, 328.

71 Howe, *Reminiscences*, 328.

72 Julia Ward Howe, "Appeal to Womanhood Throughout the World," *The Voice of Peace*, September 1874, 92–93. This was a reprint of her original essay published in 1870.

73 Clifford, *Mine Eyes Have Seen the Glory*, 86–187; Curti, *Peace or War*, 115–116; and Howe, *Reminiscences*, 326–336.

74 Howe, "Mother's Day," *The Voice of Peace*, April 1873, 3.

75 Howe, "Mother's Day," *The Voice of Peace*, April 1873, 3.

76 Clifford, *Mine Eyes Have Seen the Glory*, 186–187; Curti, *Peace or War*, 115-116; Howe, *Reminiscences*, 326–336; and "Mothers' Peace Day Celebration," 139.

77 Doherty, "Alfred H. Love," 48–49, 73 74, 88, 101–104.

78 Howe, *Reminiscences*, 336.

79 Howe, "Mother's Day," 3.

80 Peace activist Mary E. Beedy referred to Howe's Mothers' Day idea as a concession to her larger dreams of an international peace conference, but an important first step nonetheless: "I do not suppose that any very positive results will be seen immediately, but it is at least a little tilling of the soil, and in due time the harvest that Mrs. Howe sowed is sure to come." Mary E. Beedy, "Women's Work For Peace," *The Voice of Peace*, January 1873, 19.

81 Howe, "Mother's Day," 3; Howe, "Letter from Julia Ward Howe," *The Voice of Peace*, April 1874, 13; Howe, "Pamphlet of the Woman's Peace Festival, Held June 2, 1873," *The Voice of Peace*, May 1874, 29; Howe, "Reply of Julia Ward Howe," *The Voice of Peace*, September 1875, 90; and Howe, "To the Friends of Peace," *The Voice of Peace*, July 1876, 50.

82 Curti, *Peace or War*, 114.

83 "Official Report of the Third Annual Meeting of the Woman's Peace Festival," *The Voice of Peace,* July 1875, 50.

84 "Official Report of the Third Annual Meeting," 49.

85 Lydia A. Schofield, "Letter to Julia Ward Howe," *The Voice of Peace,* September 1875, 89–90.

86 Emphasis added. Howe, "Reply of Julia Ward Howe," 89–90.

87 Doherty, "Alfred H. Love," 58–68; and "What Women May Do to Promote Peace on Earth," *The Peacemaker and Court of Arbitration,* September 1885, 63.

88 "Mother's Influence for Peace," *The Peacemaker and Court of Arbitration,* July 1883, 95.

89 "Observance of Mothers' Day," *The Voice of Peace,* June 1880, 43; "Mother's Day," *The Peacemaker and Court of Arbitration,* July 1883, 14; "Mother's Day for Peace," *The Peacemaker and Court of Arbitration,* June 1903, 128; "Mothers' Day for Peace—June 2, 1903," *The Peacemaker and Court of Arbitration,* August 1903, 182; "Mothers' Peace Day," *The Peacemaker and Court of Arbitration,* May 1904, 108; and "Mothers' Peace Day Celebration," *The Peacemaker and Court of Arbitration,* 139.

90 Over the course of forty years, roughly half of the published accounts of Mothers' Day observances included a reference to a mother's training of children and/or the indictment to not raise sons to become "food for powder."

91 Curti, *Peace or War,* 116–117.

92 "Mothers' Day for Peace, June 2nd, 1904," *The Peacemaker and Court of Arbitration,* July 1904, 167; "Mothers Day for Peace," *The Peacemaker and Court of Arbitration,* July 1906, 161; "What Philadelphia is Doing for Peace Day," *The Peacemaker and Court of Arbitration,* May 1909, 99; and Doherty, 89.

93 "What Philadelphia is Doing for Peace Day," *The Peacemaker and Court of Arbitration,* 99.

94 "Motherhood the Crowning Glory," *The Peacemaker and Court of Arbitration,* May 1909, 116.

95 Alfred Love, "In Memory of Julia Ward Howe," *The Peacemaker and Court of Arbitration,* January 1911, 2.

96 Doherty, "Alfred H. Love," 162.

97 The historical accounts of Blakeley's life use the holiday's possessive singular spelling. Mary Houghton, email correspondence with author, June 8, 2008; Frank Passic, email correspondence with author, July 15, 2008.

98 John Kobler, *Ardent Spirits: The Rise and Fall of Prohibition* (New York: G. P. Putnam's Sons, 1973), 168.

99 The men tore up the wooden sidewalk in front of the home. Blakeley readily identified the men who were then forced to pay for the damages. Frank Passic, "Juliet Calhoun Blakeley," *Morning Star (MI),* May 3, 1993.

100 Passic, "Juliet Calhoun Blakeley," *Morning Star;* and Mary Houghton, email correspondence with author, June 8, 2008.

101 Passic, "Juliet Calhoun Blakeley," *Morning Star.*

102 Passic, "Grandma Blakeley Active in Underground Railroad," *Morning Star*, May 11, 2003.

103 Evans, *Born for Liberty*, 126–130; and Skocpol, *Protecting Soldiers and Mothers*, 326–327.

104 Kobler, *Ardent Spirits*, 136.

105 Sheila Rothman, *Woman's Proper Place: A History of Changing Ideals and Practices, 1870 to the Present* (New York: Basic Books, 1978), 68.

106 Kobler, *Ardent Spirits*, 131–167; Rothman, *Woman's Proper Place*, 66–69; and Skocpol, *Protecting Soldiers and Mothers*, 326.

107 Mary Houghton, email correspondence with author, June 8, 2008; and Frank Passic, email correspondence with author, July 15, 2008.

108 Roger C. Storms, *Partisan Prophets: A History of the Prohibition Party* (Denver, Colorado: National Prohibition Foundation, 1972), 5; and Passic, "Juliet Calhoun Blakeley," *Morning Star*.

109 Storms, *Partisan Prophets*, 17.

110 Passic, *A History of Health Care Facilities in Albion*, February 2000, accessed on October 31, 2013 at www.albionmich.com.

111 Passic, "Juliet Calhoun Blakeley," *Morning Star*.

112 Although Hering was married, I have not confirmed whether he had children. Published eulogies and accounts of his life never reference the presence of children or mention his role as a father. If he did have children, it may be significant that his peers did not praise him as a father.

113 Mother's Day International Association, *The Mother's Day Movement*, 3; Wolfe, "The White Carnation," 175–176; Wolfe, *Behold Thy Mother*, 190–199, 205 ; and "Glenn Positive Miss Sasseen the Founder," *Henderson [KY] Gleaner*, April 19, 1912.

114 Susan S. Towles to Thos. E. Owen, "MARY TOWLES SASSEEN WAS THE FOUNDER OF MOTHERS' DAY," 16 August, 1929; "U.S. Issues Big Stamp of Whistler's Painting to Commemorate Holiday," clipping from an unknown paper circa 1934, Mother's Day File, Henderson County Public Library, Henderson, Kentucky.

115 Towles to Owen, August 16, 1929, Mother's Day File.

116 By the late nineteenth century, it was not unusual for a young single woman to seek a career in primary education. School boards had recognized the ideal fit between women and the teaching profession; not only were women seen as equipped with a "natural disposition" suited for educating young children, but they were willing to work for lower salaries than their male counterparts. By 1880, an estimated nine out of ten professional women were teachers. Peter G. Filene, *Him/Her/Self: Gender Identities in Modern America* (Baltimore: Johns Hopkins University Press, 1998), 35; and Rothman, *Woman's Proper Place*, 57–60

117 Mary Towles Sasseen, *Mother's Day Celebration* ([Kentucky]: the author, 1893), 5.

118 Dot Rouse, "Kentucky's Annual Gift to Mothers," *Rural Kentuckian*, May 1986, 15; "U.S. Issues Big Stamp of Whistler's Painting to Commemorate Holiday," Mother's Day File.

119 Historian J. J. Glenn also wrote of Sasseen's love and devotion to her mother. "Glenn Positive Miss Sasseen the Founder," April 19, 1912; and Rouse, "Kentucky's Annual Gift to Mothers," 15.

120 Towles to Owen, August 16, 1929, Mother's Day File.

121 Sasseen, *Mother's Day Celebration*, 4.

122 Sasseen, *Mother's Day Celebration*, 7.

123 Sasseen, *Mother's Day Celebration*, 7.

124 Available histories only comment on her singular success in spreading the popularity of Mother's Day to Springfield, Ohio. While visiting her sister, Sasseen convinced the superintendent of public schools to adopt the celebration. In 1894, Springfield passed a citywide resolution designating the nearest Sunday to April 20 as Mother's Day. Towles to Owen, August 16, 1929, Mother's Day File; and Rouse, "Kentucky's Annual Gift to Mothers," 16.

125 Rouse, "Kentucky's Annual Gift to Mothers," 15–16; and Towles to Owen, August 16, 1929, Mother's Day File.

126 Audrey Boyers Walz, *The Story of Mothers' Day* (Mount Morris, NY: Allied Printing, [1943?]), 2; and Charles P. McCann, *Mother's Day Began with the Eagles*, [1940?], 1 (courtesy of the Fraternal Order of Eagles, Aerie # 4357, Buckhannon, West Virginia). In 2008, members of the aerie read directly from McCann's history of Frank Hering's primary role in establishing the holiday during the 100th anniversary of Anna Jarvis's first Mother's Day service in 1908. The commemoration was held at the International Mother's Day Shrine in Grafton, West Virginia.

127 Theodore Marvin Greenhoe, *In Memory, Frank E. Hering, 1874–1943*, [1943?], University of Notre Dame Archives, University of Notre Dame, Notre Dame, Indiana; and McCann, *Mother's Day Began with the Eagles*, 1. Due to the hazy eligibility rules of college football in the nineteenth century, Hering served as both the head football coach and team captain. He reportedly took to the field in a number of positions. Scholars also credit Hering with introducing the field goal into the game. Michael Bonifer and L. G. Weaver, *Out of Bounds* (New York: Piper, 1978), 18; and Jason A. Kelly, "Echoes: As ND as football, Mother's Day and Community Service," *Notre Dame Magazine* (Autumn 2009), accessed on October 31, 2012 at www.magazine.nd.edu/news/12240.

128 McCann, *Mother's Day Began with the Eagles*, 1.

129 Walz, *The Story of Mothers' Day*, 2. Parts of Canada, Mexico, South America, China, and Japan also celebrated Mother's Day by 1911. Mother's Day International Association, *The Mother's Day Movement*, 3; and Wolfe, *Behold Thy Mother*, 190–199, 205.

130 Wolfe, "The White Carnation," 246–248

131 McCann, *Mother's Day Began with the Eagles*, 2.

132 Bob Hansen, *The Eagles* (Milwaukee, Wisconsin: Fraternal Order of Eagles, 1960), 6; and Skocpol, *Protecting Soldiers and Mothers*, 424, 428–430.

133 Greenhoe, 1; Hansen, *The Eagles*, 7; Roy Lubove, *The Struggle for Social Security, 1900–1935* (Cambridge: Harvard University Press, 1968), 137; and Skocpol, *Protecting Soldiers and Mothers*, 430.

134 Emphasis added. Walz, *The Story of Mothers' Day*, 4.

135 Anna Jarvis to Oscar Monrad, February 4, 1924, Mother's Day File.

136 McCann, *Mother's Day Began with the Eagles*, 2; and Walz, *The Story of Mothers' Day*, 2. The American War Mothers did not include any reference to role of Jarvis, Howe, Blakeley, Sasseen, or Anna Jarvis in its published history of Mother's Day. Margaret N. McCluer and Adelaide Riffle, *Memoirs of "Mothers' Day" by American War Mothers: "Mothers' Day" Its Origin and Ways of Observing* (American War Mothers, 1925), 14–23.

137 Walz, *The Story of Mothers' Day*, 3–4; Greenhoe, *In Memory*, 1; McCann, *Mother's Day Began with the Eagles*, 1; and McCluer and Riffle, *Memoirs of "Mothers' Day,"* 14.

138 Walz, *The Story of Mothers' Day*, 3–4. In reality, the American War Mothers was far from an objective observer. As explored in chapter 4, the organization had a personal interest in the celebration of Mother's Day, especially in depriving Anna Jarvis of her exclusive status as holiday founder, in order to use the holiday in its political and charitable works.

139 Jarvis to Monrad, February 4, 1924, Mother's Day File.

CHAPTER TWO: ANNA JARVIS AND HER MOTHER'S DAY MOVEMENT

1 The following sources provide background on the history of Thanksgiving: Matthew Dennis, *Red, White, and Blue Letter Days: An American Calendar* (Ithaca: Cornell University Press, 2002), 81–118; Diana Muir, "Proclaiming Thanksgiving throughout the Land," in *We Are What We Celebrate: Understanding Holidays and Rituals*, ed. Amitai Etzioni and Jared Bloom (New York: New York University Press, 2004), 194–212; Elizabeth H. Pleck, *Celebrating the Family: Ethnicity, Consumer Culture, and Family Rituals* (Cambridge: Harvard University Press, 2000), 21–42; and Anne Blue Wills, "Pilgrims and Progress: How Magazines Made Thanksgiving," *Church History* 72, no. 1 (March 2003): 138–158.

2 Muir, "Proclaiming Thanksgiving," 196.

3 That holiday was not consistently observed each year by every state, however. Dennis, *Red, White, and Blue Letter Days*, 95; Pleck, *Celebrating the Family*, 22; Wills, "Pilgrims and Progress," 144, 147.

4 Mother's Day International Association, *The Mother's Day Movement*, [1912?], 3, Mother's Day Collection, International Mother's Day Shrine, Grafton, West Virginia; and Howard Wolfe, "The White Carnation" (1984), 2, Howard Wolfe Collection, International Mother's Day Shrine, Grafton, West Virginia.

5 Dennis, *Red, White, and Blue Letter Days*, 87.

6 Wolfe, "The White Carnation," 4.

7 Wills, "Pilgrims and Progress," 148

8 Wolfe, "The White Carnation," 158.

9 Howard Wolfe, *Behold Thy Mother: Mothers Day and the Mothers Day Church* (Kingsport, Tennessee: Kingsport Press, 1962), 190–192.

10 Eleanor McNulty, "Miss Anna Jarvis Recounts the Founding of Mother's Day," *Children: The Magazine for Parents*, May 1927, 30.

11 Mother's Day International Association, *The Mother's Day Movement*, 3; and Wolfe, "The White Carnation," 89.

12   Untitled Mother's Day International Association address, n.d., Mother's Day Collection, International Mother's Day Shrine, Grafton, West Virginia.

13   Dennis, *Red, White, and Blue Letter Days*, 104.

14   McNulty, "Miss Anna Jarvis Recounts," 30.

15   The primary academic accounts of Mother's Day include: James P. Johnson, "Death, Grief and Motherhood: The Woman who Inspired Mother's Day," *West Virginia History* 39 (1978): 187–194; James P. Johnson, "How Mother Got Her Day," *American Heritage* 30 (April/May 1979): 16–19; Kathleen W. Jones, "Mother's Day: The Creation, Promotion and Meaning of a New Holiday in the Progressive Era," *Texas Studies in Literature and Language* 22, no. 2 (Summer 1980): 175–196; and Leigh Eric Schmidt, *Consumer Rites: The Buying and Selling of American Holidays* (Princeton: Princeton University Press, 1995), 244–293.

16   Jones, "Mother's Day," 176–177; and Johnson, "How Mother Got Her Day," 16–19.

17   Quoted in Linda W. Rosenzweig, *The Anchor of My Life: Middle-Class American Mothers and Daughters, 1880–1920* (New York: New York University Press, 1993), 22.

18   As a member of the Board of Trustees of the International Mother's Day Shrine, I have personally heard all the local stories about the Jarvis family from a variety of community members.

19   Wolfe, *Behold Thy Mother*, 248–263. Johnson attributes Lillian's visual handicap to small-pox, not scarlet fever. "How Mother Got Her Day," 15, 19.

20   Anna Jarvis, "Recollections of Ann M. Jarvis," [1905?], Draft A and Draft B, Anna Jarvis Papers, West Virginia and Regional History Collection, West Virginia University, Morgantown, West Virginia; and Johnson, "Death, Grief, and Motherhood," 187–194.

21   Nancy Schrom Dye and Daniel Blake Smith, "Mother Love and Infant Death, 1750–1920," *The Journal of American History* 73, no. 2 (September 1986): 353; Carroll Smith-Rosenberg, *Disorderly Conduct: Visions of Gender in Victorian America* (Oxford: Oxford University Press, 1985), 64–66; and Rosenzweig, *The Anchor of My Life*, 17.

22   Ada Robinson to Anna Jarvis, May 15, 1905, Anna Jarvis Papers, West Virginia and Regional History Collection, West Virginia University, Morgantown, West Virginia.

23   Rosenzweig, *The Anchor of My Life*, 193–194; and Smith-Rosenberg, *Disorderly Conduct*, 64–66.

24   Jarvis, "Recollections of Ann M. Jarvis," Draft A.

25   Frank Lewis to C. V. Miller, June 21, 1950, and April 1, 1950, Clay Miller Papers, West Virginia and Regional History Collection; and Frank Lewis, "Mary Baldwin College address," May 15, 1950, Clay Miller Papers, West Virginia and Regional History Collection.

26   Like her mother, Anna Jarvis also taught Sunday school at Andrews Methodist Episcopal Church. B. F. Martin to Dr. James Reeves, September 2, 1891, Anna Jarvis Papers, West Virginia and Regional History Collection, West Virginia University, Morgantown, West Virginia; Howard Wolfe, "The Second Sunday" (1983), 33, Howard Wolfe Collection, International Mother's Day Shrine, Grafton, West Virginia; and Wolfe, *Behold Thy Mother*, 260.

27   Dr. James Edmund Reeves to Anna Jarvis, n.d., and August 24, 1891, Anna Jarvis Papers, West Virginia and Regional History Collection, West Virginia University.

28   Reeves to Jarvis, n.d., and August 24, 1891, Anna Jarvis Papers.

29   Dr. James Edmund Reeves to Ann Reeves Jarvis, August 27, 1891, Anna Jarvis Papers, West Virginia and Regional History Collection, West Virginia University, Morgantown, West Virginia.

30   Dr. James Edmund Reeves to Anna Jarvis, August 12, 1891, Anna Jarvis Papers, West Virginia and Regional History Collection, West Virginia University, Morgantown, West Virginia.

31   Reverend B. W. Hutchinson to Anna Jarvis, August 23, 1892, Anna Jarvis Papers, West Virginia and Regional History Collection, West Virginia University, Morgantown, West Virginia.

32   Anna Jarvis to William D. Marks, resignation letter, April 26, 1894, Anna Jarvis Papers, West Virginia and Regional History Collection, West Virginia University, Morgantown, West Virginia; Johnson, "How Mother Got Her Day," 16; and Bette Marsh, "Civic Group to Honor Mother's Day Founder," *Philadelphia Daily News*, May 6, 1949. Jarvis initially excelled at Fidelity Mutual Life Insurance Company. She earned accolades from her colleagues in 1896 for her essay titled "The Beneficence of Life Insurance." Interestingly, Jarvis originally submitted the essay to company president L. G. Fouse under a male "nom de plume," but he quickly attributed the essay's authorship to Jarvis. The general understanding is that Jarvis left the company in the early twentieth century to dedicate herself to her Mother's Day movement. Letters in the Anna Jarvis Papers, however, suggest that Jarvis harbored a degree of resentment against the company by 1908. Jno. F. Edwards to L. G. Fouse, June 16, 1896, and June 19, 1896, Anna Jarvis Papers, West Virginia and Regional History Collection, West Virginia University, Morgantown, West Virginia; and "The Fidelity Mutual's Bright Staff have a Reunion in the Company's New Building," *Philadelphia Times*, July 3, 1896.

33   Lillian Jarvis also commented on her sister's undue influence over her brother when it came to the management of his assets. E. L. Jarvis to Clinton A. Sowers, 12 September, 1923, Anna Jarvis Papers, West Virginia and Regional History Collection, West Virginia University, Morgantown, West Virginia; "Woman an Aid in Ending Taxi Strike," *Public Ledger [Philadelphia]*, November 14, 1913; Wolfe, *Behold Thy Mother*, 260.

34   Johnson, "How Mother Got Her Day," 16.

35   Hand-written transcription of the legal contract transferring power of attorney of Granville E. Jarvis's estate to Anna Jarvis, February 17, 1902, Anna Jarvis Papers, West Virginia and Regional History Collection; and Anna Jarvis to Ann Reeves Jarvis, July 13, 1903, Anna Jarvis Papers, West Virginia and Regional History Collection.

36   Hand-written transcription of the legal contract transferring power of attorney of Granville E. Jarvis's estate to Anna Jarvis, February 17, 1902, Anna Jarvis Papers, West Virginia and Regional History Collection; and Anna Jarvis to Ann Reeves Jarvis, July 13, 1903, Anna Jarvis Papers, West Virginia and Regional History Collection.

37   Schmidt, *Consumer Rites*, 248.

38   Regrettably, the name of the sender is undecipherable. [Unknown] to Anna Jarvis, March 19, 1905, Anna Jarvis Papers, West Virginia and Regional History Collection, West Virginia University, Morgantown, West Virginia. Although referred to as a "poor child," Lillian Jarvis was thirty-eight years old in 1905. There are additional letters from others individuals regarding Lillian's destructive behavior and mental instability. James Johnson contributes Lillian Jarvis's declining mental health as another consequence of her contraction of smallpox as a child. "Death, Grief, and Motherhood," 191.

39 Jarvis, "Recollections of Ann M. Jarvis," Draft A.

40 Jarvis, "Recollections of Ann M. Jarvis," Draft A; and Johnson, "Death, Grief, and Motherhood," 192.

41 She did arrange informal memorials in honor of her mother in the immediate years after her death. Jarvis hosted a simple gathering of friends in her home in 1906 to mark the anniversary of mother's passing and sent three hundred white carnations to members of Andrews Methodist Episcopal Church, in Grafton, West Virginia, in memory of her mother. She organized a larger commemoration at the church the following year designed again in tribute to her own mother. Norman F. Kendall, *Mothers Day: A History of its Founding and its Founder* (Grafton, WV: D. Grant Smith, 1937), 5–6; and Wolfe, "The Second Sunday," 43–44.

42 Russell H. Conwell, *The Romantic Rise of a Great American* (New York: Harper and Brothers Publishing, 1924), 216–217; Johnson, "How Mother Got Her Day," 19; Kendall, *Mothers Day*, 41; and Wolfe, *Behold Thy Mother*, 190–199.

43 Mother's Day International Association, *The Mother's Day Movement*, 3; Wolfe, *Behold Thy Mother*, 190–199, 205–206; and Wolfe, "The White Carnation," 8c, 50–52, 79–81, 175–176.

44 Mother's Day International Association, *Mother's Day Community Program* (1924) Mother's Day Collection, International Mother's Day Shrine, Grafton, West Virginia; and Mother's Day International Association, *The All Nation Mother's Day* (1924) Mother's Day Collection, International Mother's Day Shrine, Grafton, West Virginia.

45 Wolfe, "The White Carnation," 172.

46 Wolfe, "The White Carnation," 53.

47 Kriste Lindenmeyer, "A Right to Childhood:" The U.S. Children's Bureau and Child Welfare 1912–46 (Urbana: University of Illinois Press, 1997), 85.

48 Mother's Day International Association, *The Mother's Day Movement*, 2.

49 Jarvis, "Recollections of Ann M. Jarvis," Draft B.

50 Jarvis, "Recollections of Ann M. Jarvis," Draft B.

51 Jarvis, "Recollections of Ann M. Jarvis," Draft B.

52 Jarvis, "Recollections of Ann M. Jarvis," Draft A.

53 The quotes, and/or the sentiment behind them, are scattered throughout both drafts.

54 Jarvis, "Recollections of Ann M. Jarvis," Draft A.

55 Kendall, *Mothers Day*, 11–12; and Wolfe, "The Second Sunday," 34.

56 Jarvis, "Recollections of Ann M. Jarvis," Draft A; and Kendall, *Mothers Day*, 9.

57 Jarvis, "Recollections of Ann M. Jarvis," Draft A.

58 Jarvis, "Recollections of Ann M. Jarvis," Draft A.

59 Jarvis, "Recollections of Ann M. Jarvis," Draft A.

60 Jarvis, "Recollections of Ann M. Jarvis," Draft A.

61 Jarvis, "Recollections of Ann M. Jarvis," Draft A.

62   Kendall, *Mothers Day*, 11–13. Kendall's Mother's Day history offers the best evidence of Ann Reeves Jarvis's maternal activism. He records the memories of those who admired her community leadership.

63   Wolfe, "The Second Sunday," 40. Olive Dadisman, curator of The Anna Jarvis Birthplace and Museum, contends that Jarvis legally established her middle name in 1912 and that the "M" actually stands for "Mother."

64   Wolfe, "The Second Sunday," 35–36, 84.

65   Wolfe, "The White Carnation," 247.

66   Wolfe, "The White Carnation," 5.

67   Wolfe, "The White Carnation," 5–6.

68   Wolfe, "The Second Sunday," 56–59.

69   Wolfe, "The Second Sunday," 56–59.

70   Wolfe, "The White Carnation," 12–14, 50–52, 110, 149–151.

71   Anna Jarvis to Oscar Monrad, February 4, 1924, Mother's Day File, Henderson County Public Library, Henderson, Kentucky; Anna Jarvis to Sue Towles, August 12, 1929, Mother's Day File, Henderson County Public Library, Henderson, Kentucky; "Don't Be Deceived of a Kentucky Barber Seeking to Get 1,000,000 for a Monument Works and New Founder on You," n.d., Mother's Day Collection, International Mother's Day Shrine, Grafton, West Virginia.

72   Wolfe, "The White Carnation," 173–174.

73   Towles was also the Henderson Public Librarian and a relative of Sasseen. Susan Towles to Thos. E. Owen (editor, *Louisville and Nashville Railroad Magazine*), 16 August 1929, Mother's Day File, Henderson County Public Library, Henderson, Kentucky.

74   "Don't Be Deceived of a Kentucky Barber," n.d., Mother's Day Collection.

75   Jarvis to Monrad, February 4, 1924, Mother's Day File.

76   Wolfe, "The White Carnation," 177.

77   Wolfe, "The White Carnation," 31.

78   Over the course of forty years, roughly half of the published accounts of Mothers' Peace Day observances in the Universal Peace Union's magazines, *The Voice of Peace* (1872–1882) and *The Peacemaker and Court of Arbitration* (1882–1913), included a reference to a mother's training of children and/or the indictment to not raise sons to become "food for power."

79   "Founder of Mother's Day Bars Greetings Abroad," *New York Times*, May 8, 1938.

80   The article uses the possessive singular spelling for Mother's Peace Day. "Mother's Day, Inc.," *Time*, May 16, 1938.

81   It is unknown if the organizers or participants of the New York Mothers' Peace Day parade directly linked the demonstration to the observance first designed by Julia Ward Howe. Wolfe, "The White Carnation," 169.

82   "Mother's Day, Inc.," *Time*, May 16, 1938.

83   Along with Blakely, Jarvis did not publicly address the claim that Robert K. Cummings first proposed a Mother's Day service in Baltimore in 1892. Frank Passic, "A Mother's Day Commemorative Envelope," *Morning Star* [Albion, MI] May 5, 2002.

84   Cong. Rec. E1823 (2004), vol. 150 (statement of Rep. Edward Whitfield); and Frank Boyett, "Henderson's Mother's Day Role to be in Congressional Record," *The Gleaner* [Henderson, KY], October 8, 2004.

85   Sasseen maintained a vase of flowers in her parlor while Jarvis reportedly kept an urn filled with palm leaves from her mother's funeral. Dot Rouse, "Kentucky's Annual Gift to Mothers," *Rural Kentuckian*, May 15, 1986; and John LaCerda, "The Tragic Founder of Mother's Day," *St. Louis Post Dispatch*, May 14, 1944.

86   Mary Towels Sasseen, *Mother's Day Celebration* (Henderson, Kentucky: Printed by Author, 1893), cover page.

87   Oscar Monrad and J. J. Glenn, correspondence, December 13, 1923, December 15, 1923, 17 December, 1923, Mother's Day File, Henderson County Public Library, Henderson, Kentucky.

88   "Mother's Day; Dispute over Origin," *North American* [Philadelphia] May 9, 1924.

89   Anna Jarvis to the Secretary of the Federation of Churches in Henderson, telegram, 7 May, 1925, Mother's Day File, Henderson County Public Library, Henderson, Kentucky.

90   The Henderson Women's Club sponsored the Kentucky Legislative resolution officially recognizing Sasseen as the founder of Mother's Day. Anna Jarvis to Mr. and Mrs. Harry Thixton, April 2, 1926, Mother's Day File, Henderson County Public Library, Henderson, Kentucky.

91   Jarvis to Monrad, February 4, 1924, Mother's Day File.

92   Anna Jarvis to city editor, *Detroit Free Press*, August 27, 1938, Anna Jarvis Papers, West Virginia and Regional History Collection, West Virginia University, Morgantown, West Virginia.

93   Wolfe, "The White Carnation," 58.

94   "Don't Be Deceived of a Kentucky Barber," n.d., Mother's Day Collection; and Marguerite H. White, *American War Mothers: Fifty Year History, 1917–1967* (Washington, D.C.: American War Mothers, 1981), 17.

95   "Says 2 Got 500,000 in Eagles' Lottery," *New York Times*, November 30, 1932; and "Not a Cent for Charity," n.d., Anna Jarvis Papers, West Virginia and Regional History Collection, West Virginia University, Morgantown, West Virginia. Hering maintained his innocence throughout the entire trial and appeal process. He claimed ignorance of any legal violations as the management of the fundraising campaign was left to a third party, B. C. McGuire, who was also indicted. Any money he received from the 1931 campaign was based on a contract he signed five years prior when he first agreed to aid the Eagles' Bazaar Department and guaranteed to cover all potential campaign losses with his own money. The federal court found Hering guilty of "causing lottery tickets to be received across state line." Frank E Hering, "The Facts in the Case: A Message from Frank E. Hering" (1932), University of Notre Dame Archives, University of Notre Dame, Notre Dame, Indiana.

96   Anna Jarvis to managing director of WLW Broadcasting Station, Cincinnati, Ohio, November 8, 1934, Anna Jarvis Papers, West Virginia and Regional History Collection, West Virginia University, Morgantown, West Virginia; "Mann Put on Trial on Lottery Charge," *New York Times*, November 29, 1932; and "Mann Found Guilty in Eagles Lottery," *New York Times*, December 4, 1932.

97 Jarvis to managing director, 8 November, 1934, Anna Jarvis Papers; and "Pardon in Eagle Lottery," *New York Times*, November 15, 1933.

98 Bob Hansen, *The Eagles* (Milwaukee, Wisconsin: Fraternal Order of Eagles, 1960), 20; Hering, "The Facts in the Case"; and Vincent Miles to Hon. Marvin McIntyre, 3 January, 1938, Franklin D. Roosevelt Library, Hyde Park, New York.

99 Anna Jarvis to Colonel Howe, November 1, 1934, Anna Jarvis Papers, West Virginia and Regional History Collection, West Virginia University, Morgantown, West Virginia; Anna Jarvis to Attorney George Nordlin, June 12, 1934, Anna Jarvis Papers, West Virginia and Regional History Collection, West Virginia University, Morgantown, West Virginia; and Anna Jarvis to Colonel Conrad H. Mann, April 26, 1934, Anna Jarvis Papers, West Virginia and Regional History Collection, West Virginia University, Morgantown, West Virginia. In his defense, Hering and the Eagles were vocal promoters of a social pension program for impoverished mothers with dependent children and the elderly before the Great Depression. Roosevelt presented him and the F.O.E. with one of the signature pens from the Social Security Act in 1935 in recognition of that early and steadfast support. Hansen, *The Eagles*, 2–7.

100 Anna Jarvis to Governor George White, July 17, 1934, Anna Jarvis Papers, West Virginia and Regional History Collection, West Virginia University, Morgantown, West Virginia; and Jarvis to managing director, November 8, 1934, Anna Jarvis Papers.

101 Wolfe, "The White Carnation," 138.

102 Wolfe, "The White Carnation," 138.

103 Jones, "Mother's Day," 178–180

104 Wolfe, "The White Carnation," 3, 11.

105 Quoted in Schmidt, *Consumer Rites*, 261.

106 Wolfe, "The White Carnation," 157.

107 Jones, "Mother's Day," 190.

108 Wolfe, "The White Carnation," 157.

109 Schmidt, *Consumer Rites*, 245–246.

110 Elizabeth H. Pleck, "Who Are We and Where Do We Come From? Rituals, Families and Identities," *We Are What We Celebrate: Understanding Holidays and Rituals*, ed. Amitai Etzioni and Jared Bloom (New York: New York University Press, 2004), 45.

111 Anna Jarvis to Edward Bok, February 25, 1908, Mother's Day Collection International Mother's Day Shrine, Grafton, West Virginia.

112 Jennifer Scanlon, *Inarticulate Longings: The Ladies' Home Journal, Gender, and the Promise of Consumer Culture* (New York: Routledge, 1995), 4, 20; and Rosenzweig, *The Anchor of My Life*, 26–28.

113 Wolfe, "The White Carnation," 156.

114 Wolfe, "The White Carnation," 156.

115 A lack of primary evidence has made it difficult to confirm the level of actual involvement of the men and women, famous or otherwise, whose names have been linked to the Mother's Day International Association. Wolfe, "The Second Sunday," 66.

116 George Watson to John Wanamaker, May 10, 1913, Gibbons Card File, The Historical Society of Pennsylvania, Philadelphia, Pennsylvania.

117 Watson to Wanamaker, May 10, 1913, Gibbons Card File.

118 Johnson, "How Mother Got Her Day," 19;

119 Johnson, "How Mother Got Her Day," 19; and Wolfe, "The White Carnation," 24, 6.

120 "Mother's Day," *Good Housekeeping*, May 1909, 645

121 G. H. Cilley to John Wanamaker, May 10, 1913, Gibbons Card File, The Historical Society of Pennsylvania, Philadelphia, Pennsylvania; Conwell, *The Romantic Rise of a Great American*, 216; Schmidt, *Consumer Rites*, 268; Wolfe, *Behold Thy Mother*, 294; and Wolfe, "The White Carnation," 4.

122 Certificate of Incorporation Notice, Charleston, West Virginia, December 21, 1912, Anna Jarvis Papers, West Virginia and Regional History Collection, West Virginia University Morgantown, West Virginia; J. T. Mitchell to Anna Jarvis, August 10, 1934, Anna Jarvis Papers, West Virginia and Regional History Collection, West Virginia University, Morgantown, West Virginia; Johnson, "How Mother Got Her Day," 19; "Civic Group to Honor Mother's Day Founder," *Philadelphia Daily News*, May 6, 1949; Wolfe, *Behold Thy Mother*, 196, 208; and Wolfe, "The Second Sunday," 60.

123 Mother's Day International Association, *The All Nation Mother's Day.*

124 John LaCerda Lacarda, "Tragic Founder of Mother's Day," *St. Louis Post Dispatch*, May 14, 1944; and Schmidt, *Consumer Rites*, 269.

125 C. V. Miller to H. S. J. Sickel, March 2, 1950, Clay V. Miller Papers, West Virginia and Regional History Collection, West Virginia University; Mother's Day International Association, *The All Nation Mother's Day*; Wolfe, *Behold Thy Mother*, 208, 260; Wolfe, "The Second Sunday, 51; and Wolfe, "The White Carnation," 8, 178.

126 Wolfe, "The White Carnation," 178–179.

127 Wolfe, "The White Carnation," 178–179.

128 Joan Brock, "Local Grandmother Helped in the Creation of Mother's Day," *The News and Observer [Raleigh, NC]* (n.d), Mother's Day Collection, International Mother's Day Shrine, Grafton, West Virginia.

129 Anna Jarvis to John Wanamaker, 29 April, 1922, Gibbons Card Files, The Historical Society of Pennsylvania, Philadelphia, Pennsylvania.

130 "PRESIDENT WILSON DID NOT ESTABLISH MOTHER'S DAY," n.d., Mother's Day Collection, International Mother's Day Shrine, Grafton, West Virginia; and Mother's Day International Association,

131 Wolfe, "The White Carnation," 79–82; Governor Woodrow Wilson to Anna Jarvis, May 1, 1911; "PRESIDENT WILSON DID NOT ESTABLISH MOTHER'S DAY," ., Mother's Day Collection; and Mother's Day International Association, "FIRST FEDERAL LEGISLATION FOR DISPLAY OF THE AMERICAN FLAG WAS BY A WOMAN FOR HOMES," May 1934, Mother's Day Collection, International Mother's Day Shrine, Grafton, West Virginia.

132 Wolfe, "The White Carnation," 246–248; and Schmidt, *Consumer Rites*, 259.

133 Emphasis added. Quoted in Schmidt, *Consumer Rites*, 256.

134 "TAKING 'THE FLOWER' OUT OF MOTHER'S DAY," n.d., Mother's Day Collection, International Mother's Day Shrine, Grafton, West Virginia.

135 "Second Sunday in May: Mother's Day Finds Promoter of Idea Poor, Hospitalized, and Still Bitter," *Newsweek*, May 8, 1944, 35–36.

136 McNulty, "Miss Anna Jarvis Recounts," 30; "Mother's Day and White Carnations," n.d., Mother's Day Collection, International Mother's Day Shrine, Grafton, West Virginia; Mother's Day International Association, *The Mother's Day Movement*, 10; Johnson, "How Mother Got Her Day," 19–20; Schmidt, *Consumer Rites*, 260; Wolfe, *Behold Thy Mother*, 264; and Wolfe, "The White Carnation," 3, 15, 177–180.

137 "TAKING 'THE FLOWER' OUT OF MOTHER'S DAY," Mother's Day Collection; Wolfe, *Behold Thy Mother*, 264; and Wolfe, "The White Carnation," 179.

138 Mother's Day International Association, *The Mother's Day Movement*, 11; and "TAKING 'THE FLOWER' OUT OF MOTHER'S DAY," Mother's Day Collection.

139 Mother's Day International Association, *The Mother's Day Movement*, 11; "Mother's Day," *New York Times*, May 7, 1922; Johnson, "How Mother Got Her Day," 20; Schmidt, *Consumer Rites*, 268; and Wolfe, "The White Carnation," 68, 177–180.

140 Punctuation added. Anna Jarvis to President Franklin D. Roosevelt [1933?], Franklin D. Roosevelt Library, Hyde Park, New York.

141 Examples of her numerous correspondences with Franklin Roosevelt are used throughout this study. Anna Jarvis to Stephan Early, March 3, 1935, Franklin D. Roosevelt Library, Hyde Park, New York; and Anna Jarvis to President Franklin D. Roosevelt, February 6, 1934, Franklin D. Roosevelt Library, Hyde Park, New York.

142 Dennis, *Red, White, and Blue Letter Days*, 105–106; Schmidt, *Consumer Rites*, 292.

143 Wolfe, "The White Carnation," 179.

144 Wolfe, "The White Carnation," 180.

CHAPTER THREE: "HONOR THY FATHER AND THY MOTHER": THE RIVALRY OF FATHER'S DAY AND PARENTS' DAY

1 42 Cong. Rec. 5971–5974 (daily ed. 9 May, 1908).

2 42 Cong. Rec. 5971–5974 (daily ed. 9 May, 1908).

3 42 Cong. Rec. 5971–5974 (daily ed. 9 May, 1908).

4 42 Cong. Rec. 5971–5974 (daily ed. 9 May, 1908).

5 42 Cong. Rec. 5971–5974 (daily ed. 9 May, 1908); and "Against a Mother's Day," *New York Times*, May 10, 1908.

6 42 Cong. Rec. 5974 (daily ed. 9 May, 1908).

7 42 Cong. Rec. 5974 (daily ed. 9 May, 1908).

8 Leigh Eric Schmidt, *Consumer Rites: The Buying and Selling of American Holidays* (Princeton: Princeton University Press, 1995), 292.

9   Barbara Ehrenreich and Deirdre English, *For Her Own Good: Two Centuries of the Experts' Advice to Women* (New York: Anchor Books, 2005), 231–291; Sonya Michel, "American Women and the Discourse of the Democratic Family in World War II," in *Behind the Lines: Gender and the Two World Wars*, ed. Margaret Randolph Higonnet, Jane Jenson, Sonya Michel, and Margaret Collins Weitz (New Haven: Yale University Press, 1987), 155–167; Jennifer Terry, "'Momism' and the Making of Treasonous Homosexuals," in *"Bad" Mothers: The Politics of Blame in Twentieth Century America*, ed. Molly Ladd-Taylor and Lauri Umansky (New York: New York University Press, 1998), 169–190; and Julia Grant, *Raising Baby by the Book: The Education of American Mothers* (New Haven: Yale University Press, 1998), 161–200.

10 Loren Stephens, "The Ties That Bind," in *The Business of Holidays*, ed. Maud Lavin (New York: The Monacelli Press, 2004), 139.

11 Ralph LaRossa and Jaimie Ann Carboy, "'A Kiss for Mother, a Hug for Dad': The Early 20th Century Parents' Day Campaign," *Fathering* 6, no. 3 (Fall 2008): 249.

12 "Tampering With Mother's Day," n.d., Anna Jarvis Papers, West Virginia and Regional History Collection, West Virginia University, Morgantown, West Virginia; "Mother's Day, Anna Jarvis, Founder, Philadelphia," n.d., Anna Jarvis Papers, West Virginia and Regional History Collection, West Virginia University, Morgantown, West Virginia; and "Trade Vandals," n.d., Anna Jarvis Papers, West Virginia and Regional History Collection, West Virginia University, Morgantown, West Virginia.

13 Stephen M. Frank, *Life with Father: Parenthood and Masculinity in the Nineteenth-Century American North* (Baltimore: John Hopkins University Press, 1998), 117.

14 Frank, *Life with Father*, 37–38.

15 Ralph LaRossa and Donald C. Reitzes, "Continuity and Change in Middle Class Fatherhood, 1925–1939: The Culture-Conduct Connection," *Journal of Marriage and the Family* 55, no. 2 (May 1993): 456.

16 Robert L. Griswold, *Fatherhood in America* (New York: Basic Books, 1993), 10–33; and Shawn Johansen, *Family Men: Middle-Class Fatherhood in the Early Industrializing America* (New York: Routledge, 2001), 1–16.

17 Frank, *Life with Father*, 9–14; John R. Gillis, *A World of Their Own Making: Myth, Ritual, and the Quest for Family Values* (Cambridge: Harvard University Press, 1996), 6, 183–190; Sharon Hays, *The Cultural Contradictions of Motherhood* (New Haven: Yale University Press, 1996), 26–28; Mary Ann Mason, *From Father's Property to Children's Rights: The History of Child Custody in the United States* (New York: Columbia University Press, 1994), 6; Ralph LaRossa, *The Modernization of Fatherhood: A Social and Political History* (Chicago: University of Chicago Press, 1997), 24–26; and Laurel Thatcher Ulrich, *Good Wives: Image and Reality in the Lives of Women in Northern New England, 1650–1750* (New York: Vintage Books, 1991), 153–155.

18 Daniel Beekman, *The Mechanical Baby: A Popular History of the Theory and Practice of Child Raising* (Westport: Lawrence Hill and Company, 1977), 77;

19 Daniel Beekman, *The Mechanical Baby*, 73; Frank, *Life with Father*, 15–16, 22; Gillis, *A World of Their Own Making*, 187–188; Hays, *The Cultural Contradictions*, 29–35; Maxine Margolis, *Mothers and Such: Views of American Women and Why They Changed* (Berkeley: University of California Press, 1984), 11–39; LaRossa, *The Modernization of Fatherhood*,

27; Jan Lewis, "Mother's Love: The Construction of an Emotion in Nineteenth-Century America," in *Mothers and Motherhood: Readings in American History*, ed. Rima D. Apple and Janet Golden (Columbus: Ohio State University Press, 1997), 52–71; and Mary P. Ryan, *Empire of the Mother: American Writing about Domesticity* (New York: Harrington Park Press, 1985), 45–70.

20   Ehrenreich and English, *For Her Own Good*, 111–154; Frank, *Life with Father*, 36, 55; and Carroll Smith-Rosenberg and Charles Rosenberg, "The Female Animal: Medical and Biological Views of Woman and Her Role in Nineteenth-Century America," *The Journal of American History* 6, no. 2 (September 1973): 332–356.

21   Rima D. Apple, *Mothers and Medicine: A Social History of Infant Feeding 1890–1950* (Madison: The University of Wisconsin Press, 1987), 5.

22   Rima D. Apple, *Perfect Motherhood: Science and Childrearing in America* (New Brunswick: Rutgers University Press, 2006), 11–33; and Sheila M. Rothman, *Woman's Proper Place: A History of Changing Ideals and Practices, 1870 to the Present* (New York: Basic Books, 1978), 98–106, 135–153.

23   Grant, *Raising Baby by the Book*, 57.

24   Peter N. Stearns, *Anxious Parents: A History of Modern Childrearing in America* (New York: New York University Press, 2003), 17–56; and Barbara Beatty, Emily D. Cahan, and Julia Grant, introduction to *When Science Encounters the Child: Education, Parenting, and Child Welfare in 20th Century American*, ed. Barbara Beatty, Emily D. Cahan, and Julia Grant (New York: Teachers College Press, 2006), 1–15. For an overview of the changing perceptions of children as economically useful in the nineteenth century to sentimentally priceless in the twentieth century, see Viviana A. Zelizer, *Pricing the Priceless Child: The Changing Social Value of Children* (New Jersey: Princeton University Press, 1994).

25   Apple, *Perfect Motherhood*, 22; and LaRossa, *The Modernization of Fatherhood*, 37.

26   Rima D. Apple, "'Training' the Baby: Mothers' Response to Advice Literature in the First Half of the Twentieth Century," in *When Science Encounters the Child*, 195–214; Grant, *Raising Baby by the Book*, 137–160; Johansen, *Family Men*, 1–16; LaRossa, *The Modernization of Fatherhood*, 144–169; and Jessica Nathanson and Laura Camille Tuley, "Introduction: Knowing Best and Talking Back," in *Mother Knows Best: Talking Back to the "Experts*," ed. Jessica Nathanson and Laura Camille Tuley (Toronto: Demeter Press, 2008), 1–12.

27   Howard Wolfe, "The White Carnation" (1984), 18, Howard Wolfe Collection, International Mother's Day Shrine, Grafton, West Virginia.

28   Wolfe, "The White Carnation" 18.

29   Wolfe, "The White Carnation," 18.

30   Wolfe, "The White Carnation," 18.

31   Robert J. Myers, *Celebrations: The Complete Book of American Holidays* (New York: Doubleday and Company, 1972), 185; and Vicki Smith, "First Father's Day Service," *Martinsburg [WV] Journal*, June 15, 2003.

32   Jane M. Hatch, *The American Book of Days* (New York: The H. W. Wilson Company, 1978), 555, 574; Myers, *Celebrations*, 184; and Schmidt, *Consumer Rites*, 276.

33 Schmidt, *Consumer Rites*, 278–279.

34 Hatch, *The American Book of Days*, 574.

35 Hatch, *The American Book of Days*, 575; and LaRossa, *The Modernization of Fatherhood*, 173.

36 LaRossa, *The Modernization of Fatherhood*, 173.

37 Hatch, *The American Book of Days*, 575.

38 LaRossa, *The Modernization of Fatherhood*, 181–182; and Schmidt, *Consumer Rites*, 278–289.

39 Leigh Eric Schmidt and Ralph LaRossa, to my knowledge, offer the only academic accounts of Father's Day history. The only weakness in LaRossa's study of Father's Day in New York City is the reliance on the *New York Times* holiday coverage as the primary historical source. It was a decision based more on necessity than choice, however, due to a lack of other sources.

40 "This Is Called 'Father's Day:' Official Flower Dandelion," *New York Times*, June 15, 1924.

41 Schmidt, *Consumer Rites*, 283.

42 "Father's Day Dawns—Over his Protest: Ties and Cigars to Be His Lot, Then Obscurity," *New York Times*, June 19, 1927.

43 Gillis, *A World of Their Own Making*, 179–200; Griswold, *Fatherhood in America*, 88–118; and LaRossa, *The Modernization of Fatherhood*, 1–20.

44 Ann Hulbert, *Raising American: Experts, Parents and a Century of Advice About Children* (New York: Alfred A. Knopf, 2003), 36–37.

45 Grant, *Raising Baby by the Book*, 174–175.

46 Gillis, *A World of Their Own Making*, 193; LaRossa, *The Modernization of Fatherhood*, 39; and Stearns, *Anxious Parents*, 4, 57.

47 Frank, *Life with Father*, 114–116, 120–132.

48 Frank, *Life with Father*, 81.

49 Christina Hardyment, *Dream Babies: Child Care from Locke to Spock* (London: Oxford University Press, 1983), 186.

50 The following sources provide a fuller discussion of the influence of Dr. John Watson and his model of child rearing: Apple, *Perfect Motherhood*, 83–106; Beekman, *The Mechanical Baby*, 134–153; Hardyment, *Dream Babies*, 159–214; Ehrenreich and English, *For Her Own Good*, 210–230; Hulbert, *Raising America*, 122–153; and Margolis, *Mothers and Such*, 51–61.

51 "Father's Day," *New York Times,* June 19, 1938; and LaRossa, *The Modernization of Fatherhood*, 136.

52 Schmidt, *Consumer Rites*, 280.

53 Schmidt, *Consumer Rites*, 280–281.

54 Anna Jarvis to Daniel Heefner, August 2, 1934, Anna Jarvis Papers, West Virginia and Regional History Collection, West Virginia University, Morgantown, West Virginia.

55 LaRossa, *The Modernization of Fatherhood*, 181–188; and Schmidt, *Consumer Rites*, 286–290.

56 Wolfe, "The White Carnation," 180; and Schmidt, *Consumer Rites*, 290.

57 LaRossa, *The Modernization of Fatherhood*, 188–191; and Schmidt, *Consumer Rites*, 289.

58 Schmidt, *Consumer Rites*, 289.

59 Apple, *Perfect Motherhood*, 50; Molly Ladd-Taylor, *Mother-Work: Women, Child Welfare, and the State, 1890–1930* (Urbana: University of Illinois Press, 1995), 84; LaRossa, *The Modernization of Fatherhood,* 46; and Richard A. Meckel, *Save the Babies: American Public Health Reform and the Prevention of Infant Mortality, 1850–1929* (Ann Arbor: University of Michigan Press, 1990), 143, 154.

60 LaRossa, *The Modernization of Fatherhood*, 45–55.

61 Elaine Tyler May, *Homeward Bound: American Families in the Cold War Era* (New York: Basic Books, 1988), 146.

62 May, *Homeward Bound*, 146.

63 Kathleen W. Jones, "Mother Made Me Do It: Mother-Blaming and the Women of Child Guidance," in *"Bad" Mothers,* 107.

64 Julia Grant, "Bringing Up Boys: Science, Popular Culture, and Gender," in *When Science Encounters the Child*, 215–225; Grant, *Raising Baby by the Book*, 161–200; Ehrenreich and English, *For Her Own Good*, 231–291; Griswold, *Fatherhood in America*, 95–118; and Terry, "'Momism,'" 169–190.

65 LaRossa, *The Modernization of Fatherhood*, 143.

66 Terry, "'Momism,'" 169–190; and May, *Homeward Bound*, 116–117.

67 LaRossa, *The Modernization of Fatherhood*, 171. See also Ralph LaRossa, Charles Jaret, Malati Gadgil, and G. Robert Wynn, "The Changing Culture of Fatherhood in Comic-Strip Families: A Six-Decade Analysis," *Journal of Marriage and Family* 62, no. 2 (May 2000): 375–387.

68 "Tampering with Mother's Day," Anna Jarvis Papers,

69 "Women: Mother's Day, Inc," *Time*, 16 May, 1938.

70 In their research on Parents' Day, Ralph LaRossa and Jaimie Ann Carboy relied mainly on the *New York Times* coverage of the holiday. They were unable to find any archival material pertaining to the Parents' Day campaign.

71 "Fewer Poor Fed At Mission Feasts," *New York Times*, December 26, 1919; and "To Play Santa to 2,000," *New York Times*, December 25, 1921.

72 "Drop Mother's Day Plans," *New York Times*, May 13, 1923; "Many Celebrations Mark Mothers' Day," *New York Times*, May 14, 1923; and "Mother's Day, Anna Jarvis, Founder, Philadelphia," Anna Jarvis Papers.

73 John LaCarda, "Mother of Mother's Day," *Coronet*, May 1945.

74 "Walker to Deliver Tribute to Parents," *New York Times*, May 1, 1932; and "Uncle Robert, 77, is Soon to Retire," *New York Times*, April 10, 1940.

75 LaRossa and Carboy assert that Spero's concerted effort to never mention Father's Day in association with his celebration of fatherhood was a means to avoid another legal entanglement over claims of copyright infringement. "A Kiss for Mom, a Hug for Dad," 252.

76 Wolfe, "The White Carnation," 169.

77 "Mother's Day, Anna Jarvis, Founder, Philadelphia," Anna Jarvis Papers.

78 "Mystery in a Suicide," *New York Times*, August 26, 1900; "To Play Santa to 2000," *New York Times*, December 25, 1921; "Get Church's Aid for Parents' Day," *New York Times*, March 8, 1926; "Parents' Day Fete Today on the Mall," *New York Times*, May 11, 1930; "Parents' Instead of Mother's Day is Celebrated by 15,000 on Mall," *New York Times*, May 13, 1935; "Uncle Robert, 77, is Soon to Retire," *New York Times*, April 10, 1940; and "Robert Spero, 86, Children's Friend," *New York Times*, December 14, 1948.

79 "Mother's Day, Anna Jarvis, Founder, Philadelphia," Anna Jarvis Papers; and Wolfe, "The White Carnation," 168.

80 Anna Jarvis to New York State Senator John McCall, February 4, 1933, Anna Jarvis Papers, West Virginia and Regional History Collection, West Virginia University, Morgantown, West Virginia.

81 Anna Jarvis to New York State Senator John McCall, February 4, 1933, Anna Jarvis Papers, West Virginia and Regional History Collection, West Virginia University, Morgantown, West Virginia.

82 "Get Church's Aid for Parents' Day," *New York Times*, March 8, 1926.

83 "Honors to Mothers Shared by Fathers," *New York Times*, May 10, 1926.

84 Beekman, *The Mechanical Baby*, 145–153; Hardyment, *Dream Babies*, 72–86, 165-195; and Hulbert, *Raising America*, 126.

85 LaRossa, *The Modernization of Fatherhood*, 272.

86 "Get Church's Aid for Parents' Day," *New York Times*, March 8, 1926; and "Uncle Robert, 77, is Soon to Retire," *New York Times*, April 10, 1940. His statement lends itself to a host of questions, especially if Jarvis's accusations of Spero's hidden business interests are true. To add to the discussion, in 1921 the *New York Times* reported Spero's recent urging for Mother's Day to become a gift giving day. "To Play Santa to 2, 000," *New York Times*, December 25, 1921.

87 Steven Schlossman, "Perils of Popularization: The Founding of Parents' Magazine," in *History and Research in Child Development*, ed. Alice Boardman Smuts and J. W. Hagen (Chicago: University of Chicago Press, 1986), 66; and LaRossa, *The Modernization of Fatherhood*, 121. A Hecht biography published by *Parents Magazine* gave him credit for helping raise an estimated 137 million children through his magazine as of 1975, the date of the biography's publication. The publication also claimed that *Parents Magazine*, as of 1975, was the only magazine fully dedicated to issues of child rearing and family life. Parents Magazine, *George Joseph Hecht: A Lifelong Commitment to Children*, ([S.I]: Parents Magazine Press,1975), 5, 9.

88 George Hecht, "Why Not Parents' Day?" *Children: The Magazine for Parents*, May 1929, 16. The title changed to *Parents Magazine* in the 1930s.

89 "Says Mothers Favor Day for Both Parents," *New York Times*, January 26, 1930.

90   LaRossa and Carboy, "A Kiss for Mom, a Hug for Dad," 253.

91   LaRossa and Carboy, "A Kiss for Mom, a Hug for Dad," 245–247; and "Uncle Robert Grati-fied," *New York Times*, April 5, 1936. The May 10 and May 11 coverage of the rally does not mention if Farley was actually in attendance.

92   "Uncle Robert Gratified," *New York Times*, April 5, 1936; "Honor to Parents to Be Paid Today," *New York Times*, May 10, 1936; LaRossa and Carboy, "A Kiss for Mom, a Hug for Dad," 244; and "Parents' Instead of Mother's Day is Celebrated by 15,000 on Mall," *New York Times*, May 13, 1935.

93   LaRossa, *The Modernization of Fatherhood*, 123.

94   LaRossa, *The Modernization of Fatherhood*, 118–133.

95   LaRossa and Carboy, "A Kiss for Mom, a Hug for Dad," 246.

96   Anna Jarvis to New York Governor Franklin D. Roosevelt, January 26, 1932, Anna Jarvis Papers, West Virginia and Regional History Collection, West Virginia University, Mor-gantown, West Virginia; Anna Jarvis to New York State Senator Duncan T. O'Brien, Feb-ruary 4, 1933, Anna Jarvis Papers, West Virginia and Regional History Collection, West Virginia University, Morgantown, West Virginia; Anna Jarvis to New York State Senator John McCall, February 5, 1933, Anna Jarvis Papers, West Virginia and Regional History Collection, West Virginia University, Morgantown, West Virginia; Anna Jarvis to Presi-dent Franklin D. Roosevelt, April 12, 1940, Franklin D. Roosevelt Library, Hyde Park, New York; and Wolfe, "The White Carnation," 60.

97   "Father Gets Share of Mother's Day: Recent Emphasis on Honor Due to Both Causes Sev-eral Ambiguous Celebrations," *New York Times*, May 9, 1932; and "Honor to Parents to be Paid Today," *New York Times*, May 14, 1933.

98   "In Mr. Whalen's Image," *Time*, May 1, 1939; LaRossa and Carboy, "A Kiss for Mom, a Hug for Dad," 247; and "Fair Stages Fetes For Mother's Day," *New York Times*, May 13, 1940.

99   "Mother's Day is Promoted," *New York Times*, March 2, 1941.

100 Parents Magazine, *George Joseph Hecht*, 1–52; and Schlossman, "Perils of Popularization," 67–72.

101 Parents Magazine, *George Joseph Hecht*, 8.

102 LaRossa and Carboy, "A Kiss for Mom and a Hug for Dad," 249. The growing circulation of *Parents Magazine* served as the foundation of Hecht's personal wealth. Schlossman, "Perils of Popularization," 77. The 1975 biography of George Hecht published by *Parents Magazine* states: "The establishment in 1941 of the National Committee for the Obser-vance of Mother's Day to work for constructive and dignified observance of the Day. Its net receipts from Mother's Day posters are entirely donated to child welfare organiza-tions." *George Joseph Hecht*, 46. By 1960, the National Committee on the Observance of Mother's Day openly coordinated its work with commercial interests, like its Father's Day counterpart. That year, the committee predicted the biggest Mother's Day suc-cess ever, due to the 60 percent increase in the population of mothers since 1940, which included grandmothers and mothers-in-laws expecting gifts. They were also encouraged by fathers enjoying higher salaries than ever and the consumer need to "trade up" in the quality of their gift purchases. "Advertising: Mother's Day Drive is Charted," *New York Times*, March 24, 1960.

103 Without accessible manuscript collections pertaining to Spero, and in the absence of his public criticism of Jarvis, no direct proof exists of Spero's personal feelings regarding her and her efforts to stop his Parents' Day movement. It is nonetheless likely that he did not look upon Jarvis with much favor. There is also no evidence that Spero had children of his own. Strangely enough, Spero was only two years Jarvis's senior, and they died within two months of each other in 1948. Jarvis to Roosevelt, January 26, 1932, Anna Jarvis to O'Brien, February 4, 1933, Anna Jarvis Papers; Jarvis to McCall, February 5, 1933, Anna Jarvis Papers; Anna Jarvis to New Hampshire Governor Francis P. Murphy, April 30, 1938, Anna Jarvis Papers, West Virginia and Regional History Collection, West Virginia University, Morgantown, West Virginia; "Tampering with Mother's Day," Anna Jarvis Papers; "Mother's Day, Anna Jarvis, Founder Philadelphia," Anna Jarvis Papers; "Trade Vandals," Anna Jarvis Papers; Anna Jarvis to President Franklin D. Roosevelt, May 17, 1935, Franklin D. Roosevelt Library, Hyde Park, New York; Jarvis to Roosevelt, April 12, 1940; and Wolfe, "The White Carnation," 60, 62. In an interesting case of the pot calling the kettle black, Jarvis ridiculed Hecht's alleged threat to sue the Parent-Teacher Association for a million dollars if they used *Parents* in the title of their organizational magazine. Jarvis to Roosevelt, April 12, 1940, Franklin D. Roosevelt Library.

104 "Mother's Day, Anna Jarvis, Founder Philadelphia," Anna Jarvis Papers.

105 Anna Jarvis to New York Assemblywoman Marguerite L. Smith, March 23, 1920, Anna Jarvis Papers, West Virginia and Regional History Collection, West Virginia University, Morgantown, West Virginia; New York Assemblywoman Marguerite L. Smith to Anna Jarvis, April 10, 1920, Anna Jarvis Papers, West Virginia and Regional History Collection, West Virginia University, Morgantown, West Virginia; Jeremiah Connor to Anna Jarvis, June 17, 1920, Anna Jarvis Papers, West Virginia and Regional History Collection, West Virginia University, Morgantown, West Virginia; Jarvis to O'Brien, February 4, 1933, Anna Jarvis Papers; and Jarvis to McCall, February 5, 1933, Anna Jarvis Papers.

106 Anna Jarvis to Governor Franklin D. Roosevelt, January 28, 1932, Anna Jarvis Papers, West Virginia and Regional History Collection, West Virginia University, Morgantown, West Virginia.

107 Wolfe, "The White Carnation," 60.

108 Jarvis to Roosevelt, April 12, 1940, Franklin D. Roosevelt Library. Grover Aloysius Whelan headed the planning and execution of the World's Fair.

109 Campbell Gibson, "Population of the 100 Largest Cities and Other Urban Places in the United States: 1790–1990," (working paper, no. 27, Population Division, U.S. Bureau of the Census, Washington, DC, June 1998), accessed on November 6, 2013 at www.census.gov/population/www/documentation/twps0027/twps0027.html.

110 "Mother's Day, Anna Jarvis, Founder Philadelphia," Anna Jarvis Papers.

111 "20,000 in Park Pay Honor to Parents," *New York Times*, May 11, 1936. An interesting connection exists between Parents' Day and educational administrators. Members of New York City's Board of Education, Parent-Teacher Association, and the superintendent of schools were recurrent speakers and invited dignitaries at the annual celebrations. This connection offers a new avenue of exploration in the meaning of parenting when it does not involve the routine labor of childcare but the educational concerns of older children. LaRossa and Carboy, "A Kiss for Mom, a Hug for Dad," 245–246.

112 "What Mothers Think of Mother's Day," *Children: The Magazine for Parents,* May 1927, 29–30.

113 LaRossa, *The Modernization of Fatherhood,* 200.

114 LaRossa, *The Modernization of Fatherhood,* 176; and Myers, *Celebrations,* 187. In 1994, President Bill Clinton advocated for a Parents' Day holiday and signed into law a resolution to create the observance. Although barely recognized, President Clinton designated the fourth Sunday in July as Parents' Day. "Parents' Day History," accessed on November 6, 2013 at www.theparentsday.com/history.html.

115 Stephens, "The Ties That Bind," 140.

CHAPTER FOUR: THE AMERICAN WAR MOTHERS AND A MEMOIR OF MOTHERS' DAY

1 Margaret N. McCluer and Adelaide Riffle, *Memoirs of "Mothers' Day" by American War Mothers: "Mothers' Day" Its Origin and Ways of Observing* (Indianapolis: American War Mothers, 1925), 20–21; "Americans All Give One Day to Mother," *New York Times,* May 13, 1918; and Susan Zeiger, "She Didn't Raise Her Boy to Be a Slacker: Motherhood, Conscription, and the Culture of the First World War," *Feminist Studies* 22, no. 1 (Spring 1996): 31.

2 "Mothers Day for the Boys in France Set for May 12," *Chicago Tribune,* May 3, 1918; and Zeiger, "She Didn't Raise," 33.

3 "Letters to Mothers Flood Mails Here," *New York Times,* June 2, 1918.

4 "From France," *The Alma Signal [KS],* June 20, 1918.

5 42 Cong. Rec. 6235, 6273–6274 (daily ed. May 9, 1918); and "Calls on Nation to Honor Mothers," *New York Times,* May 12, 1918.

6 "Americans All Give One Day to Mother," *New York Times,* May 13, 1918; "Services for Mothers' Day Will Be Held," *San Francisco Chronicle,* May 12, 1918; "Victory Prayers on May 12," *New York Times,* May 5, 1918; "A Plea for Prayer by the Founder of the Women's National Prayer Battalion," *Atlanta Constitution,* May 12, 1918; and "42,000 Soldiers to Pray in Unison," *New York Times,* May 12, 1918.

7 Jean Bethke Elshtain, *Women and War* (New York: Basic Books, 1987), 182–193; Margaret Randolph Higonnet, Jane Jenson, Sonya Michel, and Margaret Collins Weitz, eds., *Behind the Lines; Gender and the Two World Wars* (New Haven: Yale University Press, 1987), 1–17; and Suzanne Evans, *Mothers of Heroes, Mothers of Martyrs: World War I and the Politics of Grief* (Montreal: McGill-Queen's University Press, 2007), 3–12.

8 Zeiger, "She Didn't Raise," 32.

9 Zeiger, "She Didn't Raise," 32–33. A copy of the illustration and text is included in the Zeiger article.

10 Zeiger, "She Didn't Raise," 32–33.

11 Zeiger, "She Didn't Raise," 20–30, 34.

12 Elshtain, *Women and War,* 183–187; and Barbara J. Steinson, "The Mother Half of Humanity: American Women in the Peace and Preparedness Movements in World War I," in

Women, War, and Revolution, ed. Carol R. Berkin and Clara M. Lovett (New York: Holmes and Meier Publishers, 1980), 259–281.

13   "Official History of the American War Mothers," accessed on November 8, 2013, www. americanwarmoms.org.

14   "American War Mothers," [1921?], 8, Alice Moore French Collection, Indiana Historical Society, Indianapolis, Indiana.

15   McCluer and Riffle, *Memoirs of "Mother's Day,"* 27.

16   Linda Schott, "The Woman's Peace Party and the Moral Basis for Women's Pacifism," *Frontiers: A Journal of Women Studies* 8, no. 2 (1985): 19; and Steinson, "The Mother Half of Humanity," 259, 261, 264.

17   Barbara J. Steinson, *American Women's Activism in World War I* (New York: Garland Publishing, 1982), 44; and Steinson, "The Mother Half of Humanity," 263.

18   Steinson, "The Mother Half of Humanity," 263

19   Schott, "The Woman's Peace Party," 21–22; and Steinson, "The Mother Half of Humanity," 263

20   "Protesting Women March in Mourning," *New York Times*, August 30, 1914; and "The Women's Manifestation," *New York Times*, August 30, 1914.

21   Zeiger, "She Didn't Raise," 11–12.

22   Schott, "The Woman's Peace Party," 8; Steinson, *American Women's Activism in World War I*, 17–44, 306–328; and Steinson, "The Mother Half of Humanity," 262–263.

23   Evans, *Mothers of Heroes*, 8.

24   Steinson, *America Women's Activism in World War I*, 180, 210.

25   Quoted in Peter G. Filene, *Him/Her/Self: Gender identities in Modern America* (Baltimore: The Johns Hopkins University Press, 1998), 118.

26   88 Cong. Rec. 4027 (daily ed. May 7, 1942) (statement of Rep. Charles A. Plumley).

27   D'Ann Campbell, *Women at War with America: Private Lives in a Patriotic Era* (Cambridge: Harvard University Press, 1984), 91.

28   "Speed Up Production, The Sullivans Plead," *New York Times*, February 9, 1943

29   "Speed Up Production, The Sullivans Plead," *New York Times*, February 9, 1943; and

30   Elshtain, *Women and War*, 191; and "Speed Up Production, The Sullivans Plead," *New York Times*, February 9, 1943; and "The Sullivan Brothers," accessed on November 9, 2013, www.arlingtoncemetry.net.

31   According to Sonya Michel, "official recognition of the significance of home and family reassured the American public that the society had not lost its grip on the essential values of civilization. Women as mothers were charged with perpetuating the culture that men were fighting for; abandoning this role in wartime would not only upset the gender balance but determine the very core of American society." "American Women and the Discourse of the Democratic Family in World War II," in *Behind the Lines; Gender and the Two World Wars*, ed. Margaret Randolph Higonnet, Jane Jenson, Sonya Michel, and Margaret Collins Weitz (New Haven: Yale University Press, 1987), 160.

32 Leila Rupp, *Mobilizing Women for War: German and American Propaganda 1939–1945* (Princeton: Princeton University Press, 1978), 95–96.

33 Barbara Ehrenreich and Deirdre English, *For Her Own Good: Two Centuries of the Experts' Advice to Women* (New York: Anchor Books, 2005), 258; Jennifer Terry, "'Momism' and the Making of Treasonous Homosexual," in *"Bad" Mothers: The Politics of Blame in the Twentieth-Century America*, ed. Molly Ladd-Taylor and Lauri Umansky (New York: New York University Press, 1998), 175–179; Michel, "American Women," 158; and Susan Douglas and Meredith Michaels, *The Mommy Myth: The Idealization of Motherhood and How It Has Undermined All Women* (New York: Free Press, 2004), 241–242.
      During World War I, 730,000 men (roughly 30 percent) failed to physically qualify for military service, which triggered a new interest in infant and child health programs. Richard A. Meckel, *Save the Babies: American Public Health Reform and the Prevention of Infant Mortality, 1850–1929* (Ann Arbor: The University of Michigan Press, 1990), 201. In 1917, the Indiana War Mothers were asked to support local "Better Baby" Campaigns designed to provide free health checks for infants and child-rearing advice for mothers. The war mothers resented the implication that their sons "were deficient according to up to date standards of human specimens" and refused to grant their endorsement. According to founder Alice Moore French, every member knew that her son was perfect and certainly worthy to be the country's "vanguard of safety in the terrible war." "American War Mothers," 5, Alice Moore French Collection.

34 Michel, "American Women," 164.

35 Rupp, *Mobilizing Women for War*, 108.

36 "Mother's Day May 14 Set: President Stresses Grief," *New York Times*, April 27, 1944.

37 Evans, *Mothers of Heroes*, 3–12; and G. Kurt Piehler, "The War Dead and the Gold Star," *Commemorations: The Politics of National Identity*, ed. John R. Gillis (Princeton: Princeton University Press, 1994), 170.

38 Steinson, *American Women's Activism in World War I*, 311–313.

39 Circular letter, [1917?], Alice Moore French Collection, Indiana Historical Society, Indianapolis, Indiana.

40 Circular letter, [1917?], Alice Moore French Collection, Indiana Historical Society, Indianapolis, Indiana.

41 Circular letter, [1917?], Alice Moore French Collection, Indiana Historical Society, Indianapolis, Indiana.

42 "American War Mothers," 3, Alice Moore French Collection; and Marguerite H. White, *American War Mothers: Fifty Year History, 1917–1967* (Washington, DC: American War Mothers, 1981), 2–4.

43 "American War Mothers," 3, Alice Moore French Collection.

44 Circular letter, December 4, 1917, Alice Moore French Collection, Indiana Historical Society, Indianapolis, Indiana.

45 "American War Mothers," 8–20, Alice Moore French Collection. At the first national convention in 1919, the national treasury totaled only $125. White, *American War Mothers*, 5.

46 Estelle Norris Ochiltree, "Brief History of American War Mothers," 1934, Franklin D. Roosevelt Library, Hyde Park, New York. Mothers of children adopted before their fifth birthday and step mothers whose relationship with stepchildren began before their twelfth birthday were eligible for membership. "Official History of the American War Mothers," accessed on November 9, 2013 at www.americanwarmoms.org.

47 "American War Mothers," 14, Alice Moore French Collection.

48 Emphasis added. "Rituals of the American War Mothers" (1928), 24, Digital Collection, Kentucky Historical Society, accessed on November 9, 2013, at www.history.ky.gov.

49 Alice French to County Mothers of Indiana, November 10, 1917, Alice Moore French Collection, Indiana Historical Society, Indianapolis, Indiana.

50 French to County Mothers of Indiana, November 10, 1917, Alice Moore French Collection.

51 "Rituals of the American War Mothers" (1928), 5, Digital Collection, Kentucky Historical Society.

52 White, *American War Mothers*, 12; Ochiltree, "Brief History of the American War Mothers," Franklin D. Roosevelt Library; and "Rituals of the American War Mothers" (1928), 6, Digital Collection, Kentucky Historical Society.

53 "Gold Star Mothers Weep At Inquiry," *New York Times*, April 6, 1923.

54 "McRae Warns of Pacifism: Tells War Mothers to Guard Children From Such Teaching," *New York Times*, November 2, 1927; "Will Back Cruiser Bill," *New York Times*, January 13, 1929; "Opposes Arms Reduction: President of War Mothers Would 'Not Invite Disaster,'" *New York Times*, September 24, 1929; "Women to Debate Ways to End Wars," *New York Times*, January 18, 1931; Ochiltree, "Brief History of the American War Mothers," Franklin D Roosevelt Library; and Piehler, "The War Dead and the Gold Star," 175–177.

55 Mrs. Charles Boll to Franklin D. Roosevelt, April 11, 1936, Franklin D Roosevelt Library, Hyde Park, New York.

56 Boll to Roosevelt, April 11, 1936, Franklin D Roosevelt Library.

57 In 1953, President Dwight D. Eisenhower amended the charter for the last time to include mothers of servicemen and women serving in Korea and any future American war. White, *American War Mothers*, 31, 37.

58 Mrs. E. May Hahn to President Franklin Roosevelt, November 11, 1944, Franklin D. Roosevelt Library, Hyde Park, New York.

59 White, *American War Mothers*, 2, 27; and "Rituals of the American War Mothers" (1928), 25, Digital Collection, Kentucky Historical Society.

60 McCluer and Riffle, *Memoirs of "Mother's Day,"* 26.

61 The cost of room and board at the American War Mother National Memorial Home remained contingent on the individual family's ability to pay. It was not unusual for the organization to defray the cost for 20 percent of those residing at the home. Ochiltree, "Brief History of the American War Mother," Franklin D. Roosevelt Library; and White, *American War Mothers*, 17–18.

62 The popular designation of mothers as "Gold Star Mothers" is also accredited to President Woodrow Wilson. "War Mother's Flag," accessed on November 9, 2013, at www. homeofheroes.com; John W. Graham, *The Gold Star Mother of the 1930s: Overseas Grave*

Visitations by Mothers and Widows of Fallen U.S. World War I Soldiers (North Carolina: McFarland & Company, 2005), 11–25; and Piehler, "The War Dead and the Gold Star," 171.

63   Suzanne Evans compares the American Gold Star mothers to the Canadian Silver Cross mothers, who were commemorated for the same World War I sacrifice. In contrast to the patriotic golden star, she argues, the silver cross symbol did not represent a specific Canadian national identity due to the cross's distinctly religious connotation. See *Mothers of Heroes*, 110-111.

64   "Rituals of the American War Mothers" (1928), 24, Digital Collection, Kentucky Historical Society.

65   In the early twentieth century, the American War Mothers had a small number of Jewish and African American members, as well as two Native American chapters. Piehler, "The War Dead and the Gold Star," 176–177; and White, *American War Mothers*, 30.

66   "Gold Star Woman of 100 Needs a Home," *New York Times*, December 18, 1921.

67   Steinson, American Women's Activism in World War I, 44; Steinson, "The Mother Half of Humanity," 263.

68   McCluer and Riffle, *Memoirs of "Mother's Day,"* 10; "Names Make News," *Time*, May 16, 1932; "Mother's Day Ceremonies From Arlington on Radio," *New York Times*, May 9, 1926; "Mothers' Day Tribute is Paid by Davison," *New York Times*, May 12, 1930; "War Mothers to Gather," *New York Times*, May 3, 1931; "Mothers Honor Unknown Soldier," *New York Times*, May 11, 1931; "War Mothers Hold Arlington Service," *New York Times*, May 15, 1933; Ochiltree, "Basic History of the American War Mothers," Franklin D. Roosevelt Library; and White, *American War Mothers*, 2, 12, 17, 21, 24–28.

69   "Mothers Honored at Nation's Capital," *New York Times*, May 9, 1932; and "Rituals of the American War Mothers" (1928), 24, Digital Collection, Kentucky Historical Society.

70   Mrs. E. May Hahn to President Franklin Roosevelt, May 17, 1944, Franklin D. Roosevelt Library, Hyde Park, New York ; and White, *American War Mothers*, 32-34.

71   Mrs. William E. Ochiltree to President Franklin Roosevelt, April 2, 1934, Franklin D. Roosevelt Library, Hyde Park, New York; President Franklin Roosevelt to Mrs. William E. Ochiltree, April 20, 1934, Franklin D. Roosevelt Library, Hyde Park, New York; Mrs. Howard C. Boone to President Franklin Roosevelt, April 26, 1937, Franklin D. Roosevelt Library, Hyde Park, New York; and Mrs. Irving to President Franklin Roosevelt, March 9, 1938, Franklin D. Roosevelt Library, Hyde Park, New York.

72   Mrs. E. May Hahn to President Franklin Roosevelt, April 23, 1944, Franklin D Roosevelt Library, Hyde Park, New York.

73   The letter was actually drafted for the president by Major B. W. Davenport, but we must assume it reflected the president's true sentiment. Franklin Roosevelt to Mrs. E. May Hahn, May 6, 1944, Franklin D. Roosevelt Library, Hyde Park, New York.

74   White, *American War Mothers*, 29-32.

75   Mrs. E. May Hahn to President Franklin Roosevelt, May 19, 1944, Franklin D. Roosevelt Library, Hyde Park, New York.

76   Howard Wolfe, "The White Carnation," (1984), 125, Howard Wolfe Collection, International Mother's Day Shrine, Grafton, West Virginia.

77 Wolfe, "The White Carnation," (1984), 237, Howard Wolfe Collection.

78 "Protect Tomb of Unknown Soldier," Anna Jarvis Papers, West Virginia and Regional History Collection, West Virginia University, Morgantown, West Virginia.

79 Wolfe, "The White Carnation," 168.

80 "Mothers at Odds on Day," *New York Times*, May 8, 1924.

81 "Mothers' Day Originator Acquitted," *New York Times*, September 14, 1925; Wolfe, "The Second Sunday" (1983), 61, Howard Wolfe Collection, International Mother's Day Shrine, Grafton, West Virginia. It's interesting to note that Jarvis later vehemently denied ever interrupting the AWM conference after a reference to the incident reappeared in a 1938 *Time* article about her Mother's Day work. "Mother's Day, Inc" *Time*, May 16, 1938.

82 "Protect Tomb of Unknown Soldier," Anna Jarvis Papers.

83 Anna Jarvis to President Roosevelt, May 7, 1936, Franklin D Roosevelt Library, Hyde Park, New York.

84 Piehler, "The War Dead and the Gold Star," 177.

85 The federal government racially segregated the trips. Six out of the forty-eight total voyages were designated for African American women. For a detailed history of the pilgrimages, see John W. Graham, *The Gold Star Pilgrimages of the 1930s*; "National Affairs: Gold Star Sailing," *Time*, May 19, 1930; "Plan War Mothers' Tour," *New York Times*, November 7, 1929; Piehler, "The War Dead and the Gold Star," 177–180; Constance Potter, "World War I Gold Star Mothers Pilgrimages, Part I," *The U.S. National Archives and Records Administration* 31, no. 2 (Summer 1999), accessed on November 9, 2013, at www.archives. gov; and White, *American War Mothers*, 21.

86 Wolfe, "The White Carnation," 58.

87 Wolfe, "The White Carnation," 58.

88 McCluer and Riffle, *Memoirs of "Mother's Day,"* 14–23.

89 Charles P. McCann, *Mother's Day Began with the Eagles* [1940?], 1, courtesy of the Fraternal Order of Eagles, Aerie # 4357, Buckhannon, West Virginia; McCluer and Riffle, *Memoirs of "Mother's Day,"* 14; Theodore Marvin Greenhoe, *In Memory, Frank E. Hering, 1874–1943*, [1943?], University of Notre Dame Archives, Notre Dame, Indiana; "The Father of Mothers' Day," *New York Times*, May 9, 1934; and Audrey Boyers Walz, *The Story of Mothers' Day* (Mount Morris, NY: Allied Printing, [1943?]), 3–4.

90 "Symbolism of the American War Mothers Medal," Franklin D. Roosevelt Library, Hyde Park, New York; and White, *American War Mothers*, 17.

91 Wolfe, "The White Carnation," 246–248.

92 Margaret McCluer served as AWM national president between 1923 and 1927. Under her administration, the AWM adopted the white carnation emblem, crowned Frank Hering the "Father of Mothers' Day," and held the first Mother's Day service at the Tomb of the Unknown Soldier. She also coauthored *Memoirs of Mothers' Day*. In 1933, she led the campaign for the Mothers' Day stamp as Chairman of the Commemorative Stamp Committee. Anna Jarvis to George Nordlin (grand worthy president of the Fraternal Order of Eagles), June 12, 1934, Anna Jarvis Papers, West Virginia and Regional History Collection, West

Virginia University, Morgantown, West Virginia; White, *American War Mothers*, 12–14, 24–25; and Wolfe, "The White Carnation," 246.

93   Mrs. W. E. Ochiltree (national president), Mrs. Howard C Boone (national first vice president), and Mrs. H. H. McCluer (general chairman of campaign for funds) to President Roosevelt, January 25, 1934, Franklin D. Roosevelt Library, Hyde Park, New York. Roosevelt was an avid stamp collector whose personal collection reached over one million. During his administration, he approved the issuance of over 150 postal stamps of major and minor significance—including stamps based on his personal sketches. David Greenberg, *Presidential Doodles: Two Centuries of Scribbles, Scratches, Squiggles and Scrawls from the Oval Office* (New York: Basic Books, 2006), 108–109; and "Roosevelt's Stamp Plan," *New York Times*, March 10, 1940.

94   Mr. M. H. McIntyre (assistant secretary to the president) to Mrs. William E. Ochiltree, February 3, 1934, Franklin D. Roosevelt Library, Hyde Park, New York; and Mrs. William E. Ochiltree to Mr. M. H. McIntyre, February 8, 1934, Franklin D. Roosevelt Library, Hyde Park, New York.

95   Mrs. William E. Ochiltree to Mr. M. H. McIntyre, February 8, 1934, Franklin D. Roosevelt Library, Hyde Park, New York.

96   Mrs. William E. Ochiltree to Mr. M. H. McIntyre, February 8, 1934, Franklin D. Roosevelt Library, Hyde Park, New York.

97   Press Release, February 17, 1934, Franklin D. Roosevelt Library, Hyde Park, New York.

98   "Art: Mother's Day Stamp," *Time*, March 19, 1934.

99   78 Cong. Rec. 7735–7736 (daily ed. May 1, 1934); and White, *American War Mothers*, 24–25.

100   White, *American War Mothers*, 25.

101   78 Cong. Rec. 6639 (daily ed. April 16, 1934); and 78 Cong. Rec. 8007 (daily ed. May 3, 1934).

102   Anna Jarvis to Postmaster General Farley, August 7, 1934, Anna Jarvis Papers, West Virginia and Regional History Collection, West Virginia University, Morgantown, West Virginia; and Wolfe, "The White Carnation," 246.

103   "Say 2 Got $500,000 in Eagles' Lottery," *New York Times*, November 30, 1932; "Mann Gets 5 Months for Eagle Lottery," *New York Times*, December 10, 1932; "Pardon in Eagle Lottery," *New York Times*, November 15, 1933; "Not a Cent for Charity," n.d., Anna Jarvis Papers, West Virginia and Regional History Collection, West Virginia University, Morgantown, West Virginia; and Wolfe, "The Second Sunday," 42.

104   Donald M. Reid, "The Symbolism of Postage Stamps: A Source for the Historian," *Journal of Contemporary History* 19, no. 2 (April 1984): 229.

105   78 Cong. Rec. 7736 (daily ed. May 1, 1934); Fred Reinfeld, *Commemorative Stamps of the U.S.A.* (New York: Thomas Y. Crowell Company, 1954), 106; "Whistler's Mother Postage Stamp," accessed on November 9, 2013 at www.stampcenter.com; and "WOMEN: Promotion," *Time*, May 21, 1934.

106   Anna Jarvis to Louis McHenry Howe, February 19, 1934, Anna Jarvis Papers, West Virginia and Regional History Collection, West Virginia University, Morgantown, West Virginia.

NOTES

107 She also ridiculed Farley's praise of James Whistler and his mother as admirable American figures, since Whistler was alleged to be distinctly anti-American and his mother lived abroad for twenty-five years. Anna Jarvis to Mr. Beverly King and Mr. Max John, June 18, 1934, Anna Jarvis Papers, West Virginia and Regional History Collection, West Virginia University, Morgantown, West Virginia; Anna Jarvis to Daniel Heefner, August 2 and August 3, 1934, Anna Jarvis Papers, West Virginia and Regional History Collection, West Virginia University, Morgantown, West Virginia; Anna Jarvis to Postmaster General Farley, August 7, 1934, Anna Jarvis Papers, West Virginia and Regional History Collection, West Virginia University, Morgantown, West Virginia; and Wolfe, "The White Carnation," 86, 246–248, 169.

108 Wolfe, "The White Carnation," 246–278.

109 White, *American War Mothers*, 3.

110 Anna Jarvis to President Franklin Roosevelt, April 19, 1938, Franklin D. Roosevelt Library, Hyde Park, New York.

111 Wolfe, "The White Carnation," 82–83.

112 Norman Kendall, *Mothers Day: A History of Its Founding and Its Founder* (Grafton, West Virginia: D. Grant Smith, 1937), 45.

CHAPTER FIVE: A NEW MOTHER'S DAY FOR MODERN MOTHERS

1 The Golden Rule Foundation, Observing Mothers Day the Golden Rule Way, (New York: The Golden Rule Foundation, 1933), 1. The Golden Rule Foundation used the non possessive plural spelling of Mothers Day though this pamphlet.

2 77 Cong. Rec. 2615 (daily ed. May 1, 1933).

3 77 Cong. Rec. 2615 (daily ed. May 1, 1933).

4 Although the Golden Rule Foundation was the parent organization of the American Mothers Committee, the two entities did not consistently view the annual Mother's Day campaign in the same way. Consequently, I do not use the two groups interchangeably. I am careful to refer to the Golden Rule Foundation when addressing the larger activities of the foundation and refer to the American Mothers Committee when specifically discussing its role within the Golden Rule Foundation and within the larger study of the holiday's history and relationship with Jarvis.

5 "Another 'Day,'" *New York Times*, May 1, 1931; and "Club Women Support Maternity Aid Drive," *New York Times*, May 9, 1931.

6 Howard Wolfe, "The White Carnation" (1984), 1, Howard Wolfe Collection, International Mother's Day Shrine, Grafton, West Virginia.

7 "Mothers Honor Unknown Soldier: Miss Jarvis, Founder of Mother's Day, Protests Ways in which it is Exploited," *New York Times*, May 11, 1931.

8 Anna Jarvis to President Franklin D. Roosevelt, 18 April, 1933, Franklin D. Roosevelt Library, Hyde Park, New York. Additional dates in which President Roosevelt received direct appeals from Anna Jarvis concerning the topic of philanthropic organizations: April 18, 1933, April 29, 1933, May 3, 1933, February 6, 1934, April 24, 1934, April 27, 1934,

204

March 7, 1935, March 21, 1935, April 4, 1935, April 22, 1935, April 15, 1936, March 18, 1938, April 8, 1938, April 18, 1938. Anna Jarvis to President Franklin D. Roosevelt, letters, Franklin D. Roosevelt Library, Hyde Park, New York.

9   Jarvis to Roosevelt, March 21, 1935, Franklin D. Roosevelt Library; and Jarvis to Roosevelt, April 15, 1936, Franklin D. Roosevelt Library.

10 Lyman L. Pierce, "Philanthropy- A Major Big Business," *The Public Opinion Quarterly* (January 1938): 140–141.

11 Lyman L. Pierce, "Philanthropy- A Major Big Business," *The Public Opinion Quarterly* (January 1938): 140–141.

12 Charles V. Vickrey, *The Golden Rule Book* (New York: The Golden Rule Foundation, 1933), 2, 19, 27.

13 Vickrey, *The Golden Rule Book*, 65.

14 Vickrey, *The Golden Rule Book*, 59–71, 93–127.

15 Vickrey, *The Golden Rule Book*, 48–49.

16 Anna Jarvis depicted Charles Vickrey as a salaried promoter of the Golden Rule Foundation. Throughout the 1930s and 1940s, however, Vickrey served as the primary voice of the foundation. The Golden Rule Foundation, *Observing Mothers Day the Golden Rule Way* (New York: The Golden Rule Foundation, 1933)1; and Howard Wolfe, "The White Carnation" (1984), 59, Howard Wolfe Collection, International Mother's Day Shrine, Grafton, West Virginia.

17 The Golden Rule Foundation, *Observing Mothers Day*, 13.

18 "Mother's Day Fund Planned for Needy," *New York Times*, March 3, 1931; and The Golden Rule Foundation, *Observing Mothers Day*, 12–20.

19 Governor Franklin Roosevelt officially endorsed the 1931 drive as well. Other supporters included progressive reformers Jane Addams and Lillian Wald, who served on the GRF National Mothers Day Committee. "Governor Endorses Movement for Wider Mother's Day Fete," *New York Times*, March 2, 1931; "Mother's Day Fund Planned for Needy," *New York Times*, March 3, 1931; "Asks Aid For Needy on Mother's Day," *New York Times*, March 27, 1931; and "Asks Aid for Needy on Mother's Day," *New York Times*, May 11, 1931.

20 Lillian D. Poling, *Mothers of Men: A Twenty-Five Year History of the American Mothers of the Year, 1935–1959* (Bridgeport, CT: Kurt H. Volk, 1959), 10–12.

21 Poling, *Mothers of Men*, 10–12.

22 Poling, *Mothers of Men*, 11.

23 Poling, *Mothers of Men*, 15.

24 The annual award was also known as the "Typical American Mother Award." "Typical Mother Broadcasts Plea," *New York Times*, May 13, 1935

25 Poling, *Mothers of Men*, 14–15; and "Typical Mother Broadcasts Plea," *New York Times*, May 13, 1935.

26 Between 1935 and 1959, the majority of recipients were white, middleclass, college educated members of a Christian denomination. The AMC selected its first African American

recipient in 1946, its first Native American recipient in 1950, and its first Asian American recipient in 1952. The range of recipients also included women of the Mormon and Jewish faith, women who never completed high school, and women who represented a full range of careers from housewife to the first female judge in the state of Massachusetts. Each recipient was active in community service with most pertaining to social causes involving women and children. Poling, *Mothers of Men*, 14–65.

27   Wolfe, "The White Carnation," 59.

28   Wolfe, "The White Carnation," 60.

29   Anna Jarvis to First Lady Eleanor Roosevelt, May 14, 1935, Anna Jarvis Papers, West Virginia and Regional History Collection, West Virginia University, Morgantown, West Virginia; and Wolfe, "The White Carnation," 58–64, 168.

30   Wolfe, "The White Carnation," 58–64, 246.

31   Jarvis to Roosevelt, April 29, 1933, Franklin D. Roosevelt Library, Hyde Park, New York.

32   Jarvis to Roosevelt, April 29, 1933, Franklin D. Roosevelt Library. William A Pearson, the Dean of Hahnemann Medical College of Philadelphia sent a telegram to the President Roosevelt requesting him to not sign the resolution on behalf of Jarvis. Pearson to Roosevelt, telegram, May 3, 1933, Franklin D. Roosevelt Library, Hyde Park, New York.

33   President Franklin D. Roosevelt, statement concerning Mother's Day, May 7, 1935, Franklin D Roosevelt Library, Hyde Park, New York; Franklin D. Roosevelt, *The Public Papers and Addresses of Franklin D. Roosevelt: The Advance of Recovery and Reform* (New York: Russell and Russell, 1934), 3:211–212; and Franklin D. Roosevelt, *The Papers and Addresses of Franklin D. Roosevelt: The Court Disapproves* (New York: Russell and Russell, 1935), 4:169.

34   Sara Delano Roosevelt served as Honorary Chairwoman of the American Mothers Committee until her death in 1941. Charles V. Vickrey to President Roosevelt, March 31, 1942, Franklin D. Roosevelt Library, Hyde Park, New York; and Poling, *Mothers of Men*, 10.

35   "Charity Charlatans," n.d., Anna Jarvis Papers, West Virginia and Regional History Collection, West Virginia University, Morgantown, West Virginia.

36   Jarvis to Roosevelt, April 24, 1934, Franklin D. Roosevelt Library; and Wolfe, "The White Carnation," 168.

37   North Dakota Governor William Langer to Honorable Judge Davies, May 2, 1934, Mother's Day Collection, International Mother's Day Shrine, Grafton, West Virginia; Howard Wolfe, "The Second Sunday" (1983), 66, 85, Howard Wolfe Collection, International Mother's Day Shrine, Grafton, West Virginia; and Wolfe, "The White Carnation," 11.

38   Jarvis to Roosevelt, April 27, 1934, Franklin D. Roosevelt Library.

39   Jarvis to Roosevelt, April 27, 1934, Franklin D. Roosevelt Library.

40   Charles V. Vickrey to Stephan Early, June 12, 1933, Franklin D. Roosevelt Library, Hyde Park, New York.

41   Poling, *Mothers of Men*, 12

42   Poling, *Mothers of Men*, 12. Jarvis never mentioned the American Mothers Committee by name during her battles with Vickrey and the Golden Rule Foundation. And she did

not live to see the American Mothers Committee's independent incorporation as the American Mothers, Inc., or the perpetuation of its annual maternal award. Moreover, Jarvis never learned of the American Mothers' official designation and promotion as the national sponsors of Mother's Day. Yet the American Mothers at least granted full credit to Ann Reeves Jarvis and Anna Jarvis as the original founders of Mother's day, unlike the American War Mothers. It is interesting to note, however, that the modern American Mothers, Inc., confuses Anna Jarvis with her mother on its official website. "History of AMI," accessed on November 11, 2013 at www.americanmothers.org.

43 Puerperal septicemia results from a bacterial infection of open wounds within the birth canal or uterus after childbirth. Kristen Barker, "Birthing and Bureaucratic Women: Needs Talk and the Definitional Legacy of the Sheppard-Towner Act," *Feminist Studies* 29, no. 2 (Summer 2003): 333; The Maternity Center Association, *Maternity Center Association, 1918–1943* (New York, 1943), 20; The Maternity Center Association, *Maternity Center Association Log, 1915–1975* (New York, 1975), 5–6; Esme J. Howard, "Navigating the Stormy Sea: The Maternity Center Association and the Development of Prenatal Care 1900–1903" (master's thesis, Yale University School of Nursing, 1994), 0–11; Richard A. Meckel, *Save the Babies: American Public Health Reform and Prevention of Infant Mortality, 1850–1929* (Ann Arbor: The University of Michigan Press, 1990), 161–165; and Sarah Twerdon, "The Maternity Center Association as a Vehicle for the Education of Motherhood," (master's thesis, Columbia University, 1947), 5–8.

44 Kriste Lindenmeyer, *"A Right to Childhood": The U.S. Children's Bureau and Child Welfare 1912–46* (Urbana: University of Illinois Press, 1997), 65; and Meckel, *Save the Babies,* 202–204.

45 Perkins wrote instructions to her husband on what to name the baby, in case she did not survive. Kristin Downey, *The Woman Behind the New Deal: The Life of Frances Perkins, FDR's Secretary of Labor and His Moral Conscience* (New York: Doubleday, 2009), 67–71; Howard, "Navigating the Stormy Sea," 23; George Martin, *Madam Secretary Frances Perkins* (Boston: Houghton Mifflin Company, 1976), 133–135; and The Maternity Center Association, *Maternity Center Association Log, 1915-1975,* 6.

46 Howard, "Navigating the Stormy Sea," 29; The Maternity Center Association, *Maternity Center Association Log, 1915–1975,* 7; and Twerdon, "The Maternity Center Association," 11.

47 Arlene W. Keeling, *Nursing and the Privilege of Prescription, 1893–2000* (Columbus: Ohio State University Press, 2007), 1–27.

48 Laura E. Ettinger, *Nurse-Midwifery: The Birth of a New American Profession* (Columbus: Ohio State University Press, 2006), 77.

49 Through its single center, the association conducted prenatal and postnatal clinics, supplemented hospital nursing services, provided twenty-four hour nursing supervision to mothers who delivered at home, and conducted maternal education courses. Howard, "Navigating the Stormy Sea," 29; The Maternity Center Association, *Maternity Center Association Log, 1915-1975,* 7–8; and Twerdon, "The Maternity Center Association," 11.

50 Lindenmeyer, *"A Right to Childhood,"* 64, 72; Alisa Klaus, *Every Child a Lion: The Origins of Maternal and Infant Health Policy in the United States and France, 1890-1920* (Ithaca: Cornell University Press, 1993), 16, 51; Meckel, *Save the Babies,* 122, 201; and Sheila M. Rothman, *Woman's Proper Place: A History of Changing Ideals and Practices, 1870 to the Present*

(New York: Basic Books, 1978), 135–153. The following sources provide detailed discussions of the tenets of scientific motherhood: Rima Apple, *Perfect Motherhood: Science and Childrearing in America* (New Brunswick: Rutgers University Press, 2006), 34–55; Rima Apple, "Constructing Mothers: Scientific Motherhood in the Nineteenth and Twentieth Centuries," in *Mothers and Motherhood*, ed. Rima Apple and Janet Goldman (Columbus: Ohio State University Press, 1997), 90–110; Daniel Beekman, *The Mechanical Baby: A Popular History of the Theory and Practice of Child Raising* (Westport, Connecticut: Lawrence Hill and Company, 1977), 109–205; Barbara Ehrenreich and Deirdre English, *For Her Own Good: Two Centuries of the Experts' Advice to Women* (New York: Anchor Books, 2005), 215–230; Christina Hardyment, *Dream Babies* (Oxford: Oxford University Press, 1984), 89–222; Sharon Hays, *The Cultural Contradictions of Motherhood* (New Haven, CT: Yale University Press, 1996), 19–50, 44; and Maxine L. Margolis, *Mothers and Such: Views of American Women and Why They Changed* (Berkeley: University of California Press, 1985), 11–107.

51 Barker, "Birthing and Bureaucratic Women," 348–352; Lindenmeyer, *"A Right to Childhood,"* 97–99; Rothman, *Woman's Proper Place*, 136–142; Molly Ladd-Taylor, *Mother-Work: Women, Child Welfare and the State, 1890–1930* (Urbana: University of Illinois Press, 1995), 167–196.

52 C. E. A. Winslow, *The Public Health Nurse: Children's Year Leaflet, No. 6* (Washington, DC: Government Printing Office, 1918), 5.

53 The Maternity Center Association, *Routines for Maternity Nursing and Briefs for Mothers' Club Talks* (New York, 1935).

54 The Maternity Center Association, *Routines for Maternity Nursing and Briefs*, 21.

55 Anne A. Stevens, "The Work of the Maternity Center Association," (paper, Transaction's 10th Annual Meeting, American Child Hygiene Association, Asheville, NC November 1919), accessed on November 11, 2013 at http://womhist.binghamton.edu/wccny/doc11.htm.

56 Howard, "Navigating the Stormy Sea," 10.

57 Howard, "Navigating the Stormy Sea," 28–52; and Twerdon, "The Maternity Center Association," 36–46.

58 Howard, "Navigating the Stormy Sea," 28–52; Keeling, *Nursing and the Privilege of Prescription*, 1–27; and Twerdon, "The Maternity Center Association," 36–46.

59 The Maternity Center Association, *Routines for Maternity Nursing*, 49.

60 Ettinger, *Nurse-Midwifery*, 77; Howard, "Navigating the Stormy Sea," 28–43; The Maternity Center Association, *Maternity Center Association Log, 1915–1975*, 11; The Maternity Center Association, *Routines for Maternity Nursing*, 49–83; and Twerdon, "The Maternity Center Association," 11, 44. Twerdon claims that the MCA actually disturbed a total of 120 million copies of *Twelve Helpful Hints* to prospective mothers, schools, libraries, and social agencies throughout the country by 1930.

61 Ettinger, *Nurse-Midwifery*, 76–83; and The Maternity Center Association, *Maternity Center Association Log, 1915–1975*, 12.

62 Rothman, *Woman's Proper Place*, 142–143.

63 Ladd-Taylor, *Mother-Work*, 167–196; and Robyn Muncy, *Creating A Female Dominion in*

American Reform 1890–1935 (New York: Oxford University Press, 1991), 124–157; and Rothman, *Woman's Proper Place*, 142–153.

64 The dispute between the AMA and what historians have defined as the "female dominion" within the child welfare and public health movement was, in part, a clash of professional codes. Although both rested their authority on claims of scientific knowledge, the male-dominated AMA sought to broaden its profit margin and hoard its medical expertise. In comparison, the female professionals leading the maternal and infant health campaigns were especially service-oriented and dedicated to popularizing medical knowledge through education and cooperation with experts in a broad range of medical and nonmedical fields. See Muncy, *Creating A Female Dominion*, 136–141.

65 Ettinger, *Nurse-Midwifery*, 72–102.

66 "A Pink Carnation—or a Life on Mother's Day?," *New York Times*, May 12, 1929.

67 The Maternity Center Association, *Maternity Center Association, 1918–1943*, 9–12.

68 "The Mother's Day Campaign," *American Journal of Nursing* 31, no. 7 (July 1931): 839; and "Fathers to Aid Mothers," *New York Times*, May 9, 1931. See also, "Another 'Day,'" *New York Times*, May 1, 1931; and "The Maternity Centre Luncheon," *New York Times*, May 3, 1931.

69 Howard, "Navigating the Stormy Sea," 21; and The Maternity Center Association, *Maternity Center Association, 1918–1943*, 9.

70 "Saving Mothers from Unnecessary Deaths," *American Journal of Nursing* 34, no. 3 (March 1934): 272.

71 "Mother's Day," *American Journal of Nursing* 31, no. 4 (August 1931): 449; and Norman F. Kendall, *Mother's Day: A History of its Founding and its Founder* (Grafton, WV: D. Grant Smith, 1937), 8.

72 Mary Krech to Miss Marguerite Le Hand, April 15, 1935 (provides listing of committee members and officers on MCA letterhead), Franklin D. Roosevelt Library, Hyde Park, New York; The Maternity Center Association, *Maternity Center Association, 1918–1943*, 82–84; and The Maternity Center Association, *Routines for Maternity Nursing*, 1.

73 Martin, *Madam Secretary Frances Perkins*, 134.

74 The Maternity Center Association, *Maternity Center Association, 1918–1943*, 10; The Maternity Center Association, *The Story of the New Mother's Day* (New York 1935), 6–15; and "The Mother's Day Campaign," 839–840.

75 The cartoon was designed by Pulitzer Prize–winning cartoonist Charles R. Macauley. The Maternity Center Association, *Publicity Kit for Mother's Day, May 10, 1931*, Maternity Center Association Papers, Archives and Special Collections, A. C. Long Health Sciences Library, Columbia University Medical Center, New York City, New York.

76 The Maternity Center Association, *Maternity Center Association, 1918–1943*, 11; and "The Mother's Day Campaign," *American Journal of Nursing*, 839.

77 "Mother's Day," *American Journal of Nursing*, 449–450; "How Would You Have Answered," *American Journal of Nursing* 31, no. 4 (April 1931): 450–451; "The Mother's Day Campaign," *American Journal of Nursing*, 426, 839–840; "Say It with Knowledge," *American Journal of Nursing* 33, no. 4 (April 1933): 348; "Saving Mothers from Unnecessary Deaths," 272;

"Mother's Day, May 13," *American Journal of Nursing* 34, no. 4 (April 1934): 342; "Are You Preparing for Mother's Day," *American Journal of Nursing* 36, no. 4 (April 1936): 374; "Nurses and Safe Maternity Care," *American Journal of Nursing* 37, no. 4 (April 1937): 392–393; and The Maternity Center Association, *The Story of the New Mother's Day*, 6–15.

78   Genevieve Parkhurst, "Every Baby Needs a Mother," *Good Housekeeping*, February 1934.

79   "The Mother's Day Campaign," *American Journal of Nursing*, 839–840; The Maternity Center Association, *The Story of the New Mother's Day*, 6–15; and The Maternity Center Association, *Campaign Suggestions for Mother's Day, May 12, 1935*, (New York, 1935).

80   The Maternity Center Association, *The Story of the New Mother's Day*, 12.

81   The Maternity Center Association, *The Story of the New Mother's Day*, 15; Rita S. Halle, "Make Motherhood Safe: It Can Be Done," *Good Housekeeping*, May 1934.

82   The Maternity Center Association, *The Story of the New Mother's Day*, 11.

83   Downey, 67–71; Howard, "Navigating the Stormy Sea," 23; Martin, *Madam Secretary Frances Perkins*, 133–135; and The Maternity Center Association, *Maternity Center Association Log, 1915–1975*, 6.

84   Frances Perkins, "Maternity Care and the Children's Bureau," in *Campaign Suggestions for Mother's Day, May 12, 1935*, (New York: The Maternity Center Association, 1935) B-3.

85   Frances Perkins, "Maternity Care and the Children's Bureau," in *Campaign Suggestions for Mother's Day, May 12, 1935*, B-3.

86   "How Would You Have Answered," *American Journal of Nursing*, 450; and The Maternity Center Association, *The Story of the New Mother's Day*, 15–24. Dr. Morris Fishbein, the author of "Choosing Your Doctor," which appeared in *The Story of the New Mother's Day*, was the editor of the *Journal of the American Medical Association* and the health magazine *Hygeia*.

87   Ettinger, *Nurse-Midwifery*, 79.

88   Ettinger, *Nurse-Midwifery*, 72–95; and Howard, "Navigating the Stormy Sea," 74–78.

89   Between 1932 and 1936, the Lobenstine clinic reported only one maternal death out of 1081 deliveries. One should note, however, that the clinic only accepted women who were fully expected to experience a normal pregnancy and delivery. Ettinger, *Nurse-Midwifery*, 83–102; Howard, "Navigating the Stormy Sea," 74–78; and Parkhurst, "Every Baby Needs a Mother."

90   "Charity Charlatans," n.d., Anna Jarvis Papers.

91   "Charity Charlatans," n.d., Anna Jarvis Papers.

92   "Charity Charlatans," n.d., Anna Jarvis Paper; and Wolfe, "The White Carnation," 75.

93   Downey, *The Woman Behind the New Deal*, 242; "A Pink Carnation—or a Life on Mother's Day," *New York Times*, May 12, 1929; and Wolfe, "The White Carnation," 58–64, 75, 168–172.

94   Wolfe, "The White Carnation," 61.

95   Anna Jarvis to President Franklin Roosevelt, May 15, 1933, Franklin D. Roosevelt Library, Hyde Park, New York ; Anna Jarvis to President Franklin Roosevelt, March 6, 1935,

Franklin D. Roosevelt Library, Hyde Park, New York; and Anna Jarvis to Eleanor Roosevelt, May 14, 1935, Anna Jarvis Papers, West Virginia and Regional History Collection, West Virginia University, Morgantown, West Virginia.

96 Wolfe, "The White Carnation," 75. Jarvis wrote a similar letter to U.S. Children's Bureau Chief Katharine Lenroot, May 14, 1935, Anna Jarvis Papers, West Virginia and Regional History Collection, West Virginia University, Morgantown, West Virginia.

97 Wolfe, "The White Carnation," 75. Jarvis wrote a similar letter to U.S. Children's Bureau Chief Katharine Lenroot, May 14, 1935, Anna Jarvis Papers, West Virginia and Regional History Collection, West Virginia University, Morgantown, West Virginia.

98 Lindenmeyer, "A Right to Childhood," 85, 88.

99 Rima Apple, "'Training'" the Baby: Mothers' Responses to Advice Literature in the First Half of the Twentieth Century," in When Science Encounters the Child: Education, Parenting, and Child Welfare in the 20th Century America, ed. Barbara Beatty, Emily D. Cahan, and Julia Grant (New York: Teachers College Press, 2006), 195–211; Apple, "Constructing Mothers," 90-110; Ehrenreich and English, For Her Own Good, 215–230; Grant, Raising Baby by the Book, 137–160; Hays, The Cultural Contradictions of Motherhood, 19–50, 44; Hardyment, Dream Babies, 89–222; and Margolis, Mothers and Such, 11–107.

100 Margaret A. O'Keefe to Children's Bureau, August 14, 1926, quoted in Barker, "Birthing and Bureaucratic Women," 338.

101 Barker, "Birthing and Bureaucratic Women," 345–346.

102 Howard, "Navigating the Stormy Sea," 50.

103 Barker, "Birthing and Bureaucratic Women," 345–352; Ettinger, Nurse-Midwifery, 72–102; Grant, Raising Baby by the Book, 84–85; Keeling, Nursing and the Privilege of Prescription, 1–27; and Karen Tice, "School-Work and Mother-Care: The Interplay of Maternalism and Cultural Politics in the Educational Narratives of Kentucky Settlement Workers, 1910–1930," Journal of Appalachia Studies 4, no. 2 (Fall 1988): 208–214.

104 Klaus, Every Child a Lion, 31–42; and Muncy, Creating A Female Dominion, 93–123.

105 The Maternity Center Association, Routines for Maternity Nursing, 7; and The Maternity Center Association, Maternity Center Association, 1918–1943, 5–7.

106 Apple, "Constructing Mothers,"103; Grant, Raising Baby by the Book, 73–77, 89–95; Howard, "Navigating the Stormy Sea," 66–73; Klaus, Every Child a Lion, 16, 146; Ladd-Taylor, 56–57; Lindenmeyer, "A Right to Childhood," 64; Meckel, Save the Babies, 138–139; and Muncy, Creating A Female Dominion, 117-123.

107 International Mother's Day Association, The Mother's Day Movement, [1912?], 2, Mother's Day Collection, International Mother's Day Shrine, Grafton, West Virginia.

108 "A Pink Carnation—or a Life on Mother's Day?," New York Times, May 12, 1929.

109 The Maternity Center Association, "If the Public Only Knew!," 5. Maternity Center Association papers, Archives and Special Collections, A,C. Long Health Sciences Library, Columbia University Medical Center, New York.

110 The Maternity Center Association, The Story of the New Mother's Day, 3; and the Maternity Center Association, Maternity Center Association, 1918–1943, 13.

111 The possessive plural spelling is original to the article. William Frederick Bigelow, "Get Ready for Mothers' Day," *Good Housekeeping*, April 1934, editorial page.

112 The Maternity Center Association, *Maternity Center Association Log, 1918–1943*, 13; and the Maternity Center Association, *The Story of the New Mother's Day*, 12.

113 The Maternity Center Association, *Maternity Center Association Log, 1918–1943*, 13; and the Maternity Center Association, *The Story of the New Mother's Day*, 12.

114 The Maternity Center Association, *Maternity Center Association Log, 1918–1943*, 13; and the Maternity Center Association, *The Story of the New Mother's Day*, 12.

115 Howard, "Navigating the Stormy Sea," 48–49.

116 Sheila Rothman, "Women's Clinics or Doctors' Offices: The Sheppard-Towner Act and the Promotion of Preventative Health Care," *Social History and Social Policy* (1981): 175–202. See also, Rothman, *Woman's Proper Place*, 142–153.

117 Emphasis added. The Maternity Center Association, *The Story of the New Mother's Day*, 27–28.

118 Ettinger, *Nurse-Midwifery*, 99, 101–102.

119 "Asks Aid For Needy on Mothers' Day," *New York Times*, March 11, 1931.

120 "Asks Aid For Needy on Mothers' Day," *New York Times*, March 11, 1931.

121 Anna Jarvis to President Franklin Roosevelt, April 17, 1933, Franklin D Roosevelt Library, Hyde Park, New York; Mary S. Krech to Marguerite Le Hand, 15 April, 1935, Franklin D Roosevelt Library, Hyde Park, New York.

122 This was not the first time that Jarvis recognized an honorary national mother. She awarded the title once to Mrs. Phoebe Hearst, the mother of newspaper man Randolph Hearst in the 1910s and to the mother of Commander Richard Byrd after his historic flight over the North Pole on Mother's Day in 1926. Nonetheless, her decision to target Sara Roosevelt during the 1930s is significant. Mary S. Krech to Marguerite Le Hand, April, 1935, Franklin D Roosevelt Library, Hyde Park, New York; President Franklin D. Roosevelt to Mary S. Krech, 13 May, 1935, Franklin D Roosevelt Library, Hyde Park, New York; and Mary S. Krech to President Franklin D. Roosevelt, May 17, 1935, Franklin D Roosevelt Library, Hyde Park, New York.

123 Anna Jarvis to James Roosevelt (secretary to the president), March 26, 1937 Franklin D Roosevelt Library, Hyde Park, New York.

124 "The Mother's Day Campaign," *American Journal of Nursing*, 839; "Fathers to Aid Mothers," *New York Times*, May 9, 1931; and Wolfe, "The White Carnation," 174.

125 Wolfe, "The White Carnation," 168.

126 Wolfe, "The White Carnation," 168.

127 Anna Jarvis, "Make Mother's Day Safe for Mother," *Quotarian Magazine*, April 1938.

128 Anna Jarvis, "Make Mother's Day Safe for Mother," *Quotarian Magazine*, April 1938.

129 Anna Jarvis to President Franklin Roosevelt, April 8, 1938, Franklin D. Roosevelt Library, Hyde Park, New York.

130 Anna Jarvis to William Brice, Jr., January 30, 1939, Anna Jarvis Papers, West Virginia and Regional History Collection, West Virginia University, Morgantown, West Virginia.

Epilogue

1 Charlotte Douglas Suru-Mago to President Franklin Roosevelt, May 5, 1944, Franklin D. Roosevelt Library, Hyde Park, New York.

2 The final telegram and letter found among Roosevelt's presidential papers were dated April and June of 1942. Both concerned the continued infringement, public deception, profiteering, and commercialization of Mother's Day by George Hecht's Mother's Day National Council, the American War Mothers, the Golden Rule Foundation, and the Maternity Center Association. Anna Jarvis to President Franklin Roosevelt, April 12, 1942, June 20, 1942, Franklin D. Roosevelt Library, Hyde Park, New York.

3 "Mother's Day, Inc," *Time*, May 16, 1938.

4 "Mother's Day, Inc," *Time*, May 16, 1938.

5 "Mother's Day, Inc," *Time*, May 16, 1938.

6 Howard Wolfe, "The White Carnation" (1984), 168–172, Howard Wolfe Collection, International Mother's Day Shrine, Grafton, West Virginia.

7 Jarvis defended her brother's estate from claims as late as 1933. Howard Wolfe, "The Second Sunday" (1983), 70–73, 97, Howard Wolfe Collection, International Mother's Day Shrine, Grafton, West Virginia; and Wolfe, "The White Carnation," 61–64. The oldest brother, Josiah Jarvis, died in 1919.

8 Wolfe, "The White Carnation," 77.

9 John LaCerda, "Tragic Founder of Mother's Day," *St. Louis Post Dispatch*, May 14, 1944; "Mother's Day Founder Loses Large Bequest," *Christian Science Monitor*, December 30, 1944; John LaCerda, "Mother of Mother's Day," *Coronet*, May 1945; Lillian Jarvis to Mr. Clinton A Sowers, September 12, 1923, Anna Jarvis Papers, West Virginia and Regional History Collection, West Virginia University, Morgantown, West Virginia; Wolfe, "The Second Sunday," 70–73, 97; and Wolfe, "The White Carnation," 61–64.

10 Wolfe, "The Second Sunday," 92; and Wolfe, "The White Carnation," 61.

11 Mother's Day International Association to Henderson Chamber of Commerce, February 4, 1924, Mother's Day File, Henderson Public Library, Henderson, Kentucky.

12 Anna Jarvis to President Franklin Roosevelt, April 18, 1938, Franklin D Roosevelt Library, Hyde Park, New York.

13 "Second Sunday in May: Mother's Day Finds Promoter of Idea Poor, Hospitalized and Still Bitter," *Newsweek*, May 8, 1944.

14 "Second Sunday in May," *Newsweek*, May 8, 1944; "Miss Lillian Jarvis Found Dead in Home by Policeman," n.d., Mother's Day File, Henderson Public Library, Henderson, Kentucky; LaCerda, "Tragic Founder of Mother's Day"; "Anna Jarvis Dead," *New York Times*, November 25, 1948; and James P. Johnson, "How Mother Got Her Day," *American Heritage* 30 (April/May 1979): 21.

15 H. S. J. Sickel to C. V. Miller, April 21, 1948, Clay Miller Papers, West Virginia and Regional History Collection, West Virginia University, Morgantown, West Virginia; "Second Sunday in May," *Newsweek*, May 8, 1944; and LaCerda, "Tragic Founder of Mother's Day."

16 Lillian Jarvis to Mr. Clinton A Sowers, September 12, 1923, Anna Jarvis Papers, West Virginia and Regional History Collection, West Virginia University, Morgantown, West Virginia.

17 A. L. Till to Anna Jarvis, June 2, 1925, Anna Jarvis Papers, West Virginia and Regional History Collection, West Virginia University, Morgantown, West Virginia; Untitled article, *Grafton [WV] News* Oct 8, 1951; H. S. J. Sickel to C. V. Miller, June 19, 1947, Clay Miller Papers, West Virginia and Regional History Collection, West Virginia University, Morgantown, West Virginia.

18 Johnson, "How Mother Got Her Day," 21; and Howard Wolfe, *Behold Thy Mother: Mothers Day and the Mothers Day Church* (Kingsport, Tennessee: Kingsport Press. 1962), 260.

19 "Second Sunday in May," *Newsweek*, May 8, 1944.

20 Jarvis's great grandniece Helen Virginia Jarvis Hutchinson lived in Fairview, West Virginia. Hutchinson was the last direct descendant of Granville and Ann Reeves Jarvis, dying in 1980 without children. Wolfe, *Behold Thy Mother*, 259–260; and Wolfe, "The Second Sunday," 95–103. The following documents provide additional details of the Anna M. Jarvis Committee's work: Sickel to Miller, April 21, 1948, Clay Miller Papers; H. S. J. Sickel to C. V. Miller, September 28, 1949, Clay Miller Papers, West Virginia and Regional History Collection, West Virginia University, Morgantown, West Virginia; and H. S. J. Sickel to Mrs. William Brent Maxwell, November 29, 1948, Clay Miller Papers, West Virginia and Regional History Collection, West Virginia University, Morgantown, West Virginia.

21 Wolfe, *Behold Thy Mother,* 208; and Oscar Schisgall, "The Bitter Author of Mother's Day," *Reader's Digest*, May 1960.

INDEX

ABOUT THE AUTHOR

Katharine Lane Antolini is assistant professor of History and Gender Studies at West Virginia Wesleyan College and serves on the Board of Trustees of the International Mother's Day Shrine in Grafton, West Virginia. She currently lives in Buckhannon, West Virginia, with her husband, Fred, and sons, John Michael and Cooper.